Urban Place

Urban and Industrial Environments

Series editor: Robert Gottlieb, Henry R. Luce Professor of Urban and Environmental Policy, Occidental College

Maureen Smith, *The U.S. Paper Industry and Sustainable Production: An Argument for Restructuring*

Keith Pezzoli, *Human Settlements and Planning for Ecological Sustainability: The Case of Mexico City*

Sarah Hammond Creighton, *Greening the Ivory Tower: Improving the Environmental Track Record of Universities, Colleges, and Other Institutions*

Jan Mazurek, *Making Microchips: Policy, Globalization, and Economic Restructuring in the Semiconductor Industry*

William A. Shutkin, *The Land That Could Be: Environmentalism and Democracy in the Twenty-First Century*

Richard Hofrichter, ed., *Reclaiming the Environmental Debate: The Politics of Health in a Toxic Culture*

Robert Gottlieb, *Environmentalism Unbound: Exploring New Pathways for Change*

Kenneth Geiser, *Materials Matter: Toward a Sustainable Materials Policy*

Thomas D. Beamish, *Silent Spill: The Organization of an Industrial Crisis*

Matthew Gandy, *Concrete and Clay: Reworking Nature in New York City*

David Naguib Pellow, *Garbage Wars: The Struggle for Environmental Justice in Chicago*

Julian Agyeman, Robert D. Bullard, and Bob Evans, eds., *Just Sustainabilities: Development in an Unequal World*

Barbara L. Allen, *Uneasy Alchemy: Citizens and Experts in Louisiana's Chemical Corridor Disputes*

Dara O'Rourke, *Community-Driven Regulation: Balancing Development and the Environment in Vietnam*

Brian K. Obach, *Labor and the Environmental Movement: The Quest for Common Ground*

Peggy F. Barlett and Geoffrey W. Chase, eds., *Sustainability on Campus: Stories and Strategies for Change*

Steve Lerner, *Diamond: A Struggle for Environmental Justice in Louisiana's Chemical Corridor*

Jason Corburn, *Street Science: Community Knowledge and Environmental Health Justice*

Peggy F. Barlett, ed., *Urban Place: Reconnecting with the Natural World*

Urban Place

Reconnecting with the Natural World

edited by Peggy F. Barlett

The MIT Press
Cambridge, Massachusetts
London, England

MIT Press books may be purchased at special quantity discounts for business or sales promotional use. For information, please e-mail special_sales@ mitpress.mit.edu or write to Special Sales Department, The MIT Press, 55 Hayward Street, Cambridge, MA 02142.

This book was set in Sabon by SNP Best-set Typesetter Ltd., Hong Kong Printed and bound in the United States of America.
Printed on recycled paper.

Library of Congress Cataloging-in-Publication Data

Urban place : reconnecting with the natural world / edited by Peggy F. Barlett.
    p.   cm.—(Urban and industrial environments)
Includes bibliographical references and index.
ISBN 0-262-02586-8 (alk. paper)—ISBN 0-262-52443-0 (pbk. : alk. paper)
1. Urban ecology. 2. Human ecology. 3. Organic living. 4. Bioregionalism.
I. Barlett, Peggy F., 1947– II. Series.

HT241.U726   2005
307.76—dc22

2005043788

10 9 8 7 6 5 4 3 2 1

Contents

Foreword

Roderick Frazier Nash

I could not see a single living thing out of the window of a bedroom that I occupied for the first eighteen years of my life. There was a windowless brick wall about 12 feet away, and it was ten stories high. There were no stars at night, and rain did not reach that far down in the alley. Once a forlorn pigeon landed briefly on my window sill and promptly pooped. The address was 40 East Tenth Street, New York, New York. As far as a nature-oriented sense of place went, there was, with respect to Gertrude Stein, no there there. I gave directions to where I lived, as most city people do, not in terms of landscape features but rather in terms of avenues, streets, and blocks.

City people seeking reconnection with the natural world have traditionally gone to the country. For nineteenth-century, end-of-the-frontier New Yorkers, "getting away from it all" meant Niagara Falls, the Adirondacks, or Long Island. For those who could afford it, the summer home offered a way back to nature; so did boys' and girls' camps. The Boy Scouts began in 1907; the first Tarzan stories appeared in 1912. Proactive people joined the outings of the Appalachian Mountain Club (1876) or the Sierra Club (1892). Some visited the new national parks such as Yellowstone (1872) or Yosemite (1890). The roots of today's ecotourism run back to these early adventures. So does the popularity of television shows like the venerable *Wild Kingdom*, *Animal Planet* and the Outdoor Life Network. The audience was, and still is, composed of almost entirely urban people who had stared for too long at brick walls. Wilderness appreciation was a product of the cities. The idea of finding naturalness in the cities seemed oxymoronic.

What is new and exciting about the book before you now is its demonstration that a meaningful relationship to nature does not necessarily depend on a rejection of the urban context. Drawing on old, intuitive knowledge and modern scholarship, the contributors to this book excite me by not surrendering to subways and pavement and shopping malls. They have discerned evidence that getting away might not entail leaving the cities so much as rediscovering them. There are also seeds of ideas here for how we can make cities of the future better from the standpoint of the human relationship to nature.

The stakes here are high. We are rapidly losing the old ways of perception and satisfaction. Making the cities of the future successful habitats for creatures whose evolutionary past is overwhelmingly wild and rural should be on the top of our urban planning agendas. Educators have a big role to play here as well. For me, it is encouraging to learn in this book how university communities can provide theoretical and practical leadership to the greening of the urban experience.

1

Introduction

Peggy F. Barlett

> Our ties to the green world are often subtle and unexpected. It is not merely that hemoglobin and chlorophyll bear striking similarities in structure, or that plants provide the pleasure of food and flowers. When people who garden find new friendships with neighbors, when a walk in the woods brings relief from pent-up tensions, or when a potted begonia restores vitality to a geriatric patient, we can begin to sense the power of these connections and their importance to physical and psychological well-being.
> —Charles Lewis, *Green Nature/Human Nature*

Alphabetic literacy created a human watershed, argues David Abram in *The Spell of the Sensuous* (1996), greatly intensifying a process of cultural estrangement from wild nature that had been underway since the advent of agriculture. In our temperature-controlled comfort, contemporary city dwellers' relations with plants and animals are often restricted to domesticated, human-dependent species. Urban culture even celebrates a sophisticated distance from the messy realities of farm and wilderness. As Woody Allen famously asserts, "I am two with Nature" (Lax 1991:39).

Moving against this dominant ethos of distance from nature, a surprisingly diverse group of urban grassroots efforts are building reconnection to place and to the natural world. Most have emerged from the environmental and sustainability movements: watershed alliances, farmers markets, community gardens, the slow food movement, and urban forest restoration efforts are examples. These activities restore a sense of place and foster a deeply meaningful renewal of relations with the earth. Their efforts resist some of the environmentally and socially destructive effects of contemporary industrial culture and economic globalization. The groups described in this book are local-level experiments in either living an alternative, less environmentally damaging way of life or moving toward the awareness of place and nature that will allow such lifeways to emerge. Each effort, though only partial, seeks to restore a sense of connection through food, greenspace, water quality, or other environmental concerns.

Why is reengagement with place so powerful? This book presents intriguing studies from medicine, public health, psychology, and landscape architecture to show that important mental and physical health impacts arise from connections with the natural world. These studies suggest that estrangement from the animate earth has negative consequences for human functioning. Evidence from natural experiments, surveys, and medical trials brings to our attention dimensions of health often ignored in the study of urban life. The cross-disciplinary dialogue among the chapters suggests there are unanticipated benefits to collective and individual well-being with the reconnection to the natural world, an often-neglected dimension of the emerging paradigm shift toward a more sustainable society.

Recent scholarly work has drawn attention to *place*, often as a counter to the massive effects of globalization on population mobility and changing relationships to locale. Especially in reference to urban areas, however, studies of place usually emphasize human interactions within the built environment, perhaps with the natural landscape as a backdrop. *Place* generally refers to meaningful architectural features and geographical sites and the human social relations enacted in them, with little or no attention to the natural systems supporting life. Relations with other species are rarely a focus of academic attention, and the impacts of health and well-being have often been missed.

Currently, growing awareness of environmental degradation in both industrialized and developing countries has eroded confidence in the adequacy of our governing paradigm of modernization, capitalist progress, and industrial growth. Seeking a more sustainable approach to the future, many writers have called for an integration of systems thinking into our daily mind-set and into public policy. Also connected to notions of bioregionalism, such a stance calls attention to the "more-than-human" world and the biological cycles with which we are interdependent. The authors in this book see the grassroots efforts described here as part of a shifting paradigm that locates humankind within the biosphere. Though urban dwellers described in these chapters engage the natural world at many different levels, they share a common direction of movement. This book explores human evolution and changing relations with the natural world as urban and peri-urban areas have expanded. In tracing the recent resurgence of U.S. community gardens, local food systems, and restorations of forests and prairies, we see how individuals often experience profound satisfactions and how new forms of community and social capital are constructed as well.

This introduction briefly traces the history of nature estrangement in urban culture and highlights the new perspectives that locate cities within their ecological systems. Emerging from grassroots efforts to build a more sustainable society, these arenas of action creatively reengage the natural world. The chapter then explores how our studies fit into and extend the recent surge of research on place. Turning to the issue of the relationship between nature and society, it will look at calls from a number of directions to alter the view of human society as separate from nature. I turn then to the issue of how nature is defined and explore the diversity in constructions of the natural world. Despite the diversity in social constructs and levels of critique, new relationships to place are integral to collective efforts to shift political and economic institutions. After looking at some of the characteristics of these collective efforts, the final section of this chapter provides an overview of the empirical and analytical contributions of our studies. As this book explores the forms and impacts of reconnection with the natural world, it highlights as well how reconnections with the natural world offer new perspectives—and new imperatives—with regard to human health.

Nature Estrangement and Urban History

To understand the origins of urban distance from the natural world, cultural anthropology points to the historical growth of political empires, the specialization of labor, and the lives of city-based elites that can become divorced from rural hinterlands. Although in many societies, sophisticated urbanites often maintained ties to recreation sites on rural estates and to the benefits of agricultural production, the arts and graces of urban life frequently flourished at a distance from biological systems (Riley 1992:28).

Anthropological theorists Allen Johnson and Timothy Earle attribute the contemporary estrangement of urban society from ecological systems to the impact of modern markets and emerging forms of social class. Commodification of resources and the degradation of the former sanctity attributed to nature combined to erode the political and ideological brakes on damage to local environments and to undermine the sustainability of production systems over time (Johnson and Earle 2000:377; Netting 1993; Rappaport 1994). The free market "dissolves a sense of interconnection with the natural world, just as it dissolves the social integument" (Johnson and Earle 2000:377).

Urban industrial contexts today present a particular challenge for restoring more systems-sensitive perspectives. "Indeed cities have been sites of assumed . . . control over ecological processes" as processes of industrialization and intensive urbanization peaked in the twentieth century (Keil and Graham 1998:100–101). Concrete jungles are inhospitable to many species that once thrived in those locales, and cities are often sources of air, water, and solid waste pollution. Modern cities make distance from nature possible for a larger group than in the past. "Cities are built in nature, with nature, through nature, yet so often appear to be external and opposed to nature" (Keil and Graham 1998:102). The built environment comes to dominate attention—even, at times, the lives of youth. There is a "kind of placelessness engendered by sheer indifference, which has reached such a point in this country that there are teenagers whose daily routes run from home to school to mall to television. They have never climbed the hill immediately behind their town, and there are children who have never gone the few miles from their homes to the sea" (Lippard 1997:44). Urban dwellers can even be so surrounded by human artifacts that some are actively uncomfortable with forms of nature outside human control (Orr 1994:131).

Urbanity can mark the epitome of the modern and is often closely connected to the national imagination; energetic young people set off from the countryside "to do great things in the city" (Kusno 2001:17). Whether we are talking about Manhattan or Jakarta, cities "concretize the modern," with their tall towers, flyover superhighways, and malls

(Smith and Bender 2001:6). Urban place is a locale as well for the enactment of human hierarchy. Distance from the natural world may be connected to power over the lower classes and their labor (Kusno 2001). The built environment in urban Indonesia, for example, expresses notions of modernity in which the poor walk on the ground, while the affluent drive on elevated highways (Smith and Bender 2001:6). Smith and Bender note that urban dwellers associate "the street" with danger and dirt. Danger highlights the social dimensions of the urban environment, while dirt evokes the degraded natural environment. Modernity celebrates the transcendence of older forms of boundedness to place, embracing technology, rationality, and control over nature as a means to development and personal success (Agnew and Duncan 1989:16; Friedland and Boden 1994; Giddens 1990).

Connection with the natural world, though at certain times and places disparaged, was not wholly abandoned in cities. Gardens preserved some elements of nature but often in a form "constrained, bent, sheared" (Lewis 1996:27). Urban designers such as Frederick Law Olmsted sought to offset the harmful effects of isolation from greenspaces among less affluent classes as well as elites. Their designs for park systems created urban "lungs" for cleaner air and psychological restoration. After being neglected in the post–World War II era, urban parks in many cities are now being restored and cherished (Lewis 1996:29).

Beyond appreciation for parks and gardens within the city, some urban dwellers in the Progressive era between 1880 and 1920 celebrated the attachment to the natural world through hiking, scouting, and "the strenuous life" (Sutter 2002). The health benefits of nature contact were particularly well articulated in some European cities (Rotenberg 1993). A romance of wilderness emerged along with efforts to protect wild areas and scenic national parks (Nash 2001; Thomas 1983). Nature tourism grew with the automobile, and "the tourist's desire to visit nature is a modern desire, but it also is driven by a deep ambivalence about modernity" (Sutter 2002:29).

The forms of reconnection explored in this book go beyond the tourist's appreciation of the far away and the exotic, drawing attention back to the ordinary experience of everyday city life. Nature in the city is experienced in leisure activities such as walks in a park, but also as a view through the window or the surroundings one passes through on the way to lunch. Contact with the natural world can be sought out through efforts to create a community garden or the health of natural systems fostered by efforts to restore a stream. Growing numbers of such grass-roots efforts provide evidence of an emerging desire for a more complex and engaged relationship with nature in its various forms.

Sustainability, Bioregionalism, and an Emerging Systems Perspective

Trees, plants, and animals are doorways to deeper systems understandings, "interconnected elements of a larger design in which people are also a thread." Engagement with the natural world gives us an opportunity "to understand our part in the complex tapestry of life." (Lewis 1996:8)

In the past 20 years, as the full environmental costs of industrial development have become more vivid, perspectives on sustainability and bioregionalism have emerged to counter the modernist tendency to ignore the realities and limitations of the natural world (Norgaard 1994). Embracing technology and science as means to dominate the earth's processes, modernity celebrates the damming of rivers for electricity generation, the efficiency of pulpwood chipper plants, and the chemical solution to crop insect infestations. A focus on sustainability seeks instead a productive and viable intersection among economic, environmental, and social domains of life (Harris and Goodwin 2001; Holmberg 1992). A broader view of desired development replaces a narrower focus on economic growth and cultural Westernization (Milton 1996). Visions of the future become multifaceted, seeking economic livelihood for whole populations in a particular locale, while attending to social equity, cultural continuity, and political participation, as well as to the environmental viability of the lifeways embraced (Evans 2002; Pretty 2002; Redclift 1987). Ensuring long-term ecosystem productivity is as important as long-term economic productivity, and both must seek a balance with long-term social sustainability and social justice. The social dimension embraces a number of Enlightenment commitments to human rights, equality, political participation, and dialogue (Dryzek 1997), as well as more recent international commitments to cultural diversity and gender equity. Such is the triple bottom line now embraced, at least in theory, by development agencies, the United Nations, and even the World Bank (Brown 2001; Hawken 1993; Hawken, Lovins, and Lovins 1999).

Some critics lament the difficulties in specifying such trade-offs in legal or scientific terms and criticize sustainability objectives as vague, impractical, or easily co-opted by powerful groups (Katz 1998:57; Redclift 1987). Sustainability rhetoric can also leave aside consideration of institutions that created the current crisis (Fischer and Hajer 1995:5; Adams 2001). It seems, however, that sustainability efforts are beginning to construct new ways of being in the world, new logics, and new meanings, though they are far from a coherent political or legal platform (Castells 2004). Renewed attention to the local is part of this change (Allen et al. 2003; Snyder 1990). Modernity emphasizes the essential transferability of ideas, people, building plans, and the sacred. With the globalization of the economy has come the mobility of people, customs, languages, architecture, and food. By contrast, the sustainability paradigm is emerging in profoundly local contexts, as small groups of people around the world reject aspects of the consumerist, growth-oriented perspective and experiment with alternatives (Norgaard 1994; Shuman 1998).

Robert Thayer points to the concept of bioregion as a focus for "relocalization" movements (2003). Bioregions are unique geographical territories identifiable by natural rather than political boundaries, supporting unique human and nonhuman living communities (p. 3). "Although by no means a unified philosophy, theory, or method, the bioregional approach suggests a means of living by deep understanding of, respect for, and ultimately, care of a naturally bounded region or territory" (p. 4). Coordinated resource management plans, Friends of Parks groups (or of other natural features), and alternative local currencies build a new sense of relationship to local natural systems. Bioregionalism highlights—even for cities—a goal of unique architectures, daily habits, and foodways that takes into account the climate, resources, and surrounding natural world (McGinnis 1999; Snyder 1990). As international systems of power constrain many aspects of national life, especially legislative approaches to environmental challenges, local experiments provide a viable forum for alternative voices (Shuman 1998; Smith and Johnston 2002).

Sustainability efforts and bioregional perspectives counter the modernist separation of urban life from nature and move toward an awareness of humans within natural systems. Writers from many points on the intellectual spectrum have called in particular for developing a relationship with other parts of the natural world as a response to the current environmental crisis (T. Berry 1988; W. Berry 1987; Macy and Brown 1998; Orr 1994; Wilson 1998). David Abram's work "awakens us to the breathing landscape" (Whatmore 2002:167). Martin Heidegger's *dwelling* "assigns importance to the forms of consciousness with which individuals perceive and apprehend geographical space" (Basso 1996: 106). Dwelling consists, more precisely, in the "lived relationships" that people maintain with places (Abram 1996; Basso 1996; Gray 1999).

This new sense of relationship with surrounding natural systems reflects a different paradigm of humans as part of the natural world (Castells 2004:169). Systems thinking is a conceptual framework deriving from ecological perspectives on the complex cycles of interrelated biological phenomena (rain, soil erosion, river silt, suffocated fish, fertile delta soils) and the social, economic, and political dimensions of these phenomena (suburban expansion, deforestation, taxation incentives to sprawl, air pollution from automobile exhaust). A systems perspective transcends local boundaries and highlights the web of bio-geo-chemical processes that surrounds and supports urban life (Moran 1990). For many city dwellers, such systems thinking is a major change, one that is fostered by the grassroots activities described in this book. As volunteers clean up a trash-filled urban stream, for example, they absorb a new concept of watershed. They learn that parking lots, driveways, and lawn chemicals affect water quality and stream insect life. People who might never have thought about mayflies or runoff water temperature develop a new relationship to the stream ecosystem and indicators of its health (Barlett 2002). Concerns about urban air quality also draw attention to the ecological matrix of life. Trees provide "services" by removing air pollutants, retaining stormwater, cooling temperatures, and providing habitat and food for other species. Restoration work of prairies and forests builds attachment to the natural world in a more grounded local way than a more diffuse embrace of nature in the abstract (Light and Higgs 1997).

Attention to the natural world therefore reawakens the urban dweller to what has been previously hidden or limited knowledge of a larger ecosystem. Such reweaving of lost connections or construction of new ones, especially for those who have no past history of attachment to the land, generates new emotional connections. Local organizations with quite diverse purposes and constituencies have found that reconnecting to the natural world has been a significant tool to support their efforts, one in which unexpectedly powerful meanings emerge for participants (Von Hassell 2002). Coming to the organizations from many motives, participants often grow in ways they did not expect. Community gardens not only provide nutritious food and conviviality with neighbors, but can build a different sense of self through a new awareness of growing cycles, weather, and human agency. As Miles, Sullivan, and Kuo report, ecological restoration builds a sense of belonging, connection to nature, and positive sense of control (1998). Charles Lewis's observations in Manhattan echo several of the authors in this book that positive new self-identities emerge in "intimate relationships with plants" (1996:56–57). Thus, in this book, we outline not only the organizations and efforts that are rebuilding relations with the natural world within cities, but also the impacts of their activities on the identities and actions of individual participants and on the social fabric in which they participate.

Nature in Recent Scholarship on Place

Place is a focus of considerable scholarship at present from a number of disciplinary perspectives. Work on place includes the anthropological "sense of place" or identification with a location "engendered by living in it" as well as the economist's sense of location that includes real estate markets (Agnew and Duncan 1989:2; Rotenberg and McDonough 1993). Place includes the sociologist's or artist's sense of locale—the setting for everyday life and polities—and the attention to place that is central to urban planning and landscape architecture; all are complementary dimensions of place.

Rarely, however, does the contemporary surge of interest in place take account of species other than human, especially within urban areas.

Within anthropology, Keith Basso's research among the Apache was among the first to articulate the importance of place. Place, for Basso, can include a subway platform, urban monuments, and street garbage, but also the pigeons, the rain, and the smell of the air. The shade of a tree can have meaning for a city dweller, even those who know nothing about the oxygen-producing, carbon dioxide–absorbing, temperature-cooling properties of trees. Basso notes that anthropologists have generally had little to say about the ways in which local groups engage with place and nature (1996:xiv). Basso's work contains minimal description of nature per se, because the rural, agricultural life of the Apache is intimately intertwined with other species. Mud, juniper tree, growing corn—all are inseparably connected with Apache material life and religious meaning. The existence of a web of relationship between the land, diverse species on it, and human individuals in conversation is taken for granted.

Setha Low brings an interest in place to urban anthropology and celebrates how anthropology, now liberated from the study of particular groups in fixed locations, can explore borders, migration, and national identity among mobile populations (Low 1996; Low and Lawrence-Zúñiga 2003). The urban anthropology of place tends to emphasize social relations and social principles, with the natural world included only as a backdrop. Low also notes that place attachment has been less the focus of research in the New World, where geographical and cultural instability call attention to how people adapt to the new (Low and Altman 1992:2). At the same time, this anthropological work on place points to the "depth and complexity with which people construct meaningful relations with their surroundings" (Low and Lawrence-Zúñiga 2003:18; Altman and Low 1992), which opens the door for attention to relations with the more-than-human world.

Doreen Massey's *Space, Place, and Gender* emphasizes that place is constructed by a social group or an individual through a process that takes meaning within political and economic realities, often through linkages with powerful groups outside a locale (1994:155). In chapter 4 of this book, Malve von Hassell describes how a community garden in New York City may replace an abandoned lot and come to be a social focus for many who live nearby. As developers or city officials seek to destroy the garden in order to build on the lot, the neighbors' attachment to the vegetables, flowers, and trees in the garden takes on new depth. The New York garden case illustrates another dimension common to place studies—the focus on diverse actors and their potentially conflicting interests and actions (Massey 1994:49). The importance of playgrounds or space to grow food may vary in importance with the ability to afford day care or fresh vegetables in the store.

Much recent work in cultural studies engages with locality as buildings, infrastructure, capital—and social activities and relationships—but omits the dimension of the natural world (Massey 1994:136).[1] Anthony Giddens (1990) also notes that modernity fosters relations with absent others, so "locales are thoroughly penetrated by and shaped in terms of social influences quite distant from them" (cited in Massey 1994:6). Place is a meaningful "setting for interaction" (Massey 1994:138), but not so clearly a setting for interaction with nonhuman species. In 2003, the Rural Sociological Society meetings were focused on space and place, yet attention to species other than human was conspicuously absent.

David Harvey's work illustrates emerging attention to environmental dimensions of place in urban research. His earlier book, *The Urban Experience* (1989b), sees locality as bound to politics and power and draws attention to the process of human activities and relationships among the buildings, infrastructure, and investment of capital that are its tangible result (see also 1989a). In *Spaces of Hope* (2000), Harvey recognizes environmental justice issues within the urban context, although he is still focused mainly on class struggle and capitalism. Within landscape architecture, manuals for planners and citizens engage with common themes of place and sustainability from an applied perspective (Beatley and Manning 1997; Platt, Rowntree, and Muick 1994; Spirn 1984). Even within the field of art, attention to the power of place has grown, but also focuses heavily on the political and economic dimensions of history (Lippard 1997).

This book seeks to contribute to the literature on place by drawing attention to different avenues for engagement with the natural world and the health implications of nature contact. Place and nature are overlapping spheres in many of the studies reported here. Not all places are designed to include other species—a small plaza may be completely paved and devoid of greenery—but often the attachment to urban places includes an awareness and enjoyment of trees, shrubs, grass, birds, bees, and flowers. In grassroots groups that seek to preserve or restore certain ecosystems, the new awareness of other species and their needs gives deeper meaning to place. For others, an already significant locale takes on new dimensions as relationships are built with other species living there. The ecological systems thinking described in many chapters opens the door to new understanding of the impacts of nature on health and well-being within the urban landscape (R. Kaplan 1984; S. Kaplan 1985; Kaplan and Kaplan 1989).

Nature and Society

Nature as we know it was invented in the differentiation of city and countryside, in the differentiation of mental and manual labor, and in the abstraction of contemporary culture and consciousness from the necessary productive social work of material life. (FitzSimmons 1989:108)

The contemporary neglect of the natural world within studies of place has deep roots in European intellectual life and the dominant modernist paradigm, though a number of writers have called for greater attention to nature and how it is culturally constructed. Raymond Williams was one of the earlier social theorists to reject the Western dualism of nature and society. Noting that humankind was included in early European conceptions of the natural world, he argues that the emergence of later Victorian era views of humans as intervening in nature presupposes that humans might find it possible not to do so (Williams 1980:75). Williams argues that nature thus came to be constructed as something separate from human social life, and it was often conceptualized as existing at the margins of industrial areas (p. 80). Images of nature as refuge, as places of healing, solace, and retreat also became common (Nash 2001). The separation of nature from human activity occurred not just because urban growth or an industrial economy expanded the urban area but, paradoxically, because there was an increasingly real interaction between the two. Slagheaps and stinking rivers were powerful evidence of the interaction, but for industrializing Europe, this interaction became distanced from perception (p. 83). Williams's view of nature as a historically changing concept, socially constructed, is now commonplace in the social sciences.

In America, Ralph Waldo Emerson confronted the abhorrence of wilderness within frontier culture, asserting both the beauty and the goodness of the wild (Nash 2001). Henry David Thoreau is associated with discourses of nature as unspoiled, wild, and distinct from the built environment of the urban (Gottlieb 2001:6). Changing urban imperatives continue to shift the construction of nature. In recent times, nature is more than ever before commoditized, either for resource extraction (logging, privatized water) or as recreation (ecotourism) (Sutter 2002). These views are "firmly rooted in a modern dualism in which nature is seen as external to society: its other" (Braun and Castree 1998:4).

FitzSimmons points out that for academic researchers, the "pervasive view that nature is external and primordial is unconsciously confirmed by our placement as intellectuals in a spatially organized society in which 'intellectual work' and 'intellectual life' are urban" (1989:107). Geography and other academic fields developed as disciplines in a context in which nature was external to society, nature existing without social meaning (FitzSimmons 1989:111). Such perspectives are still common among "rootless academics," who embrace a cosmopolitan placelessness (Zencey 1996:15; Barlett and Chase 2004).

Recent critical theory in geography, sociology, and other fields has expanded this perspective, however, broadening our understanding of the social construction of nature (Agnew and Duncan 1989; FitzSimmons 1989; FitzSimmons and Goodman 1998; Freudenburg, Frickel, and Gramling 1995). " 'Nature' resides in place, whether in a city, suburb, rural area, or designated wilderness area" (Gottlieb 2001:44). What is defined or experienced as "nature" is affected by cultural practices that define appropriate interactions with and investments in the natural world (Braun and Castree 1998:17). It is the changes in such definitions and patterns of interactions that form the ethnographic and experimental basis for the chapters in this book.

What Is the Natural World?

What we call nature is, in a sense, the sum of the changes made by all the various creatures and natural forces in their intricate actions and influences upon each other and upon their places. (W. Berry 1987:7)

The arenas of action documented in the chapters that follow bring to life a range of ways in which people open to deeper relationships with other species and natural phenomena such as thunderstorms. Although definitions as clear as that of Wendell Berry just cited are not always articulated, most individuals (and most authors) in this book use the term *nature* to summarize the plants and animals and biological processes around them with varying degrees of attention to how phenomena are socially constructed. Sometimes we emphasize "green nature," the grass, trees, and shrubs that soften the concrete landscape. Sometimes we talk about nature as a shorthand for much more complex systems understandings, more like Berry's. Sometimes our different foci when we talk about nature reflect different methodological designs or disciplinary vocabulary. We hope these studies will contribute to cross-disciplinary fertilization and a more nuanced language in future research.

In addition to disciplinary approaches, we acknowledge the diverse standpoints of individuals and groups as they interact with nature. Our studies see the social construction of nature as varying from culture to culture and individual to individual within the same city (Thomashow 1995:3). The social life of the urban area is made up of many overlapping groups and social relationships, articulating affiliations both acknowledged and invisible, by neighborhood and ethnicity, race and class, religion and lifestyle. Daily life experience in the city—from the curriculum of schools to the existence of neighborhood greenspace—affects the awareness of the natural world, an awareness constrained and affected by the power relations of urban social organization. For example, it is obvious that well-educated residents of wealthy neighborhoods have different options in supporting watershed restoration or local greenspace acquisition. The impact of bankers' decisions to fund new housing projects can determine a neighborhood's quality of life and even a child's ability to learn about intact ecosystems through personal observation. And the necessity to work three jobs to make ends meet is perhaps even more of a constraint on the opportunity to engage with the natural world. Our studies do not attempt to develop a comprehensive analysis of social life, community, and power as urban groups form new connections with other species, but we recognize that relations with the natural world are affected by these social group configurations.

Habits of thinking about natural phenomena are also affected by the attitudes and practices of family and peers and by our past histories with less urban environments. Does summer fishing in a nearby pond remind us of the river where we grew up? Are picnics a scene of combat with ants and mosquitoes or of peaceful family sociability? Are sites for former picnics now front lawns of the wealthy? In addition, the human relationship with the natural world can have negative as well as positive dimensions. Few of us relish our relationships with rats or roaches; we may love squirrels, but not in our own attic. Other dimensions of nature contact are invisible, such as the changed temperature of a shaded sidewalk to the hurried passerby who does not notice. And when noticed, the power of wind or thunderstorms may be unmarked in urban discourse, as discussed by Robert Rotenberg in chapter 9. What we notice, what noticings are shared, what relations with other species are celebrated or vilified or simply dismissed, and what actions flow from these conceptions all vary within the urban situation. This variation exists not only from individual to individual and group to group, but across time— across both the city's history and the personal life span.

As our chapters depict some of the ways locality is invigorated with deeper understandings of nature, however it is constructed, one of the significant parallels among the studies is the way that common concerns transcend lines of color, class, and power. We see awakenings to nature, systems thinking, environmental concern, and forms of civic action embraced by very different groups. Although urban dwellers engage with other species in diverse ways, with diverse understandings, and from diverse standpoints, there are themes of common ground in the concern for sustainability, bioregion, local control over resources, resistance to external power structures, and a reembedding of the human species within biological systems. This book presents a cross-section of initiatives throughout urban and peri-urban settings that retrace, celebrate, and revive linkages with other species and demonstrate alternative ways in which people seek meaningful relationships with the natural environment. We look forward to further analyses of the diversity of such meanings and relationships and the societal ramifications of such initiatives.

Relations with Nature

What do new relationships with the natural world mean for participants in these groups? Some make tentative steps to overcome fears of bugs, germs, and dirt. Others exult in mystical encounters with deer, bears, or butterflies but are still newcomers to the concept of ecological systems. Still others find new scientific knowledge about their bioregions brings them to nonrational and even spiritual understandings of themselves and the universe.

The studies in this book document several layers of connection to nature:

- *Knowledge*—about local plants, animals, and natural phenomena (such as the dietary preference of the blue heron for a neighbor's Japanese koi or the invasive ivy that chokes a nature preserve)
- *Emerging emotional attachment* (such as to the trees and wildflowers of a local park)
- *Purposeful action* that engages with other species (such as a homeless child's harvest of tomatoes at a shelter)
- *New personal choices and ethical action* (such as a new decision about meat consumption based on the impact of large livestock facilities on coastal ecosystems)
- *Commitments to political action* emerging from an affective bond (such as efforts to save an urban forest or challenge zoning preferences)

In addition to the qualities of relationship that range from casual awareness to strong emotional commitment are forms of engagement from simply viewing nature outside a window, to incidental exposure while otherwise focused, to active forms of engagement such as planting trees or feeding birds. Our growing knowledge of the health impacts of this range of engagements with nature are discussed by the authors in part II of this book.

Since a relationship involves at least two entities, it implies the separation of an individual human from hawk, tree, or river. This view is supported by some religious traditions that emphasize human dominance over other species. Many cultures around the world and many of the individuals who take part in the arenas of action described here embrace a more intertwined and complex view (Dryzek 1997; Nash 2001; Thomas 1983). For some urban dwellers, the bond with nature extends the sense of self toward an identification with other species, a softening of the boundaries of separation. Deep ecologists and many conservationists reject the human primacy in the web of life and are motivated by an ethic of care and respect for the intrinsic value of diverse species (Dryzek 1997:156; Devall and Sessions 1985; Milton 2002).

Some environmental efforts are bedeviled by such decisions. Are some forms of nature more beneficial? Judgments about whether a riverine ecosystem is somehow intrinsically better than a bike trail or whether a forested public park allows more connection with nature than a grassy back yard are important issues, but generally beyond the scope of this book. The research presented in the chapters of part II shows clearly that important psychological benefits accrue to a wide variety of contacts with nature. This book signals that much work remains to distinguish the impacts of different experiences in nature on different individuals. As we gain appreciation for self-sustaining ecosystems, clearly the forest or river has the potential to allow more species to survive and interact separate from human impact. At the same time, we are learning that even quite dense urban areas can support a rich array of species, ecosystems, and natural phenomena.

Contact with the natural world not only shifts identity and attachment to place, but it can also teach important lessons about change and stability. Plant rhythms—following the sun, sprouting, dying back—are "elemental life qualities to all who listen" (Lewis 1996:64). The natural cycles of plants provide a reassuring stability, very different from the erratic growth of suburbs or the changing high-tech landscape. Through gardening, as with other rituals, one connects with the currents of dynamic change while touching as well the timeless eternal (Rappaport 1971).

Shierry Nicholsen argues that some people resist the possibility of "deeper entwinement with the natural world" out of vulnerability and fear, perhaps anxiety, and sometimes even panic over the environmental destruction we perceive (Nicholsen 2002:91). Compassion can be too painful at this historical moment or too closely connected to self-sacrifice (p. 52). Williams is less charitable, describing among British elites a hypocritical reverence for nature: "Established at powerful points in the very process which is creating disorder, they change their clothes at week-ends, or when they can get down to the country; join appeals and campaigns to keep one last bit of England green and unspoilt; and then go back, spiritually refreshed, to invest in the smoke and the spoil" (Williams 1980:81). Williams's point, that wealthy individuals can journey to refreshing nature experiences outside the city while supporting an economic system that makes such experiences ever more precarious, draws our attention back to the differences of power and position within the city. But we also note that over the past twenty years, the context for such ethical dilemmas has changed. The emerging sustainability paradigm and international efforts to challenge corporate power and steer globalization in new directions constructs both oppositional and alternative mandates, both with growing appeal. Not only are grassroots groups offering alternatives to the "smoke and spoil," but even some large corporations seek to find the triple bottom line of sustainability.

Understandings of nature, built on the reverence for the wild of Thoreau and Emerson, are for the groups described here part of awakenings to place and bioregional sensibilities. As groups seek to diminish environmental harms, there is often, as well, a "culturally achieved meaningfulness of a particular way of life" (Torgerson 1995:189). As urban places come to be seen as part of living systems, not only are new individual identities created and new knowledge shared and celebrated, but a new basis for political action emerges as well.

Political and Economic Dimensions of Grounding in Place

People-plant relationships, which are innate, presage a movement toward the concept embodied in the Hebrew words *tikkun olam*: healing, repair, and transformation of the world around us. (Lewis 1996:62)

A sensibility of place and bioregion is essential to several critiques of economic development and to imagining green alternatives to modernization and globalization (Agnew and Duncan 1989:3; Dirlik 1998:10; Gottlieb 2001; Pretty 2002). Sustainability efforts often expand or directly challenge modernist notions of the sophisticated urban life

(Norgaard 1994; Milton 2002). Massey notes that specific meaningful locales can become useful in political struggles (1994:151) and David Harvey notes that tangible solidarities rooted in affective and knowledgeable communities can become connected to global ambitions that reach out across space (Allen et al. 2003:62). Thayer documents as well the use of bioregional identification as a way to rally around certain values, especially to resist external control (Thayer 2003:63; Castells 1997): "Today, however, a new equilibrium is being reached between communities of *interest*, which tend to be global, and communities of *place*, which tend to be local" (Thayer 2003:65; Castells 1997, 2004).

One example of the ways in which place connects to healing and repair is the new urban agricultural movement that highlights the foodshed, the area from which foodstuffs are obtained. The concept draws attention to the environmental costs of long-distance food transport and the sometimes harmful impact of conventional industrial food production on soil, air, water, farm families, workers, and local businesses. One result is the growing market for locally grown and processed foods in many urban areas, as described by Susan Andreatta (chapter 5) and Elizabeth Barham, David Lind, and Lewis Jett (chapter 6) in this book. Alternative agriculture reweaves production and consumption (Apffel-Marglin and Parajuli 1998) and "invite[s] other languages of attachment" (Whatmore 2002:167; see also Pretty 2002). It also draws attention to the political structures that have brought into being or helped to hide the negative consequences of industrial agriculture (Allen et al. 2003). Several chapters in this book explore economic and political arrangements, both national and international, that have encouraged or even compelled the inattention to place.

Foodshed awareness can lead also to collective action for policies that help consumers buy locally, such as food labeling initiatives or space for farmers markets (Andreatta 2000; Barham 2002, 2003). Concerns about water quality or air pollution can lead to efforts toward higher gasoline taxes, new zoning rules, or urban planning strategies. These movements step beyond resistance, embracing the old while also, as DeLind and Ferguson articulate, "building something new . . . a celebration of hope against fear" (1999:197). In her work with the Michigan State University food service, Laura DeLind sees efforts to build local agriculture as political resistance not only to the multinational agrofood industry, but also to certain uses of technology and to some local business interests (DeLind and Link 2004). New local alliances and an emerging consumer-farmer partnership replace older political configurations. Though groups may vary greatly in their level of engagement with politics, corporate critique, or attention to social equity, these kinds of efforts are growing in momentum. In New York State for example, Thomas Lyson documents that community gardens expanded from 550 in 1978 to 1,500 in 2000 (Lyson 2004). Local farmers markets numbered only 6 in 1964 but increased to 269 by 2002. Community-supported agriculture did not exist in 1964, but by 2002 there were 80 such farmer-consumer partnerships reported in New York (Lyson 2004:97). Remarkable growth in agro-food initiatives are echoed in many other states (Allen et al. 2003).

Because the dynamism of these efforts comes from neither national political parties nor manifesto-driven revolution nor the bureaucratic centers of multinational power, they have yet to receive much attention (Barlett 2001; Bornstein 2004; Castells 2004). Rarely portrayed in the mass media, these thousands of local efforts are the experimental proving ground of a cultural transformation that is an essential part of the shift to a new paradigm of progress, one that uses the framework of sustainability. In *Livable Cities?* Evans argues that these countertrends to globalization rescue us "from the paralyzing conviction that the contemporary global economy has no room for agency in the service of livelihood and sustainability" (2002:23).

These movements show some differences from past progressive political action—and particularly New Left groups—of the 1960s (Boggs 1993). Many such efforts at political renovation began with a romantic attachment to a heroic vanguard, were based on a social rootlessness that encouraged a scattered and elitist style of politics, sought analyses of local events in international formulas, and promoted political action with no base of local support (p. 168). In contrast, the efforts that seek more sustainable solutions today attend to "decentralized forms of work, renewable energy, remodeling of technology," and engaged, participatory, organizational structures (p. 73). Benefiting from the resistance to bureaucracy that emerged in the 1960s movements, many sustainability efforts reject technocratic expertise in favor of an idealistic renewal of civic society (including the embrace of popular wisdom) and seek space for inward reflection as well as direct action (pp. 170–173).

Several of the chapters of this book draw our attention to such reflection and to the individual experience and emotional reaction created by reconnection with the natural world. In others, political action and resistance to current economic and political trends are highlighted. Psychological restoration or the physical impacts of nature on health and healing are also a focus. Combining attention to discourse and behavior, to individual experience and collective action, to societal health and individual well-being, this book seeks a broad engagement with issues of place.

Several important arenas of action unfortunately could not be included in this collection. Watershed alliances and riverkeeper efforts have mushroomed around the country and draw together very diverse groups of people. Another significant shift has occurred among religious denominations and congregations. Not only in the scriptural interpretations of humans in relation to the natural world but also in sustainability efforts, faith communities are an important sector of grassroots action. There is also intriguing research on contact with animals, from keeping pets to bird watching. Gender issues emerge in several chapters but are not a focus of analysis, nor are particularities by region, ethnicity, race, or class. We hope this book will stimulate further study in these and other directions.

About the Book: The Impact of Reconnection with the Natural World

I know some people would say that the other kind of nature—trees, hills, brooks, animals—has a kindly effect. (Williams 1980:67)

Although urban gardeners and prairie restorers know they enjoy their work, few of us appreciate the full extent of the "kindly effect" of nature. Bringing health and well-being into our understanding of the power of place and reconnection to the natural requires a conversation across the boundaries of traditional academic disciplines. Just as cross-disciplinary dialogue was a delight for the Emory University faculty described in chapter 2, the cross-disciplinary dialogue of this book has been deeply enriching for the participants and our understanding of the issues. Some chapters emphasize the local richness of participants' experience, while others emphasize context and the political economy of the grassroots effort. Our different methodological tools are also visible here: historical and archival research, interviews, observations, surveys, and experiments. The authors are diverse as well: some are actively involved in fostering connection to place through organizations, projects, or university programs. Others have focused more on research and outreach via publications and lectures.

Part I, "Arenas of Reconnection," contains eight chapters that survey a range of contexts in which we see urban reconnection with the natural world. Part I documents the broad range of nature reconnection and the extent to which urban areas around the country are affected. The first of the three sections highlights examples of newly found connections to place, followed by a section with accounts of more established programs, and then by two explorations of the ways meanings of nature are reconstructed within the urban setting. In the first section, participants' enthusiasm and delight figure in the accounts by Peggy Barlett and Susan Stuart (chapters 2 and 3) as they describe connections (or reconnections) to place among programs directed at two very different groups. The Piedmont Project at Emory University in Atlanta (chapter 2) aims to foster environmental literacy and sustainability efforts on campus by providing support and new, place-based experiences for faculty. Stuart describes a California project that pioneered the introduction of therapeutic gardens into domestic violence shelters (chapter 3). Project GROW provided healing moments at a very stressful time for women and children in the shelters, as well as for the staff. The psychological restoration found in the gardens was enhanced by the empowerment of learning new skills and discovering new foods. Improved nutrition and the beautification of the surroundings were benefits for center employees and also for residents.

Appreciation for nature's beauty is part of the Piedmont Project as well, although faculty emphasize more the importance to them of learning about nature in a supportive community and the vitality of cross-university exchange. Follow-up interviews revealed that awareness of place, both the wild and the built environments, increased dramatically, and affective bonds with the natural world were strengthened. New systems thinking was also evident, some individuals changed their personal habits, and others expanded their political action in ways that deepened engagement with sustainability issues. Both chapters highlight the interweaving of aesthetic and sensory experience for participants, expanded meanings assigned to both nature and the human community, and the excitement of new knowledge, both scientific and personal. Through the words of participants themselves, these two chapters explore many dimensions of significance in attachment to the natural world.

The next cluster of four chapters, "Elaborating New Forms of Connection," focuses on more established, long-term movements: community gardens, local food systems, and ecological restoration projects. Malve von Hassell (chapter 4) explores some of the political, economic, environmental, and religious components of the vibrant community gardening movement in the Lower East Side ("Loisaida") of New York. These gardens are created and defended by very diverse groups of residents, with distinct agendas, economic interests, and meanings of the spaces they embrace. For the most part, the predominantly Hispanic and lower-income residents of the Lower East Side share common emotional connection to place with many other groups in this book. Von Hassell's description of the annual Rites of Spring pageant shows how community gardens became a "battleground for the emergence of new sets of ideas of living in cities" (2002). Community gardens are a form of "revitalization movement" that partially rejects the market economy while also embracing aspects of environmentalism. The gardeners negotiate individualized expressions of relationship with nature and ecofeminist spirituality with the conflicting political agendas of the grassroots movement. For von Hassell, community gardens seek not a return to an older way of life but are indeed the construction of something new.

Also joining the old with the new are the many efforts around the United States and across the globe to construct more sustainable agricultural systems. Growing awareness of the environmental and human costs of the current agrofood industry has led urban consumers in many areas to seek local alternatives. Susan Andreatta's work with farming communities in North Carolina gives her insight into the emerging connections between urban consumers and the land and people who produce local food. Chapter 5 explores the new connections to place promoted by the international Slow Food Movement, the advent of community-supported agriculture, and farmers markets. In Andreatta's account of Project Green Leaf in North Carolina, we see how economically as well as ethnically diverse populations are drawn into a personal relationship with farmers who provide fresh, local food. A reconnection to the natural world transcends ethnic and racial groups and diverse life circumstances and has the potential to become the basis for a "transformative social force" (Buttel 1992:12).

Elizabeth Barham, David Lind, and Lewis Jett (chapter 6) explore the emergence of regional cuisines and place-based labeling programs as a means by which consumers can assure themselves that the food they buy contributes to the values and policies they support. Defining first the concept of foodshed, the chapter outlines the many types of local food projects emerging across the country and draws attention to the issues of economic equity, democratic values, and food security that accompany environmental concerns in many of these efforts. Barham and colleagues describe a new effort in Missouri to develop unique place-based products and note that local chefs in St. Louis restaurants are important brokers in reshaping consumer tastes. Food captures the imagination and plays a role in an emerging sense of local identity and politics, cutting across the various dimensions (environmental, economic, social) of sustainability. Both chapters draw links between food production, health, and quality diets.

In chapter 7, Robert Ryan and Robert Grese recount the impact of volunteering in urban restoration projects. Prairies, forests, and parks have been the focus of restoration efforts in many areas, and the chapter shows that volunteers value highly the opportunity to help nature and to feel useful. Volunteers' experiences not only expand their knowledge of native species and deepen their emotional connections to sites where they work, but also lead to political efforts to defend and preserve natural spaces around the city. Echoing the Atlanta study in chapter 2, Ryan and Grese call attention to the cognitive, affective, and practice aspects of attachment to place. In addition, this chapter looks at some of the ways that different cultural expectations and preferences about nature create challenges for restoration work and notes some of the solutions, such as landscaped "cues to care." In this chapter, as in several others, small celebrations or rituals are an interesting component of projects that build meaning in place.

The two chapters in the following cluster, "Reclaiming Meanings," show how cultural and political contexts influence the interpretation of relations with the natural world. In Barbara Lynch and Rima Brusi's account of Latino gardens in New York (chapter 8), historical meanings of Puerto Rican identity and island politics are recreated and adapted in the small houses and patios (*casitas*) built on nearby vacant lots. The Latino gardens mediate between the built and the unbuilt environments. Neither solely of the physical world nor of the social, neither clearly indoors nor out, they emphasize that what is considered natural or artificial can be contested. The casita landscape with its small building and yard offers its own unique contribution to our understandings of relations with nature in parks and wild spaces. Latino gardens also draw our attention to conflicting meanings and renegotiations of community; not all neighbors appreciate the illegal casitas or the social life of the gardens around them.

Chapter 9 by Robert Rotenberg provides a contrasting perspective on meaning in nature. While Puerto Ricans in New York seek to create a safe space in their gardens, Rotenberg's discussion of the sensibility of the sublime draws our attention to relatively unsafe dimensions of the experience of nature. His research in Vienna highlights for him the ways in which the U.S. discourse about nature in the city emphasizes control, sanitation, and governmentality. Although experiences of the sublime—the encounter with forces beyond oneself that engender awe or terror—are available in urban encounters with wild animals or extreme weather, Rotenberg argues there is a poorly developed cultural framework within which to value these emotions. In the light of the fact that the sublime was once considered as important to human experience as the encounter with beauty, a less muted experience of the sublime may allow deeper and more vibrant interactions with nature in the city.

In part II, four chapters help us understand the implications for human health and functioning of connections to the natural world. The significance of the many arenas of cultural engagement with ecological processes explored in part I is sharpened by the findings of medical and psychological research that an estrangement from the animate earth has consequences for individual physical health, mental well-being, and social life. Contact with "nearby nature" (parks, gardens, backyards, street trees) has positive effects on healing and psychological functioning. William Sullivan and his colleagues have conducted natural experiments of Chicago inner-city dwellers living without contact with trees, shrubs, or grass and compared their lives to those whose homes look out on nearby nature. Reported in chapter 10, these studies show that nature affects personal safety, sense of community, levels of household conflict, and crime. Natural settings have positive consequences for our mental resources as we face the stresses of urban life. Sullivan explores the links between these current findings and our evolutionary heritage.

Howard Frumkin (chapter 11) extends our understanding of how health and illness are affected by features of place, from contact with the natural world to the way entire metropolitan areas are designed and built. Whether in quicker surgical recovery in hospitals, easier pain control in clinical settings, or fewer sick calls among prisoners whose cells look out on farmland and trees, the evidence for the value of nature contact is compelling. Similarly, buildings, parks, and cities can all be designed to enhance health—or in ways that overlook it. Both Frumkin's and Sullivan's work suggest that, given human evolutionary history, an urban environment devoid of connections to the natural world is detrimental to mental and physical functioning. Frumkin also draws attention to methodological issues, raising the question, "How do we know what makes a good place?" His chapter points the way to future research on nature contact, buildings, public places, and urban form.

In chapter 12, Rachel Kaplan and Stephen Kaplan review a range of studies in psychology and landscape architecture and propose a model of the kinds of nature contact that support our functioning as reasonable people. Their model explains why connections to the natural world are restorative and help individuals become clear-headed, resilient, and cooperative. Reviewing a broad spectrum of benefits and diverse settings, Kaplan and Kaplan show how the environment can support basic human needs. Chapter 12 echoes the perspectives of place attachment in other chapters but develops a more complex model, focused on cognitive functioning and information processing. In highlighting the importance of opportunities for meaningful action in relationship to nature, as a key component of the reasonable person model, their work illuminates yet another dimension of satisfaction likely to be experienced in many of the examples of action throughout the book.

The final chapter, by Jules Pretty and Peggy Barlett, draws together the implications of the book for our understandings of nature and health in the urban environment. Calling for vigorous engagement with policy and urban planning, the chapter develops an understanding of the health imperatives in these accounts of urban reconnections with the natural world.

Conclusion

In our efforts to understand the varied faces of urban reconnections to nature, we have drawn together the voices and experiences of many different individuals and groups, from California to New York, from North Carolina to Missouri. Taken together, the accounts collected here point to a constructive and dynamic middle ground between individualism and community, between urban and rural life, between private plots (and private scholarship) and public space (and public action), between production and consumption, and between geographical mobility and commitment to place. By joining research on individual health and human functioning to emerging social movements and grassroots sustainability efforts, we highlight some joyful and positive dimensions of our responses to current cultural dilemmas, dimensions that are often overshadowed by the attention to environmental degradation and crisis.

Urban gardeners, like farmers market shoppers, Slow Food convivia members, park volunteers, and many academics, embrace a creative spirit and an artistic sensibility together with the pragmatic, dirty process of growing food, making compost, planting trees, and challenging received academic wisdom. We find ourselves in communities of vision that identify with others across the country, and even globally. Community garden coalitions, organic market advocates, and greenspace preservationists courageously face the overwhelming power of global and regional forces, enacting visions of a different future. The contradictions and potential complementarities of spontaneity and planned, strategic action, of leadership and grassroots involvement, of political compromise and idealistic commitments, all echo through the chapters in this book. By grounding ourselves in *place*, we have been privileged to explore and inspired to see the many opportunities for the re-shaping of human communities in deeper connection with the natural world.

Acknowledgments

This Introduction benefits from the generous sharing of ideas that have occurred in several fora over the past two years; I am particularly grateful to the other authors in the book for their helpful suggestions. I thank Bradd Shore, Hudita Mustafa, Howard Frumkin, Laurie Patton, Bobbi Patterson, Steve Walton, Sharon Parks, and David Abram for their help in developing the Emory symposium that stimulated the ideas in this book. The Emory University Departments of Anthropology and Religion, the Hightower Fund, the Gustafson Seminar, and the Academic Exchange Series all played a role in encouraging this work. I thank Robert Rotenberg, Malve von Hassell, Rachel Kaplan, Robert Gottlieb, Clay Morgan, Allison Adams, Jeff Samotny, Sandra Minkkinen, and Beverly H. Miller; all have contributed with their generous support, good ideas, and editorial assistance. Special thanks are due to Sharon Parks and Larry Daloz of the Whidbey Institute for introducing me to the power of place and sparking the interests that led to this volume.

Notes

1. Some important scholarly works on issues of place that have for the most part overlooked connection with the biological web of life are Agnew and Duncan (1989), Auge (1995), DeCerteau (1984), Friedland and Boden (1994), Gieryn (2000), Gupta and Ferguson (1997), Tilley (1994), Tuan (1977), and Whatmore (2002).

References

Abram, David. 1996. *The Spell of the Sensuous*. New York: Vintage.

Adams, W. M. 2001. *Green Development: Environment and Sustainability in the Third World*. 2nd ed. New York: Routledge.

Agnew, John A., and James S. Duncan, eds. 1989. *The Power of Place: Bringing Together Geographical and Sociological Imaginations*. Winchester, Mass.: Unwin Hyman.

Allen, Patricia, Margaret FitzSimmons, Michael Goodman, and Keith Warner. 2003. Shifting Plates in the Agrifood Landscape: The Tectonics of Alternative Food Initiatives in California. *Journal of Rural Studies* 19(1):61–75.

Altman, Irwin, and Setha M. Low. 1992. *Place Attachment*. New York: Plenum.

Andreatta, Susan. 2000. Marketing Strategies and Challenges of Small-Scale Organic Producers in Central North Carolina. *Culture and Agriculture* 22(3):40–50.

Apffel-Marglin, Frederique, and Pramod Parajuli. 1998. Geographies of Difference and the Resilience of Ecological Ethnicities: "Place" and the Global Motion of Capital. *Development* 41(2):14–21.

Auge, Marc. 1995. *Non-Places: Introduction to an Anthropology of Supermodernity*. New York: Verso.

Barham, Elizabeth. 2002. Towards a Theory of Values-Based Labeling. *Agriculture and Human Values* 19:349–360.

Barham, Elizabeth. 2003. Translating Terroir: The Global Challenge of French AOC Labelling. *Journal of Rural Studies* 19:127–138.

Barlett, Peggy F. 2001. Global/Local Paradox: Emerging Visions of Sustainability Among Grassroots Groups. International Conference on the Effects of and Responses to Globalization. Atlanta: Halle Institute, Emory University. Available at: http://www.emory.edu/OIA/Halle/publications.html.

Barlett, Peggy F. 2002. The Emory University Walking Tour. *International Journal of Sustainability in Higher Education* 3(2):105–112.

Barlett, Peggy F., and Geoffrey W. Chase. 2004. *Sustainability on Campus: Stories and Strategies for Change*. Cambridge, Mass.: MIT Press.

Basso, Keith H. 1996. *Wisdom Sits in Places: Landscape and Language among the Western Apache*. Albuquerque: University of New Mexico Press.

Beatley, Timothy, and Kristy Manning. 1997. *Ecology of Place: Planning for Environment, Economy, and Community*. Washington, D.C.: Island Press.

Berry, Thomas. 1988. *The Dream of the Earth*. San Francisco: Sierra Club Books.

Berry, Wendell. 1987. *Home Economics*. San Francisco: North Point Press.

Boggs, Carl. 1993. *Intellectuals and the Crisis of Modernity*. Albany: SUNY Press.

Bornstein, David. 2004. *How to Change the World: Social Entrepreneurs and the Power of New Ideas.* New York: Oxford University Press.

Braun, Bruce, and Noel Castree, eds. 1998. *Remaking Reality: Nature at the Millennium.* New York: Routledge.

Brown, Lester R. 2001. *Eco-Economy: Building an Economy for the Earth.* New York: Norton.

Buttel, Frederick H. 1992. Environmentalization: Origin, Processes, and Implications for Rural Social Change. *Rural Sociology* 57(1):1–27.

Castells, Manuel. 1997. *The Rise of the Network Society.* Malden, Mass.: Blackwell.

Castells, Manuel. 2004. *The Power of Identity.* 2nd ed. Malden, Mass.: Blackwell.

DeCerteau, Michel. 1984. *The Practice of Everyday Life.* Berkeley: University of California Press.

DeLind, Laura, and Anne E. Ferguson. 1999. Is This a Women's Movement? The Relationship of Gender to Community-Supported Agriculture in Michigan. *Human Organization* 58(2):190–200.

DeLind, Laura, and Terry Link. 2004. Place as the Nexus of a Sustainable Future: A Course for All of Us. In *Sustainability on Campus: Stories and Strategies for Change.* Peggy F. Barlett and Geoffrey W. Chase, eds. Pp. 121–138. Cambridge, Mass.: MIT Press.

Devall, Bill, and George Sessions. 1985. *Deep Ecology: Living as If Nature Mattered.* Salt Lake City: Peregrine Smith Books.

Dirlik, Arif. 1998. Globalism and the Politics of Place. *Development* 41(2):7–13.

Dryzek, John S. 1997. *The Politics of the Earth: Environmental Discourses.* New York: Oxford University Press.

Evans, Peter, ed. 2002. *Livable Cities? Urban Struggles for Livelihood and Sustainability.* Berkeley: University of California Press.

Fischer, Frank, and Maarten A. Hajer, eds. 1995. *Living with Nature: Environmental Politics as Cultural Discourse.* New York: Oxford University Press.

FitzSimmons, Margaret I. 1989. The Matter of Nature. *Antipode* 21(2):106–120.

FitzSimmons, Margaret, and David Goodman. 1998. Incorporating Nature: Environmental Narratives and the Reproduction of Food. In *Remaking Reality: Nature at the Millennium.* Bruce Braun and Noel Castree, eds. Pp. 194–220. New York: Routledge.

Freudenburg, William R., Scott Frickel, and Robert Gramling. 1995. Beyond the Nature/Society Divide: Learning to Think about a Mountain. *Sociological Forum* 10(3):361–393.

Friedland, Roger, and Dierdre Boden. 1994. *NowHere: Space, Time, and Modernity.* Berkeley: University of California Press.

Gieryn, Thomas F. 2000. A Space for Place in Sociology. *Annual Review of Sociology* 26:463–496.

Giddens, Anthony. 1990. *The Consequences of Modernity*. Stanford, Calif.: Stanford University Press.

Gottlieb, Robert. 2001. *Environmentalism Unbound: Exploring New Pathways for Change*. Cambridge, Mass.: MIT Press.

Gray, John. 1999. Open Spaces and Dwelling Places: Being at Home on Hill Farms in the Scottish Borders. *American Ethnologist* 26(2):440–460.

Gupta, Akhil, and James Ferguson. 1997. Culture, Power and Place: Ethnography at the End of an Era. In *Culture, Power, and Place*. Akhil Gupta and James Ferguson, eds. Pp. 1–32. Durham, N.C.: Duke University Press.

Harris, Jonathan M., and Neva R. Goodwin. 2001. Introduction. In *A Survey of Sustainable Development: Social and Economic Dimensions*. Jonathan M. Harris, Timothy A. Wise, Kevin P. Gallagher, and Neva R. Goodwyn, eds. Pp. xxvii–xxxv. Washington, D.C.: Island Press.

Harvey, David. 1989a. *The Condition of Postmodernity: An Enquiry into the Origins of Cultural Change*. New York: Blackwell.

Harvey, David. 1989b. *The Urban Experience*. Baltimore, Md.: Johns Hopkins University Press.

Harvey, David. 2000. *Spaces of Hope*. Berkeley: University of California Press.

Hawken, Paul. 1993. *The Ecology of Commerce: A Declaration of Sustainability*. New York: Harper.

Hawken, Paul, Amory Lovins, and L. Hunter Lovins. 1999. *Natural Capitalism: Creating the Next Industrial Revolution*. Boston: Little, Brown.

Holmberg, Johan, ed. 1992. *Making Development Sustainable: Redefining Institutions, Policy, and Economics*. Washington, D.C.: Island Press.

Johnson, Allen W., and Timothy Earle. 2000. *The Evolution of Human Societies: From Foraging Group to Agrarian State*. 2nd ed. Stanford, Calif.: Stanford University Press.

Kaplan, Rachel. 1984. Impact of Urban Nature: A Theoretical Analysis. *Urban Ecology* 8:189–197.

Kaplan, Rachel, and Stephen Kaplan. 1989. *The Experience of Nature: A Psychological Perspective*. Cambridge: Cambridge University Press.

Kaplan, Stephen. 1995. The Restorative Benefits of Nature: Toward an Integrative Framework. *Journal of Environmental Psychology* 15(3):169–182.

Katz, Cindi. 1998. Whose Nature, Whose Culture? Private Productions of Space and the "Preservation" of Nature. In *Remaking Reality: Nature at the Millennium*. Bruce Braun and Noel Castree, eds. Pp. 46–63. New York: Routledge.

Keil, Roger, and John Graham. 1998. Reasserting Nature: Constructing Urban Environments after Fordism. In *Remaking Reality: Nature at the Millennium*. Bruce Braun and Noel Castree, eds. Pp. 100–125. New York: Routledge.

Kusno, Abidin. 2001. Violence of Categories: Urban Design and the Making of Indonesian Modernity. In *City and Nation: Rethinking Place and Identity*. Michael Peter Smith and Thomas Bender, eds. Pp. 15–50. New Brunswick, N.J.: Transaction Publishers.

Lax, Eric. 1991. *Woody Allen: A Biography*. New York: DaCapo Press.

Lewis, Charles A. 1996. *Green Nature/Human Nature: The Meaning of Plants in Our Lives*. Urbana: University of Illinois Press.

Light, Andrew, and Eric Higgs. 1997. The Politics of Corporate Ecological Restorations: Comparing Global and Local North American Contexts. In *Articulating the Global and the Local*. Ann Cvetkovich and Douglas Kellner, eds. Pp. 102–125. Boulder, Colo.: Westview.

Lippard, Lucy. 1997. *The Lure of the Local*. New York: New Press.

Low, Setha M. 1996. The Anthropology of Cities. In *Annual Review of Anthropology*. Palo Alto, Calif.: Annual Reviews.

Low, Setha M., and Irwin Altman. 1992. Place Attachment: A Conceptual Inquiry. In *Place Attachment*. Irwin Altman and Setha M. Low, eds. Pp. 1–12. New York: Plenum.

Low, Setha M., and Denise Lawrence-Zúñiga. 2003. *The Anthropology of Space and Place: Locating Culture*. New York: Blackwell.

Lyson, Thomas A. 2004. *Civic Agriculture*. Medford, Mass.: Tufts University Press.

Macy, Joanna, and Molly Young Brown. 1998. *Coming Back to Life: Practices to Reconnect Our Lives, Our World*. Gabriola Island, B.C., Canada: New Society Publishers.

Massey, Doreen. 1994. *Space, Place, and Gender*. Minneapolis: University of Minnesota Press.

McGinnis, Michael V. 1999. *Bioregionalism*. New York: Routledge.

Miles, I., William C. Sullivan, and Frances E. Kuo. 1998. Ecological Restoration Volunteers: The Benefits of Participation. *Urban Ecosystems* 2:27–41.

Milton, Kay. 1996. *Environmentalism and Cultural Theory: Exploring the Role of Anthropology in Environmental Discourse*. New York: Routledge.

Milton, Kay. 2002. *Loving Nature: Toward an Ecology of Emotions*. New York: Routledge.

Moran, Emilio, ed. 1990. *The Ecosystem Approach in Anthropology: From Concept to Practice*. Ann Arbor: University of Michigan Press.

Nash, Roderick. 2001 [1967]. *Wilderness and the American Mind*. 4th ed. New Haven, Conn.: Yale University Press.

Netting, Robert McC. 1993. *Smallholders, Householders: Farm Families and the Ecology of Intensive, Sustainable Agriculture*. Stanford, Calif.: Stanford University Press.

Nicholsen, Shierry Weber. 2002. *The Love of Nature and the End of the World: Unspoken Dimensions of Environmental Concern*. Cambridge, Mass.: MIT Press.

Norgaard, Richard B. 1994. *Development Betrayed: The End of Progress and a Coevolutionary Revisioning of the Future*. New York: Routledge.

Orr, David W. 1994. *Earth in Mind: On Education, Environment, and the Human Prospect*. Washington, D.C.: Island Press.

Platt, Rutherford H., Rowan A. Rowntree, and Pamela C. Muick. 1994. *The Ecological City: Preserving and Restoring Urban Biodiversity*. Amherst: University of Massachusetts Press.

Pretty, Jules. 2002. *Agri-Culture: Reconnecting People, Land and Nature*. London: Earthscan.

Rappaport, Roy A. 1994. Disorders of Our Own: A Conclusion. In *Diagnosing America*. Shepard Forman, ed. Pp. 235–311. Ann Arbor: University of Michigan Press.

Rappaport, Roy A. 1971. Ritual, Sanctity, and Cybernetics. *American Anthropologist* 73(1):59–76.

Redclift, Michael. 1987. *Sustainable Development: Exploring the Contradictions*. New York: Routledge.

Riley, Robert B. 1992. Attachment to the Ordinary Landscape. In *Place Attachment*. Irwin Altman and Setha M. Low, eds. Pp. 13–35. New York: Plenum.

Rotenberg, Robert. 1993. On the Salubrity of Sites. In *The Cultural Meaning of Urban Space*. Robert Rotenberg and Gary McDonough, eds. Pp. 17–29. Westport, Conn.: Bergin and Garvey.

Rotenberg, Robert, and Gary McDonough, eds. 1993. *The Cultural Meaning of Urban Space*. Westport, Conn.: Bergin and Garvey.

Shuman, Michael. 1998. *Going Local: Creating Self-Reliant Communities in a Global Age*. New York: Free Press.

Smith, Jackie, and Hank Johnston. 2002. *Globalization and Resistance: Transnational Dimensions of Social Movements*. New York: Rowman and Littlefield.

Smith, Michael Peter, and Thomas Bender. 2001. *City and Nation: Rethinking Place and Identity*. New Brunswick, N.J.: Transaction Publishers.

Snyder, Gary. 1990. *The Practice of the Wild*. New York: Farrar, Straus, and Giroux.

Spirn, Anne Whiston. 1984. *The Granite Garden: Urban Nature and Human Design*. New York: Basic Books.

Sutter, Paul S. 2002. *Driven Wild: How the Fight against Automobiles Launched the Modern Wilderness Movement*. Seattle: University of Washington Press.

Thayer, Robert L., Jr. 2003. *LifePlace: Bioregional Thought and Practice*. Berkeley: University of California Press.

Thomas, Keith. 1983. *Man and the Natural World: Changing Attitudes in England, 1500–1800.* New York: Oxford University Press.

Thomashow, Mitchell. 1995. *Ecological Identity.* Cambridge, Mass.: MIT Press.

Thomashow, Mitchell. 2002. *Bringing the Biosphere Home.* Cambridge, Mass.: MIT Press.

Tilley, Christopher. 1994. *A Phenomenology of Landscape: Places, Paths, and Monuments.* Providence, R.I.: Berg.

Torgerson, Douglas. 1995. Images of Place in Green Politics: The Cultural Mirror of Indigenous Traditions. In *Living with Nature.* Frank Fischer and Maarten A. Hajer, eds. Pp. 186–203. New York: Oxford University Press.

Tuan, Yi-Fu. 1977. *Space and Place: The Perspective of Experience.* Minneapolis: University of Minnesota Press.

Von Hassell, Malve. 2002. *Struggle for Eden: Community Gardens in New York City.* Westport, Conn.: Bergin and Garvey.

Whatmore, Sarah. 2002. *Hybrid Geographies: Natures, Cultures, Spaces.* Thousand Oaks, Calif.: Sage.

Williams, Raymond. 1980. Ideas of Nature. In *Problems in Materialism and Culture: Selected Essays.* Pp. 67–85. London: Verso.

Wilson, E. O. 1998. *Consilience: The Unity of Knowledge.* New York: Vintage.

Zencey, Eric. 1996. The Rootless Professors. In *Rooted in the Land: Essays on Community and Place.* William Vitek and Wes Jackson, eds. Pp. 15–19. New Haven, Conn.: Yale University Press.

I

Arenas of Reconnection

Discovering Relationships with the Natural World

2

Reconnecting with Place: Faculty and the Piedmont Project at Emory University

Peggy F. Barlett

An end-of-semester curriculum development project for faculty in urban Emory University is perhaps an unlikely context for a deepening connection with place. Since 2001, the Piedmont Project has drawn together cohorts of roughly 20 faculty from diverse fields across the university to learn about environmental issues and sustainability. Development of new courses or course materials begins with a two-day introductory workshop, including lectures on ecology, public health, environmental justice, and an overview of campus environmental efforts. Midday woods walks provide some recreation and an opportunity for experiential learning. The lectures, discussions, outdoor time, and workshop materials all highlight connections between environmental dimensions of Atlanta, the campus, and broader national and international issues of sustainability.

In formal evaluations immediately after the workshop, participants in the first three cohorts gave the Piedmont Project a level of approval not common among Emory faculty:

"I learned a ton in there."

"A wonderful group of colleagues."

"It was an intellectual feast."

"[The] discussion . . . was inspiring, informative, and joyful."

"Everything we did was important to me."

"This was the best faculty development activity I've participated in at Emory."

Why was the Piedmont Project so satisfying? Interviews with faculty a year after their participation revealed that one of the most valuable components of the workshop was an enhanced sense of place. Place clearly has two overlapping dimensions for Piedmont Project faculty; it refers to both the natural world of woods, streams, and less disturbed ecosystems and to the built environment of Atlanta and the campus. Growing attachment to these dimensions of place and new understandings of how urban place is intertwined with biological and ecological processes seem to be central to the impact of the project and to go beyond new course development. The workshop is a time when awareness is seized, "when individuals step back from the flow of everyday experience and attend self-consciously to place" (Basso 1996:106).

Such enthusiasm for place contrasts with the dominant ethic of higher education that values a cosmopolitan placelessness (Zencey 1996). Professors "are expected to owe no allegiance to geographical territory . . . [they are] supposed to belong to the boundless world of books and ideas and to eternal truths, not the infinitely particular world of watershed, growing seasons, and ecological niches" (p. 15). Such a commitment to placelessness responds to the mobility of academic positions and the nomadic life that many experience. It also reflects the deep familiarity that some faculty have with cities and places far from where they teach, an expertise that may be part of why they were hired in the first place. David Orr, however, sees such emphases as "indoor thinking, careerism" (1994:28) and a barrier to greater environmental awareness in higher education. Such values are transmitted to students, who are commonly educated "to be mobile, rootless, and autistic toward their places" (Orr 2004). Thus, the enthusiasm for the Piedmont Project reflects a shift away from conventional academic reward systems. Indeed, participation itself reflects a willingness to resist the university politics that tend to devalue teaching over research and to emphasize specialization and productivity. As we will see below in their own words, faculty find intellectual and personal nourishment from the opportunity to engage with environmental issues, and the diminishment of their own "autism" seems to provide deep satisfaction.

The Piedmont Project participants reported ways that their experience built, renewed, or deepened their relations with the natural world. Low and Altman separate three dimensions of place attachment: the cognitive (knowledge, thought), the affective (emotion, feelings), and practice (action, behavior) (1992:4–5). All three dimensions of place attachment emerge in the accounts of Piedmont Project participants, often from a particular emphasis on one or another dimension that was strengthened or engaged by the experience. Low and Altman's framework is helpful to organize what participants say about the impact of the project, though I do not intend to imply that all participants organize their experience in this way.

The interviews also revealed that context is important. Emory faculty emphasize that their engagement with the Piedmont Project, a combination of intellectual and embodied learning, is enhanced when it occurs within a safe and supportive group.[1] Other aspects reported to build an appreciation for place and expand the learning process are the opportunity to learn the names of species, face-to-face narratives, and connections with ethics and personal values.

Each of these aspects of the process of building awareness of place emphasizes interconnection and relationship and echoes other research on connections to the natural world. The importance of a supportive group context has been noted in many environmental literacy efforts (Barlett and Chase 2004; Bowers 1999; Thomashow 2002). Barry Lopez also articulates the importance of naming as a means of teaching about relationships, both between listeners and storytellers and between humans and the surrounding more-than-human world (1988). David Abram's analysis of human presence in narrative emphasizes that the breath and spirit of the storyteller enhance listeners' awareness of the aliveness of the natural world (1996). And many sustainability efforts on campuses around the country report that the reintegration of ethics and personal values into professional life is deeply rewarding to faculty and staff (Aronowitz 2001; Barlett and Chase 2004; Sabin 2002). Though there are undoubtedly other aspects of the Piedmont Project that contribute to its impact on participants, these four dimensions of the workshop experience—the power of the group, the naming of species, the use of narrative, and the integration of work and values—have emerged as enhancing the cognitive, affective, and practice dimensions of place attachment. Such insights may help explain some of the power in similar experiences of growing reconnection with the natural world around the country.

Part of building a stronger relationship with the natural world is awareness of the interrelationship of humans, the earth's biological systems, and the impacts of urban life. As Piedmont Project participants try to make sense of how their disciplinary competencies intersect with sustainability challenges, they develop an enhanced awareness on many levels of ecological processes in the urban landscape, and larger global and regional implications as well. Project planners hoped such broadened systems thinking would emerge in many different kinds of academic course work, but the Piedmont experience suggests that it has in some cases carried over into other areas of personal and professional life as well. This chapter explores the practice dimension of a growing attachment to place, as well as the many ways the project supports connections to place through an intertwining of the cognitive and affective domains.

The Piedmont Project Approach to Environmental Literacy

The immediate goal of the Piedmont Project is to fulfill the university's commitment to environmental literacy (Mumford 2001) by bringing environmental issues into the formal curriculum. The format is based on the multiyear success of the Ponderosa Project at Northern Arizona University (Chase and Rowland 2004) and provides incentives and a support network for 18 to 20 faculty a year to explore environmental issues in their own fields.[2] Each participant is paid a small stipend and commits to developing a new course or a new module for an existing course. Participants commit to attending the two-day opening workshop, spending approximately three weeks over the summer in course development, and sharing their experiences in a follow-up lunch and field trip in August and a dinner the following March.

Influenced by bioregional perspectives, the workshop's planners draw resource people from both inside and outside the university to introduce environmental issues through a focus on the local context of Atlanta. Faculty hear an ecological lecture about the Piedmont bioregion and its native trees and plants. They learn about on-campus efforts to construct more environmentally sound buildings and to preserve remaining stands of hardwood forest. Discussions cover concerns about campus actions that affect local watershed protection, erosion, and water pollution. Another lecture links patterns of solid waste disposal and sewer overflows to political processes, neighborhoods, and Atlanta's racial history. A lecture on the health consequences of urban sprawl also emphasizes that the form of the built environment can harm health as well as be a benefit (see chapter 11; Fitzpatrick and LaGory 2000:48).

The noon woods walk on the first day highlights an old-growth forest with huge beech trees and rare wildflowers, hidden behind a dense scrub of invasive privet. The ecologist leading the walk is one of the faculty members who successfully lobbied to shift the construction of the building in which the workshop is held in order to protect the forest. The second day's walk takes place across the street, in a small forest preserve along a major creek, and teaches about stream degradation in urban areas and the challenges of forest restoration.

This chapter presents information gathered in open-ended interviews with all 37 Piedmont Project participants from the first two years. Lasting from a half-hour to two hours, the interviews were scheduled roughly one year after the summer experience to discover what participants remembered from the workshop, what still resonated for them, and if the experience had affected any aspects of their lives in addition to their courses. Other data in this chapter are taken from verbal feedback and an e-mail survey immediately after each annual workshop and from an e-mail survey of all three cohorts carried out in the fall of 2003. In the second year, five administrators took part, and instead of a course change, their projects focused on campus operations such as paper use, energy consumption, or building renovation. Their responses are included in the analysis here where appropriate.

The Piedmont Project has been very successful in stimulating curricular change. Participants came from the full range of liberal arts fields, from English, history, philosophy, theater, art, and music to sociology, anthropology, chemistry, biology, and environmental studies. Professors from five language departments as well as physical education were involved. Professional school faculty from law, business, theology, and public health made up a fifth of the total. A number of faculty found that once they immersed themselves in the particular issues they wished to learn, many more opportunities emerged to incorporate environmental issues into their teaching. Responses from 51 Piedmont Project faculty participants from the three years revealed that 59 percent had changed two or three courses, not just the one planned, for a total of 69 undergraduate and 22 graduate courses. A surprising number changed how they taught as well. Three-fourths responded that they used more experiential teaching methods as a result of the Piedmont Project, adding field trips, outdoor exercises, linkage to current events, and new writing assignments. Their own research and writing were affected. Of the faculty participants, 53 percent reported publishing an article or making a professional presentation as a result of their engagement with environmental issues. Said one, "I'm surprised I'm writing so much about place. I thought it would be teaching [that would be altered], but writing . . ."

About half the Piedmont Project participants in the first year were drawn from faculty with prior interests or specializations in environmental issues. Later years drew more newcomers. But knowledge depth in a particular environmental field did not lessen the environmental learning from the program; most faculty felt they learned a great deal, often in areas they had not thought about before. Only one or two participants in each cohort expressed dissatisfaction, usually from the program's failure to provide curricular resources in their specific areas. Faculty came from all academic ranks, from lecturers to endowed chair professors, and spanned the full age range. One-third were women.

Building Community

New bonds of community and connection with others across university boundaries are the most common aspects of the project that stand out a year later for participants:

"The best part was meeting other faculty. It builds the collegial environment."

"The intense, sustained interaction with colleagues from different departments, ranks, and roles in the university. People coming together for a range of reasons, to discuss sustainability. I really took pleasure in the sustained interaction."

Figure 2.1
Small group discussions during the Piedmont Project (photo by Peggy Barlett).

"The excitement of having all those people in all those disciplines interested in environmental issues, that was a *huge* thing for me."

It is significant that words like *enjoyment, pleasure, satisfaction,* and *excitement* were commonly used in response to the question, "When you think back on the two-day Piedmont workshop, what stands out for you?" Clearly, the workshop was a pedagogical exercise beyond most faculty members' expectations and constructed "centers of human significance and emotional attachment" (Tilley 1994:15).

For some participants, there was a sense of surprise to find so many knowledgeable, committed people across the university who shared an interest in environmental issues. It reduced a sense of anomie and isolation and reassured some that their concerns were shared. This sentiment was expressed by newcomers and long-time faculty alike. The interdisciplinarity of the dialogue enhanced participants' grasp of the complexity of environmental and sustainability issues and the importance of collaborative intellectual engagement in response. A few emphasized how their academic fields were normally cut off from the rest of the campus: "I'm a little isolated, so that was a nice feature for me."

"Specifically, we became a functioning subunit of the whole intellectual community. We had all the principles of sustainability on the table in front of us all. Now, how do we bring our *expertise* to bear?"

The relatively egalitarian, democratic activities of the workshop fostered a climate of trust, a sense of safety. The workshop's leaders promoted a pattern of respectful engagement through alternating large-group discussions and small-group breakout sessions. The workshop combined abstract environmental issues with concrete pedagogical challenges and fostered a willingness to think together without competitive hierarchy (Barlett and Eisen 2002).

"One of the best benefits I've seen in Piedmont Project is that it provides a forum for people to talk, learn, without needing to be 'the expert.' It's a place to actually be safely curious."

Several participants reported gaining new hope from the experience. The interactions generated optimism that "we can create something new together." This statement reflects the way the experience of community is connected to potentialities of action, as well as to affective attachment.

Simply gaining new knowledge about environmental issues was important to many. The cognitive component of the workshop supported their intellectual curiosity and was satisfying because it was new, enriching. "I never took ecology," said a natural scientist. "And to sit down and hear from experts was a wonderful thing . . . the knowledge of ecosystems and the interplay of us and the environment." However, the way in which community was also emphasized by nearly all the participants suggests that the context of a supportive group enhances the cognitive learning of environmental issues and the meaningfulness of that experience.

Place: In the Woods

Piedmont Project faculty commented on their new awareness of the built environment of Emory and Atlanta, but foremost in their accounts was the power of the lunchtime woods experiences.

"But the most fun was the experiential thing. . . . It was something new. And being in a city with woods; that's really unusual. The experience was operating on many levels."

"It was eye-opening to me."

"Really educational."

"Being outside together . . . it was great. I'd love to see tons more."

"*This* nature was what deepened. That's why I loved the walk—drinking in the new environment *here*."

How faculty learned was also important. The education in the woods walks was embodied, sensory, and rich. It combined fun, outdoor exercise, and hands-on learning in a way that evoked past childhood time in nature. "Getting out in nature and putting names with the things, learning special things about what we saw—it was *wonderful*! It revived an interest from my childhood."

Figure 2.2
Field experience to a nearby park (photo by Anne L. Hall).

For several faculty, the woods walks awakened a dormant engagement with the natural world that had been very important in early years. Several were reminded that they had once thought of being ecologists or botanists, and one rediscovered the love of the outdoors felt in scouting. Adult life, family obligations, and academic pressures had driven these experiences underground, and the embodied learning of the woods walks brought back important memories, a common dimension of attachment to place (Low and Lawrence-Zúñiga 2003:20).

The time in the woods slowed the hectic academic pace. The celebration of the remaining stands of forest was playful and also somewhat reverent. For a few, the time in nature joined the academic life with spiritual commitments. One participant commented that finding peace in nature was a lifelong pattern, but it had never been before connected to professional activities with colleagues. Being able to share religious language for experiences in nature with a theology professor was gratifying, said one scientist. Another said, "Looking at the trees—and just slowing down, taking our time—it was invaluable to me. It changed my perspective." Those who reported the woods walks to have had a profound impact were more likely to adopt more experiential teaching methods in their classes.

Many faculty commented specifically on the value to them of learning to name and identify local trees and rare wildflowers.

"The nature walks—I remember really enjoying that. Telling me what the trees here are called. Different types of forest—trees, rare plants—it was very entertaining."

"I knew nothing about the South when I came here. . . . This was one of the best things for me: learning about the trees."

"The most fun, memorable part was going on the hike. Learning to identify native plants. . . . It really *did* change the way I think. Down toward the Village [the campus-edge shopping district], I notice now the row of magnolias, and I think, 'There's a planted row. And we have our own species of magnolia—*grandiflora*—that we saw in Hahn Woods.'"

Barry Lopez suggests that naming both evokes and strengthens relationships. Showing the connection of one thing to the whole "holds the human imagination" (Lopez 1988:149). To explain the power of spending time in nature with children, Lopez says, "An extrapolation from a single fragment of the whole is the most invigorating experience I can share with them. I think children know that nearly anyone can learn the names of things; the impression made on them at this level is fleeting. What takes a lifetime to learn, they comprehend, is the existence and substance of myriad relationships: it is these relationships, not the things themselves, that ultimately hold the human imagination" (1988:149). Echoed a language professor: "The lectures and explanations, and I guess I should say the *names*, definitely showed me I should learn factual things. It becomes more concrete and maybe means more to me."

These comments support the work of scholars who have highlighted the restorative experience of time in nature (see chapter 13; R. Kaplan 1984; S. Kaplan 1995; Kaplan and Kaplan 1989; Talbot and Kaplan 1986). As Jacobson argues, building a relationship with nature "conjures up the sacred eternal" (Jacobson 2002:194). Time in the natural world also counteracts the speed-up and "compression" of a globalized society (Robertson 1992, cited in Milton 1996:164–166), thereby providing a kind of time out, a pause, in the rhythm of the university life. The restorative quality of the woods walks brought a vitality to the whole workshop, as well as building attachment to place. Faculty enjoyed the new knowledge learned, enhanced especially by the opportunity to learn new names, leading to a new awareness of teaching method.

"[It was] really educational. I *could* have learned that, I suppose, from reading but I *wouldn't*. I may not act on it, but I realized I *should* be more concrete in my courses."

Stories and Breath

In a symposium at Emory University in 2002 that formed the genesis of this book, David Abram spoke of the importance of a living narrator as a critical dimension of connection to the natural world. A sense of place, with a connection to the animate world, is both an oral and aural experience. Abrams argued that connection to other species is evoked by the breath of the narrator, whose voice as well as story content heighten a sensibility of the aliveness of the world around. The spoken breath—

echoing the gust of wind, the anima of spirit—supports the sharing of mind and echoes the shared ecosystem around us. Knowledge has historically been held in stories where animal characters often provide a timelessness, an association with the natural world, and an easy mnemonic for oral lessons. Basso also has found that the landscape can carry stories and reinforce an intimacy with place through its daily reminders (1996). Narratives that bind us to the city, to the place that we live, said Abram, can counteract the deadening sensibilities of a globalized, dis-placed, digital culture.

David Abram argues that current global environmental crises make a renewal of this layer of oral/aural language and the accounts of place that they convey "absolutely necessary." Children need to see adults engaging with story, using the breath, bringing knowledge together with human presence in the landscape. The practices of a more environmentally aware society are embedded in bodies and in the sensory experience of people in the community—people in communication. A focus on the ecology of sensory experience and kinesthetic, embodied ways of experiencing the natural world are connected to our survival as a species (Abram 1996).

These insights suggest a number of fruitful directions for research, and they suggest another possible understanding of the power of the Piedmont Project. Although participants had readings and heard lectures, what they remember most are the shared conversations and the learning in the woods. What has evoked new engagement with campus and Atlanta landscapes seems to be more what they learned from the stories of presenters and less from their handouts. As many hint in their memories of the experience, it is the combination of knowledge and emotion and the context of a growing sense of community that results in something new. The guidance and enthusiasm of the ecologist storyteller enhanced the woods walks. It is perhaps the sharing of breath in the sense of active narration and engaged participatory listening, as well as the sensory experience of the woods, that allows a more self-conscious attention to place.

In addition, the stories that accompany the Piedmont Project readings, lectures, and discussions contribute to a sense of comfort with environmental issues and their implications for daily life. The oral/aural component of narrative in the workshop seems to build a sense of competence as well, as participants come to "read" the landscape of Atlanta and to act on it, as discussed below. Narrative and personal encounter have been noted to strengthen environmental learning and psychological comfort in other settings (Dwyer et al. 1993; Geller 1994; Silko 1996), making people more receptive to change.

Place: University and City

The power of connection to place goes beyond the species living in woods and creeks to the relationship of the earth's living systems with the built environment of Atlanta and Emory. The workshop lecture on sprawl, health, air quality, and transportation issues connected many of the most difficult aspects of faculty daily life to larger issues of global climate change, the U.S. obesity epidemic, and deforestation. The presentation on campus sustainability efforts brought forward changing policies in building construction, a campuswide environmental mission statement, and other efforts to weave environmental issues into the fabric of everyday campus life. A growing awareness of Atlanta and Emory was reported by many participants in response to the question, "Did the Piedmont Project change in any way your sense of place or your connection with this place?"

"I think about land use and city planning more."

"I never drive down Buford Highway without thinking about what Howie said about that walkway."

"Now, I never have a visitor in town without pointing out Baker Woods, pointing out the old forest on Clifton Road. . . . My sense of place, the urgency of ecological responsibilities in Atlanta right now, was informed."

"I have a heightened perception, sense of Emory as a campus. I go with friends and point the greenspaces out. I'm more conscious of that."

"On my way home, I go past Peavine Creek, and it feels like a creek I have responsibility for. In my neighborhood . . . it's Emory's creek."

These dimensions of place intersect and build on each other, joining perceptions of the natural world with the built environment. Place attachment provides a kind of rootedness and stability (Thomashow 2002:76) as daily contact with creeks, buildings, or shuttles serves as reminders of the environmental lessons of the project.

Piedmont Project participants also learn that the community includes individuals with active engagement in protecting and restoring the woods and in seeking appropriate policies and practices on campus. The linkage of interdisciplinarity and the democratic sharing of expertise go one step further into a history of human agency on campus. This is a new awareness for some faculty. It echoes Low and Altman's assertions that place attachment, through opportunities to relax from formal roles, can foster creativity and imagination about aspects of one's life (1992:10). Said one previously unengaged faculty member, "[The workshop] alerted me to people out there working." Said another, "I'm excited about the momentum—people [acting] around the campus."

Part of the impact of the project is the intersection of intellectual curiosity with ethics and personal values.

"It matters to me that I sense a certain *moral commitment* [among participants]. This was not just CV fodder. . . . Everyone who signed up for this workshop believed these things *really matter*. It let me throw myself into it."

"Very quickly, I felt I belonged with them and they with me. Even though it wasn't mentioned much, we had a kind of a cause. We all cared really passionately about something, and I enjoyed being part of that movement, that cadre. I felt more effective because we were banding together."

Another faculty member mused, "I had had a lot of doubts about my life . . . teaching rich kids," and course revision for the project allowed a way to integrate personal values, "which is very positive for me personally." One faculty member struggled with a desire to know more about Emory's surroundings that conflicts with the reward system in his profession for "maintaining a portable currency. . . . The base emotion is toward indifference to the current campus. . . . Maybe how we identify as a *person* and as a professional are separate, and maybe with environmental issues, they're brought together."

The accounts suggest that the Piedmont Project shifted "people's relationship to the world, motivated by concern and subsequent involvement," as Heidegger would expect (Gray 1999:449). A part of the satisfaction of the workshop was a sense of shared commitment and the fact of engagement by the university with critical urban problems and issues. People feel they can contribute something of value and are not condemned to passivity (Nicholsen 2002:166).

"I get a sense of satisfaction of being part of an institutional process dedicated to positive ends. It feels good to be a part of an environmentally friendly institution."

Connections to Practice

The Piedmont Project expands faculty awareness of the biological cycles that support human existence and of the full ecosystem costs of contemporary urban lifeways, thereby bringing environmental challenges into sharper focus. Grounding these issues in local places and seeing connections to ethics and personal responsibility fosters for some participants a reflection on daily life (Thomashow 2002). Such expanded consciousness serves the university's goal of building environmental literacy among employees as well as students and is an essential precursor to the creativity that will bring societies—including universities—into more environmentally sustainable practices. In nearly a third of the Piedmont Project interviews, evidence emerged of a growing systems perspective. For example, one faculty member who rides a bike to work talked about how the Piedmont Project changed his sense of geography: "Travelling along the major watersheds—I can feel that."

"[I'm] worrying more now about what I throw out. Wondering where does it go? I see the street lined with washers, dryers, stoves, air conditioning, hoses. Sooner or later, that all has to be a problem."

A newcomer to Emory notes, "My neighborhood has terrible sidewalks and that's an individual concern, but now I see the issue of walking versus driving, and it has a broader, institutional contextualization."

One administrator recounted a campus effort supported by others for economic reasons that he advocated instead because "this is a more responsible way; it's a *green* thing to do—to think about the long-term impacts. . . . The Piedmont Project was a reinforcement of the perspective I was developing. I think differently about what comes across my desk." Said another,

"I saw that our growth [as a college] had economic ties to the town, and it began to dawn on me. Sustainable living—other forms of living. Beyond saving money, this [sustainable campus project] is about the palpable, lived, learning outside the classroom. I realized we ought to work to make this place [the college] a sustainable way of living."

Almost half of the participants reported some kind of new action flowed from their new or strengthened awareness of environmental issues. A few talked about changes in current household behavior, such as more careful recycling, planting more indigenous species in the yard, saving electricity, considering a pervious surface for a new driveway, and reducing grassed lawn. Many cautioned that the effects of the Piedmont Project were combined with other life influences in these new behaviors. However, one family began to include hikes and other nature experiences as part of family vacations, something they had not done prior to Piedmont and a direct result of the sense of fun rekindled by the woods walks. For others, past household decisions became a focus for reflection: "I got really upset about where I'm living [in a distant suburb]. . . . I ask myself now: 'What was I thinking?' I didn't see the big picture. It made me sad."

Several people reported undertaking new local political action. "I talked to my hiking group about environmental issues. It was [somewhat sheepishly] *empowering*! Expressing views and hearing others' views—I didn't do that before."

"I got involved because I had been in Piedmont," said one young professor whose suburban community faced controversy over a housing project planned for a nearby farm. Raising issues of density, sprawl, and green space, she transmitted Piedmont lessons to neighbors and eventually organized a citizens' group to support more thoughtful local planning. "It [the Piedmont Project] made a really, really big impact."

Another faculty member reported that learning more about neighborhood walkability and its connection to health helped him participate for the first time in county and state civic groups: "It changed my priorities." He and his wife had previously not seen the need to be engaged in an organizational way; "it increased our neighborhood activism."

Conclusion

The Piedmont Project introduces an experience of place that is new for most participants in this curriculum development workshop. The enthusiasm with which faculty embrace and build on it in their work and their personal lives offers an opportunity to understand more fully dimensions of place attachment that occur in many chapters of this book. For some urban residents, developing a relationship with the natural world allows cognition and action to join with meaning.

It is interesting that neither academic discipline nor longevity at Emory seemed to make much difference among Piedmont Project participants in the importance given to the interdisciplinary community and experiences in nature. Among both newcomer faculty and those who had lived in Atlanta for decades were individuals excited to learn the names of trees or the health consequences of urban sprawl. Only among the small group (less than a fifth) who were already teaching environmental subjects or carrying out research in these areas was the new knowledge relatively unimportant; these individuals emphasized more the value of community and the joy of the woods walks, and a few also reported feeling more deeply connected to Atlanta or the campus. Since Piedmont Project faculty are self-selected, their experiences are not generalizable to all professors, but prior interest in environmental issues might also have worked against the impact of the program, since information might be less new or the experience less stimulating. As we have seen, the combination of the two-day workshop and several summer weeks of independent reading and course revision, together with an end-of-summer field trip and a spring check-in dinner, had an impact far beyond curriculum change.

The components of the Piedmont Project affect the diverse group of faculty and administrators in many different ways. For some, most satisfying is the intellectual stimulation, and particularly the science, the facts, the issues they now understand. Transcending the silos of knowledge in the university builds partnerships. For others, the connection of environmental concerns with social justice is central. Once they hear about the differential impact of Atlanta's sewer or landfill woes on racial and income groups in the city, environmental issues have more meaning. Others begin with an aesthetic engagement with the natural world. They have a passionate attachment to landscapes where they grew up, and they come to transfer some of that connection to the land around Emory. Some people love to connect the local issues with the wider international ones. Others love the reverse—to see global greenhouse gas emissions as tied to the existence of local sidewalks or campus shuttles. Both contribute to a sense of "rootedness and stability in a world of dynamic environmental change" (Thomashow 2002:76).

Interestingly, for all of these groups, the naming of trees and wildflowers is often mentioned spontaneously as an important gift of the Piedmont Project. Though Pretty (2002:23–24) and Thomas (1983) argue that systematic botanical knowledge has historically undermined local knowledge of nature, naming for the faculty at Emory provides a language of reengagement. As in many universities, faculty come from many locales and from other countries as well and thus lack any local solidarity based on a shared taxonomy. Learning the names—oak, beech, bloodroot—eases the transfer of knowledge from the workshop to other outdoor opportunities to become more familiar with nature. The workshop's scientific education helps create group knowledge, shared understandings that deepen the human relationships.

Conveyed through narrative and experiential learning, the naming of species shifts teacher to learner and simultaneously evokes the challenge of teaching—a primary, day-to-day preoccupation for faculty. As they learn about environmental issues, their curiosity and excitement are validated by the other members of the group. For some, new scientific and social facts are connected with personal values and ethics. Self-consciously reflecting on their own embodied, sensory learning in nature brings stimulating insights about methods of teaching. As participants experience a deeper connection to the natural world, they also have a means to bring that to their students, thereby combining the professional and personal around issues of societal urgency.

Some faculty at Emory embraced the Piedmont Project out of a simple desire to get help in changing their courses. In the end, the program spoke to deeper frustrations with the closed, disciplinary focus of much of academic life and the hunger to talk of significant issues in informal settings. Since sustainability efforts in higher education focus most commonly on campus operations, the Piedmont Project experience suggests that curriculum development can be a fruitful alternative that strengthens knowledge of environmental issues, systems thinking, and experiential learning. With its grounding in the local, place-based faculty development also enhances positive experiences with the university itself. The Piedmont Project embodies a liberal education (for professional school faculty as well as for college instructors), supporting personal as well as intellectual growth, for faculty and for students.

In the process, the experience of place—the woods, the city, the campus—comes to hold new meanings. Whether a recognition that most of Atlanta's forests are second or third growth, that the stream they love has signs of degradation, that the campus is home to fox and beaver, that hundreds of people die each year from the city's smog—the engagement with the natural world has changed. Naming the oak or the bloodroot seems to be connected for some with taking pride in a green building. A sense of reverence for majestic beech trees combines with admiration for taxonomic expertise and for the campus committee work that kept the trees from destruction. A deeper relationship to place fosters an ethic of care for both local species and the emerging community of concerned faculty and administrators. Knowledge and emotion are then, for almost half, connected to practice and emerge in new personal actions, large and small, toward a more sustainable way of life. New forms of action reinforce and extend the learning from the Piedmont Project and, often, the connection to place. These dimensions of place attachment are enhanced by the power of the group, an emerging sense of community that is the most valued aspect of the program. The trust and respect for each others' efforts as scholars and administrators broadens to include efforts as citizens and family members. The breath, the spoken word, carries the message and grounds it in place.

"Seems to me that's, like, the university at its highest level—that's what it's all about. Moments like this don't happen very often."

"The overall sense of satisfaction. I wouldn't have anticipated that . . . it's just wonderful. Unexpected."

Acknowledgments

The Piedmont Project benefited greatly from the experience and guidance of facilitators Geoffrey Chase and Paul Rowland, both at the time from Northern Arizona University. The many contributions of cofacilitators Arri Eisen, Sally Pete, and Jim Wynn made the project possible, and I am very grateful for their partnership. Funding was provided by Emory University's University Teaching Fund, Program for Science and Society, Center for Teaching and Curriculum, and the Office of the Provost. I am also grateful to Marc Miller, Tong Soon Lee, Chris Beck, Barry Ryan, and Faidra Papavasiliou for their efforts on behalf of the Piedmont Project and to each of the interviewees for their cooperation and precious time. Special thanks are due to Bobbi Patterson, Rachel Kaplan, Stephen Kaplan, Tim Bryson, Laurie Patton, Malve von Hassell, Arri Eisen, and Kay Milton for their helpful comments on earlier drafts of this chapter.

Notes

1. Dualisms between mind and body, built environment and natural environment, humans and nonhumans emerge in almost every Piedmont Project interview from open-ended questions about what people remembered and the impact of the program. This project was not focused on whether or how some participants transcended these dualisms, and therefore this analysis represents my own understandings of their accounts.

2. The Ponderosa Project was established to build environmental literacy at Northern Arizona University under the leadership of Geoffrey Chase, Paul Rowland, and others (Chase and Rowland 2004). For five years, a summer program like the one described for the Piedmont Project brought together faculty and administrators, and over one hundred new or revised courses were added to the curriculum. The Ponderosa Project was part of a shift in the university's identity at that time, as it distinguished itself among the other Arizona schools as "the environmental university."

References

Abram, David. 1996. *The Spell of the Sensuous*. New York: Vintage.

Aronowitz, Stanley. 2001. *The Last Good Job in America: Work and Education in the New Global Technoculture*. New York: Rowman and Littlefield.

Barlett, Peggy F., and Geoffrey W. Chase. 2004. *Sustainability on Campus: Stories and Strategies for Change.* Cambridge, Mass.: MIT Press.

Barlett, Peggy F., and Arri Eisen. 2002. The Piedmont Project at Emory University. In *Teaching Sustainability at Universities: Towards Curriculum Greening.* Walter Leal Filho, ed. Pp. 61–78. Frankfurt: Peter Lang.

Basso, Keith H. 1996. *Wisdom Sits in Places: Landscape and Language among the Western Apache.* Albuquerque: University of New Mexico Press.

Bowers, Chet. 1999. The Role of Education and Ideology in the Transition from a Modern to a More Bioregionally-Oriented Culture. In *Bioregionalism.* Michael Vernon McGinnis, ed. Pp. 191–204. New York: Routledge.

Chase, Geoffrey W., and Paul Rowland. 2004. The Ponderosa Project: Infusing Sustainability in the Curriculum. In *Sustainability on Campus: Stories and Strategies for Change.* Peggy F. Barlett and Geoffrey W. Chase, eds. Pp. 91–106. Cambridge, Mass.: MIT Press.

Dwyer, William O., et al. 1993. Critical Review of Behavioral Interventions to Preserve the Environment: Research since 1980. *Environment and Behavior* 25(3):275–321.

Fitzpatrick, Kevin, and Mark LaGory. 2000. *Unhealthy Places: The Ecology of Risk in the Urban Landscape.* New York: Routledge.

Geller, E. Scott. 1994. The Human Element in Integrated Environmental Management. In *Implementing Integrated Environmental Management.* T. V. Crawford and H. Halwasser, eds. Pp. 5–26. Blacksburg, Va.: Virginia Polytechnic Institute and State University.

Gray, John. 1999. Open Spaces and Dwelling Places: Being at Home on Hill Farms in the Scottish Borders. *American Ethnologist* 26(2):440–460.

Jacobson, David. 2002. *Place and Belonging in America.* Baltimore, Md.: Johns Hopkins University Press.

Kaplan, Rachel. 1984. Impact of Urban Nature: A Theoretical Analysis. *Urban Ecology* 8:189–197.

Kaplan, Rachel, and Stephen Kaplan. 1989. *The Experience of Nature: A Psychological Perspective.* Cambridge: Cambridge University Press.

Kaplan, Stephen. 1995. The Restorative Benefits of Nature: Toward an Integrative Framework. *Journal of Environmental Psychology* 15(3):169–182.

Lopez, Barry. 1988. *Crossing Open Ground.* New York: Scribners.

Low, Setha M., and Irwin Altman. 1992. Place Attachment: A Conceptual Inquiry. In *Place Attachment.* Irwin Altman and Setha M. Low, eds. Pp. 1–12. New York: Plenum.

Low, Setha M., and Denise Lawrence-Zúñiga. 2003. *Anthropology of Space and Place: Locating Culture.* New York: Blackwell.

Milton, Kay. 1996. *Environmentalism and Cultural Theory: Exploring the Role of Anthropology in Environmental Discourse.* New York: Routledge.

Mumford, Karen G. 2001. Developing a Campus-Wide Environmental Policy: "It's All About Process." In *Conference Proceedings, Greening of the Campus 4: Moving to the Mainstream.* Pp. 267–270. Muncie, Ind.: Ball State University.

Nicholsen, Shierry Weber. 2002. *The Love of Nature and the End of the World: Unspoken Dimensions of Environmental Concern.* Cambridge, Mass.: MIT Press.

Orr, David W. 1994. *Earth in Mind: On Education, Environment, and the Human Prospect.* Washington, D.C.: Island Press.

Orr, David W. 2004. Review of David Sobel, Place-Based Education: Connecting Classrooms and Communities. Orion Society web site, Accessed July 18, 2004. http://www.oriononline.org/pages/ob/index_ob.html.

Pretty, Jules. 2002. *Agri-Culture: Reconnecting People, Land and Nature.* London: Earthscan.

Sabin, Paul. 2002. Academe Subverts Young Scholars' Civic Orientation. *Chronicle of Higher Education,* Feb. 8.

Silko, Leslie Marmon. 1996. Landscape, History and Pueblo Imagination. In *The Ecocriticism Reader: Landmarks in Literary Ecology.* Cheryll Glotfelty and Harold Fromm, eds. Pp. 268–269. Athens: University of Georgia Press.

Talbot, Janet F., and Stephen Kaplan. 1986. Perspectives on Wilderness: Reexamining the Value of Extended Wilderness Experiences. *Journal of Environmental Psychology* 6(3):177–188.

Thomas, Keith. 1983. *Man and the Natural World: Changing Attitudes in England, 1500–1800.* New York: Oxford University Press.

Thomashow, Mitchell. 2002. *Bringing the Biosphere Home.* Cambridge, Mass.: MIT Press.

Tilley, Christopher. 1994. *A Phenomenology of Landscape: Places, Paths, and Monuments.* Providence, R.I.: Berg.

Zencey, Eric. 1996. The Rootless Professors. In *Rooted in the Land: Essays on Community and Place.* William Vitek and Wes Jackson, eds. Pp. 15–19. New Haven, Conn.: Yale University Press.

3

Lifting Spirits: Creating Gardens in California Domestic Violence Shelters

Susan M. Stuart

A little girl in an Oakland-area domestic violence shelter jumps for joy because she has helped to grow strawberries, something she has never experienced before. A domestic violence victim in San Diego describes feeling less isolated and worried when she works in the community garden created by the shelter where she lives. A middle-aged immigrant woman in Orange County, a shelter graduate and volunteer, talks about how gardening reminds her of her childhood and helps her pass her culture on to her daughter, who never lived in Vietnam. A young Caribbean immigrant and domestic shelter resident in Los Angeles says that she likes to garden because she can get fresh vegetables and herbs while learning about nature and the seasons.

These stories and many more like them were taken from the experience of Project GROW, a unique California-based pilot program that explored the idea that gardens and healthy food could enrich the lives of both the residents and staff of grassroots domestic violence shelters. At the heart of the project was an effort to link the food security of shelter programs with healing and empowerment goals for the lives of the women and children whom they serve.

From spring 1999 to December 2000, approximately 1,500 women and children, not including agency staff, participated in some aspect of Project GROW. Many were exposed for the first time to gardening, new types of fruits and vegetables, new cooking techniques, farmers markets, and community-supported agriculture (CSA). These activities provided fresh opportunities for therapy, recreation, education, and cultural exchange. They also allowed the participants a means to reconnect with nature or in some cases, particularly in the case of children, to establish a relationship with nature for the first time.

Plants, Horticulture, and Healing

For centuries, gardens have been thought to encourage mental and physical healing. The monastery gardens of medieval Europe, evolving from the ancient gardens of Persia, Egypt, and Asia, were believed to provide a place of serenity and comfort and to have curative powers. According to Gerlach-Spriggs, Kaufman, and Warner, restorative gardens went into a decline throughout much of Europe from the fourteenth to the seventeenth centuries as a result of the decline of monasticism, the arrival of the plague, and social and political upheaval, only to be rediscovered during the 1700s combining "hygienic and therapeutic goals" (1998: 7–16).

The belief that gardens could promote good health and healing was institutionalized on this side of the Atlantic beginning in the 1800s, when they became a part of some psychiatric and medical institutions. Lewis notes that in 1812, Benjamin Rush, a physician and signer of the Declaration of Independence, wrote that mental patients who spent time outdoors in gardening activities made more progress in their recovery than those who were confined to the hospital (1994:14). In the late nineteenth and early twentieth centuries, gardening became a part of rehabilitative activities in tuberculosis sanitariums and veterans' hospitals and a "planned activity linked to patients' therapeutic regimen . . . when occupational therapy came into its own in the twentieth century" (Gerlach-Spriggs et al. 1998:28).

In the 1960s, horticultural therapy programs were developed at the Menninger Clinic in Topeka, Kansas, at Michigan State University, at the Rusk Institute for Rehabilitation Medicine in New York City, and at Clemson University in South Carolina. The first U.S. horticultural therapy master's degree program was founded at Michigan State University in 1953, and the first undergraduate program (growing out of the work of the Menninger Foundation) was established at Kansas State University in 1972 (Gerlach-Spriggs et al. 1998:31). Horticultural therapy is now used in all types of settings throughout the country: in hospitals, hospices, nursing homes, rehabilitation centers, juvenile detention programs, and prisons.

Beginning in the 1970s, scholars began to research the impacts of plants and horticultural activities on humans (Coulter 1999; Lohr and Relf 2000; Relf and Lohr 2003). Since that time, researchers from a variety of disciplines have explored the therapeutic and social effects in specific populations and settings. To date, researchers have not specifically studied the therapeutic and social effects of natural settings, garden environments, or horticulture on the survivors of domestic violence or domestic violence programs. However, research has been done on public housing residents, hospital patients, older people in long-term care, workers, British garden owners, school children, juvenile offenders, children with attention deficit disorder (ADD), inner-city children, visitors to botanic gardens, and college students, among others.[1] A growing body of evidence produced by these studies indicates that gardens and green environments may promote physical, psychological, and social well-being.

The work of Sullivan, Kuo, and others discussed elsewhere in this book, found that a green environment was associated with positive effects on social interactions, domestic conflict, and possibly crime rates in urban neighborhoods (Sullivan and Kuo 1996; Kuo and Sullivan 2001). Another study (Kweon, Sullivan, and Riley 1998) found that elders who lived in housing with trees in their common area had more positive interactions with neighbors than those with paved outdoor areas.

The literature on community gardening also contains relevant information on the social, environmental, and communal aspects of gardening. A comprehensive study conducted among 376 households in Great Britain found that perceived benefits included (reported by over 40 percent) an enhanced environment, relaxation, fresh air and exercise, working with plants, closeness to nature, and the provision of cut flowers. Personal creativity, obtaining fresh produce, and better social interactions were reported by approximately 20 percent of respondents. The most frequently reported benefits of gardens to environmental quality were a more beautiful environment and more relaxation (Dunnett and Qasim 2000).

A study of community gardens in a poor neighborhood on the Lower East Side of Manhattan found that community gardens served as spaces for food and socialization and helped to strengthen a sense of community and security (Schmelzkopf 1995). Research in Philadelphia (Blair, Giesecke, and Sherman 1991) comparing adult gardeners to nongardeners found that gardening was associated with higher rates of vegetable consumption, a sense of satisfaction, and higher levels of participation in community projects. A comparison of immigrant and nonimmigrant gardeners in San Jose, California (Lee 2002) found that immigrant gardeners with horticultural experience or fewer years in the United States were able to acculturate more easily and connect to their homeland through gardening.

A study of U.S. entrepreneurial community gardens (Feenstra 1999) found positive impacts that included increasing self-esteem, personal satisfaction and stability, as well as neighborhood beautification and crime reduction. Research on the socioeconomic impacts of community gardens (Patel 1991) found that besides providing a source of fresh produce, improved diets, and cost savings, community gardens were a place for social interaction, neighborhood improvement, and community building. Gardeners in the study described feelings of enjoyment and self-sufficiency.

Domestic Violence Shelters: A New Arena for Gardening and Food Advocacy

On a daily basis, thousands of domestic violence victims throughout California receive education, support, and a roof over their heads from a vast network of nonprofit grassroots shelter programs. Some of these agencies provide services on a short-term, emergency basis, and others organize housing, counseling, and support services for up to two years. Women from all ethnic groups, most between the ages of 18 and 50, find their way to these shelters, sometimes alone but often with children.[2] Most are low income and dependent on their own resources, socially and economically.

Domestic violence shelters are often in bleak physical environments, completely devoid of any sign of nature. Despite the fact that most of

California has a climate that makes it possible to garden throughout the year, most shelters do not have food or flower gardens and may lack even the requisite lawn, shrubbery, and scraggly pot of flowers. Even in cities with an abundance of greenery, domestic violence shelters are often surrounded by a world of concrete and asphalt and are essentially separated from the natural world.

Food Insecurity and Stress among Domestic Violence Victims

Before entering shelters, many battered women have been living lonely, secluded lives. As one shelter resident put it, "At home we didn't know anyone." All kinds of experiences have been limited, including educational and work opportunities. The effects of social isolation and poverty are seen in two women who had never eaten in a restaurant before being taken on an outing by shelter staff; by a woman who said she had never been "allowed" by the abuser to do simple things like carve a pumpkin at Halloween; by a group of women who cooked an artichoke for the first time during shelter communal cooking activities; and by the woman who said she did not think that she was "capable" of gardening before she entered the shelter.

Women are often leaving a situation where they have had limited food choices or difficulty simply putting food on the table due to poverty or conflicts over the family diet that were part of a pattern of abuse. Some domestic violence victims speak of negative feelings about food resulting from family violence at mealtimes or of eating disorders caused by the stress of a violent home. A woman and her teenaged daughters who talked about how tired they were of eating the same monotonous daily diet of pork, potatoes, and beans dictated by the batterer illustrates this point. Variety in the family diet came only when "my soon-to-be-ex would be in a good mood; he'd bring chips, chocolate, candy, or soda." Shelter life was a great relief for the family, partly because they were able to try new foods. One of the daughters joyfully said, "We're actually eating. Before, Mom would force me to eat dinner." And her mother added, "I didn't want her to be like me and not eat and not be able to hold it down."

The poor quality of foods in most low-income neighborhoods combined with little knowledge of nutrition, lack of time to prepare meals in high-stress circumstances, and overreliance on high-fat, high-sugar snacks as comfort foods all contribute to unhealthy eating by large numbers of women who enter domestic violence programs. One shelter director said that her clients had been reliant on "diets heavy in meats and potatoes over fruits and vegetables; and Pop-Tarts for breakfast." A director of another agency summed it up this way: "People who have poor diets don't know different foods."

Food and Gardens in Domestic Violence Shelters

Historically, fresh food and gardening have not been a major focus of activities in typical shelter programs because of competing demands of crisis intervention, tight budgets, and short resident stays. Domestic violence shelters serve food-insecure women and children on a daily basis while they grapple with their own agency food insecurity. Shelter food programs are cobbled together from a number of sources including Federal Emergency Management Agency (FEMA) vouchers, government food commodity programs, donations, and wholesale and retail groceries. Shelters rely heavily on canned and processed foods, and fresh fruits and vegetables are rarely seen at shelter meals. Donations frequently include nonnutritious junk foods that contribute to unhealthy eating patterns for both staff and clients.

Most shelter staff and volunteers lack education and training in nutrition and horticulture. According to one agency director, "Many [staff] are former clients so in that sense they have moved out of being on welfare." Likewise, many staff members have had little exposure to a broad range of foods. To illustrate this point, a shelter director said that she had a staff member who had never before eaten an apple.

Most shelters are located in older, poorly maintained, rented buildings, surrounded by uninviting physical environments. They are often in expensive or highly developed urban neighborhoods where garden space is dear. Insecure rental arrangements, tight program budgets, and demanding schedules make it difficult for grassroots agencies to justify investing a lot of time and effort into the improvement of shelter surroundings.

The Seeds and Development of Project GROW

In 1997, the Urban and Environmental Policy Institute's Center for Food and Justice (CFJ), formerly called the Community Food Security Project, produced an analysis describing the potential for domestic violence shelters to develop gardening projects that could provide horticultural therapy, increase food security, and promote economic development (Mohr 1998). Inspired by the findings of this study, CFJ organized a series of workshops, sponsored by the California Department of Health Services, Maternal and Child Health Branch, Domestic Violence Section (MCH/DVS), and attended by state-funded domestic violence program staff, to explore the food insecurity issues of domestic violence victims and agencies and to learn more about the possibilities of developing food and gardening initiatives in shelter settings. The positive response of the domestic violence agency staff to the workshops (e.g., "most exciting new concept I'd heard in ten years") led to the creation of Project GROW, a 21-month pilot program, funded by MCH/DVS. CFJ provided coordination, technical assistance, evaluation, and documentation for the project.

The idea that food needs to be both a source of basic nutrition and healthier eating was seen as complementing the concept that the growing of food (and other community food security strategies for accessing and preparing food) could be a source of knowledge, therapy, and empowerment. Additionally, gardens were seen as a way to reconnect shelter residents to the source of the food that sustains them and to the never-ending multitude of sights, sounds, flavors, and fragrances of nature. And finally, the pilots were designed to create an important new linkage between community food security and domestic violence constituencies. Although not intended as a program goal at the outset, the quality of the food and food-related and gardening activities for agency staff became a factor in the development of the pilots. The improvement of the shelter's physical environment, although seen as implicit in the creation of gardens, was not a primary focus of the pilot program. Eventually, however, it became an important feature and emphasis in a number of projects.

The nine Project GROW pilots, chosen through a competitive grants process, were situated in different climates, gardening zones, and regions reflecting California's geographical and human diversity. Five of the projects were in metropolitan areas. They varied in size, emphasis, and the length of time that residents remained in the shelter. Some programs stressed nutrition and cooking, while others focused on horticultural therapy, gardening education, food production, or job training.

In some cases, gardens were installed at the shelter, and in other cases they were established off-site, in partnership with other in-house agency programs or community organizations. Whatever their focus, all of the shelters either expanded a small existing garden or developed a new garden, and most of the pilots emphasized some food production. All of the programs—despite the difficulties posed by security and confidentiality requirements—worked with local consultants and developed relationships with community partners such as Cooperative Extension (Master Gardener program and the Expanded Food and Nutrition Education Program, EFNEP), CSAs, Plant-an-Extra-Row projects, Project Lean (Leaders Encouraging Physical Activity and Nutrition), the American Horticultural Therapy Association, the California Nutrition Network, and local gardeners, farmers, and environmental organizations.

As part of program evaluation, we designed and conducted surveys or in-depth structured interviews with 81 residents, 60 women, and 21 children.[3] As shown in table 3.1, this number represented 5 percent of the total population of program participants. Questions were customized depending on program emphasis (gardening, nutrition/cooking, or food security). In one pilot that placed an agency-wide emphasis on the garden program, we surveyed or interviewed 27 program graduates, staff, and volunteers using the same format. Upon completion of the project, we conducted additional in-depth interviews with 18 administrators and coordinators across all sites to try to determine the impact of the program on the agencies. Thirty-two of the 60 resident women had children with them at the shelter. Data were made available for the length of stay for 64 of those interviewed or surveyed; the average was 9.4 weeks.

Table 3.1
Ethnicity of resident participants in Project GROW

Ethnicity	Women		Children		Total	
	Project GROW	Interviewed or surveyed	Project GROW	Interviewed or surveyed	Project GROW	Interviewed or surveyed (% of total)
African American	154	10	207	9	361	19 (23%)
Asian/ Pacific Islander	15	3	30	0	45	3 (4%)
Hispanic/ Latino	124	20	158	4	282	24 (30%)
Native American	12	3	15	0	27	3 (4%)
White	388	22	315	6	703	28 (34%)
Other	10	2	9	2	19	4 (5%)
Unknown	48		6		54	0
Total	751	60	740	21	1491	81 (100%)

Healing Gardens

We wanted to know if the mere presence of a garden or the participation in a garden program had any positive effect on the lives of the shelter residents. Did it make any difference in the way they felt? Did they enjoy just sitting in the garden? Did they learn anything new about horticulture or food? Did they appreciate being able to eat fresh produce? Did they feel it had any positive benefit for their children? We asked a subgroup of women and teenage residents—8 self-identified African Americans, 3 Asians, 14 Latinas, 3 Native Americans, and 16 whites—in six pilots (nearly all of whom resided in metropolitan areas or smaller cities) who had spent time in the garden or participated directly in gardening activities about the effects of these experiences.[4]

Because we knew that they were recovering from physical and emotional trauma and contending with strange, new surroundings and multiple sources of stress, such as looking for housing and jobs and applying for various sources of assistance, we were prepared for the possibility that they might be too busy or distracted to find a source of healing in the garden and related activities. Yet a majority of this group said that the main effects of the gardening experience were the psychosocial and therapeutic benefits (mentioned by 29 out of 44 people, or 66 percent). These aspects were considered more important than both the educational effects (34 percent) and the ability to obtain fresh food from the garden (16 percent).

Furthermore, 93 percent (41 out of 44) said that they intended to garden in the future. One of the pilot programs found similar data using its own survey tool. Staff asked a combined group of shelter residents and neighborhood participants at their community garden project how the garden program had helped or benefited them. Nine out of 16, over 50 percent, mentioned psychosocial and therapeutic benefits. Furthermore, this held true for all ages and ethnic groups in both sets of data (50 percent of the neighborhood participants were Spanish speaking).

Gardens as Psychological and Physical Retreats

Again and again in interviews and surveys, women emphasized that the garden program had been a powerful antidote to sadness and depression and a source of stress relief and relaxation. Activities such as planting, weeding, and watering seemed to be a way to remove themselves from their enormously wearing life difficulties for just a little while:

"Releases stress."

"Makes me forget my problems."

"[In the garden] we don't have time to worry."

"Like a tranquilizer."

"Controls anxiety."

"Really helped me with stress and depression."

"Relaxing, found it hard to talk about things except the garden [itself]."

"[I'm] happy gardening."

"Fun and relaxing."

"Problems are forgotten. It's like watching a movie."

"Helps lift everyone's spirits."

Figure 3.1
Women say they can forget their problems for a while when working in the garden (photo by Michelle Mascarenhas).

Some said that the physical act of touching the soil was by itself therapeutic:

"It's peaceful putting my hands in the dirt."

"I loved the way we got our hands in the soil."

"Puttering in the soil . . . as if the earth absorbs negativity."

Others told us that the garden was a calm retreat from the outside world:

"It's peaceful . . . and very beautiful just to sit and look at. It just takes you away."

"I've liked just sitting in the garden. It's very peaceful."

"[I feel] tranquility, to be able to think of other things apart from my problems."

Sometimes the garden was a symbol of the monumental life changes families were going through:

"The garden says you're in a different place [in your life]."

"The garden gives me air. I breathe fresh air. It relaxes me. I return to life. I stop now and notice the flowers."

"I've learned that as with plants, life is a process that takes time."

"Seeing new growth on the trees makes me feel hopeful."

Simply being able to get out of the house and enjoy the outdoors was new and special for many women ("nice to be outdoors" and "didn't imagine gardening is so much fun"). Several neighborhood women who participated in a shelter's community garden project echoed the comments of the shelter residents when they talked about how gardening helped them with the stresses of their home lives:

"It's different here. I feel comfortable. It's very tough being in this hole that I'm in. I come [to the garden] to participate, work the soil, sing. I have more motivation."

"I go out and water and kind of just meditate. . . . We can come any time we want to water and plant. It's nice to have a place to be by yourself. . . . I'm growing stuff at home now. My ex-boyfriend has destroyed my plants four times. But I keep replanting them."

"It has helped me with stress and to get me out of the house."

The effect of the garden experience on women who spent three hours or fewer in the garden per week ($N = 19$) compared with women who spent six hours or more ($N = 20$) are summarized in table 3.2. The results indicate that women who spent more time in the garden perceive more psychological effects. For instance, whereas 58 percent of the women who had spent three or fewer hours in the garden per week reported the effect of therapeutic or positive feelings, 85 percent who spent six hours or more reported those same types of feelings. (Table 3.2 reports the multiple responses from some women.)

Shelter Environments and Gardens

Although shelters offer temporary safety, some women complained about regimentation and cramped communal conditions. They said that getting outside to take in a little bit of the natural world was a release from the

Table 3.2
Effect of time in garden reported by resident ages 14 or older

Response to garden experience	3 hours or less per week		6 hours or more per week	
	N = 19	% of responses	N = 20	% of responses
Therapeutic or positive feelings	11	42	17	50
Learned about food or gardening	5	19	9	26
Other (e.g., fresh food, improved environment)	7	27	8	24
No effect	3	12	0	0
Total	26	100	34	100

restrictive shelter environment ("liked the change of scenery," "get more energy by being outdoors rather than watching TV," and "felt peaceful, a little bit of freedom").

Gardening soothed the adjustment to the shelter for one woman: "Right after I got here, on 'lock down' the first three days. . . . We weren't allowed to make phone calls or go anywhere. Gardening took my mind off of what I was going through." She said she wanted to have a house with her "own little yard and space," and added, "We could heal." Another woman talked about how her shelter's rules and regulations (some in place because of concerns about security) reminded her of being controlled by the batterer: "A lot of us are on guard because of our past. It's not the shelter's fault. Just the situation I'm coming from. . . . It's good therapy to be outside, makes you feel happier." Sometimes the garden was a retreat from poorly maintained shelter living spaces: "In the shelter if everyone doesn't clean, things don't operate equally. There are ants, and worst, if some ignore their cleaning rules, animals appear. I like to be in the garden."

And yet for many, shelters remained safe havens, and the garden was representative of that ("love living here"). One program graduate, an immigrant who had no relatives or friends to turn to when she left the

Figure 3.2
Blighted urban locales were transformed by the creation of food and flower gardens (photo by Michelle Mascarenhas).

batterer, said that she had arrived "in heaven" in the first days at the shelter. She did not have to worry about where she would sleep or eat, and felt it was harder once things had settled down and she had to think about her future—"no papers [immigration], money or jobs." Gardening gave her something physical to do to take her mind off these issues: "Doing something with your hands instead of thinking crazy thoughts takes a lot of stress off. There's nothing to do here to get your mind off of things." Another woman, alluding to the fact that the women sometimes gardened as part of mandatory activities, said: "I need the structure. I need the rules. I couldn't be happier. . . . Going to the shelter was a *huge* thing."

Children

The garden programs sometimes helped to structure and elevate the level of activities for children. One administrator in a shelter that created a horticultural therapy program solely for children noted, "Children get put last. So it is important." Sixteen of 32 women, when asked about garden program effects, mentioned positive effects for their children. They frequently talked about how good it made them feel to see their children able to play and learn from the gardening and cooking activities. Separate children's activities in the garden also served as a form of child care in some programs, allowing mothers time for other things such as counseling groups.

Sometimes women were too busy to spend much time in the garden, but they enjoyed it vicariously through their children. Others said that the garden program helped them to be a better parent and relate to their children:

"The best experience was sharing with my daughter and observing how the little seed grows into vegetables."

"I never thought I'd be gardening. I do more things with my kids now."

"My kids will tell you that I don't yell at them as much."

"They [children] are more careful with plants. It helped me to set up boundaries with them."

Because children's well-being was uppermost in the minds of their mothers, seeing them being able to play peacefully and grow and learn about nature, nurturing, and healthy foods was itself a form of healing. One mother said, "I feel the gardening program has made my children become more gentle with plants and flowers; also they have learned all things grow with care and love." Another woman who could not spend times outdoors because of a health condition that made her sensitive to the sun talked about enjoying the experience through her child: "I like watching him come outside and swing and dig in the dirt. I think it's good for him. Let him be a kid. He can feel like we're okay doing something healthy." And still another said, "Kids love helping out in the garden. It's peaceful for me."

A woman with a teenager who normally had great difficulty focusing because of a learning disorder said that her son spent long hours in the garden because "plants don't talk back, they don't blame him." The ability to move back and forth quickly among a variety of tasks in the

Figure 3.3
Women say they found it healing to share the gardening experience with their children (photo by Michelle Mascarenhas).

garden also seemed to work well for him. Another mother said, "The children point out all the vegetables we grow at the garden when we go to the market. They want me to buy more vegetables and fruit."

Sixteen children ages 12 and under were asked how they felt in the garden. Nearly all expressed positive feelings ("happy," "fun," "excited"). Children were most interested in the food they received from the garden and the gardening tasks they performed; they also seemed to be more excited about gardening than teenagers were. In fact, of the small group of teenagers who were interviewed, most expressed a clear preference for other kinds of food activities such as cooking or shopping at the farmers' market. This fits with studies of adolescents and natural settings that have suggested that there is a kind of hiatus during the teen years when young people have less appreciation for nature and tend to "favor places where they can be with their peers and activities that convey excitement and action" (Kaplan and Kaplan 2002).

Small children in the pilots were especially proud of their new physical activities and the food they had helped produce. One child said, "I helped make them strawberries." When asked what she grew in the garden a little 4 year old shouted, "I grew PUMPKINS, STRAWBERRIES, lettuce, seeds, lambs ear, BASIL, BASIL, beans and corn, flowers, tomatoes, chard . . ."

The smallest children sometimes compared the plants to themselves, to their problems, and to the world around them. One lively 4 year old said, "If I'm a seed, and I'm down in the ground, it feels warm. It feels good because you can eat dirt if you're a seed. It feels good and snug."

Little children described their feelings very directly. Sometimes they interpreted feelings to mean physical sensations:

"I feel happy and hot."

"I just feel glad and stuff."

"I feel happy because I feel nothing."

"I like the smell of mulch."

Older children sometimes sounded like adults, perhaps reflecting a kind of maturity acquired in response to difficult lives. Two 11 year olds talked about the garden's making them feel "calm" and "releasing stress."

Self-Sufficiency and Empowerment

Another common theme among both women and children was the sense of empowerment and psychological nourishment that came from nurturing living things, watching plants grow and produce food, and experiencing the mystery of natural processes:

"It is something to see your results. You see the seed, then the flower, and then the *chiles* come."

"Appreciate seeing something grow from seed to maturity, to harvest."

"It is good to learn to grow our own vegetables, not only to learn to eat them."

"Feeling of pride of eating from the garden something that I grew."

"Enjoyed planting things and watching them grow."

"It nice to take the time to care for and nurture something."

"My favorite part was taking care of it. The plants need love."

"Gardening gets you back to nature."

Children especially enjoyed the sense of achievement and mastery that came from controlling their environment:

"I feel happy because one day I'm going to look and say I did this."

"It was really fine when the garden began. When we were pulling things out. Then it began to look really good. The kids were *really* helping. The kids felt that they could help the other people."

Memories of an Earlier Place in Time

Most women and children did not have the freedom, space, or time to garden in the years immediately prior to coming to the shelter, although about half of those who were asked spoke of childhood gardening experiences or some experience raising houseplants.[5] For many, having a garden represented a small luxury that they had never been able to afford. For those who had gardened as children, the experience was a way to reconnect to memories of a better place and time or a way to hold on to their cultural heritage. For those who had children of their own, it offered a form of continuity to grandparents and great-grandparents, sometimes in another country.

Immigration into California of people with horticultural skills has steadily risen. A study of the experience of community gardeners in San Jose, California, showed that many immigrants have the knowledge to grow their own food (Dotter 1994). This was reflected in the comments of immigrants participating in Project GROW who talked about gardening in their family backgrounds. One immigrant in a San Diego county shelter said, "I always wanted to garden but didn't have space. At my grandparents' in Mexico, I watched them garden corn, wheat, squash, beans, sugar cane, lemon, pomegranate, flowers, and herbs." Another woman, a graduate of her shelter program who remembered gardening with grandparents as a child in Vietnam and began to garden again as a result of the pilot program, said that gardening was a way to escape from the special difficulties of being an immigrant and to stay connected to her cultural heritage:

"It's so stressful in America. This is needed to relax you. Nature. Soft noises. . . . Most Vietnamese people have farmed. Ninety percent of Vietnamese people grow something at their house or their apartment. . . . I love to grow herbs. In Vietnamese food, you have to have green and red. We grow all those herbs. My daughter loves to garden. She doesn't remember Vietnam. She has her own plants and calls me out to see how they're doing."

But it was not only immigrants who had memories of gardening. Women from all ethnic groups and backgrounds talked about the gardens of their childhood. A Yurok woman talked about how the garden experience triggered memories of being a little girl: "Grandma used to have a garden. She'd pick the flowers and sell them to tourists." An African American woman who had not gardened as an adult until she came to the shelter said, "I grew up in the country in Illinois. My grandmother gardened. I really enjoy it now. . . . When I get my own place, I will definitely garden, to beautify my home and to grow vegetables." A white woman from Bakersfield said, "When I was a little girl my mom used to grow tomatoes and peppers."

And for some, gardening was totally new:

"I always wanted to garden. I knew nothing before I came here."

"At first I didn't like it because I never done it before."

Changes in Shelter Spaces and Neighborhoods

The addition and expansion of gardens helped to beautify and rehabilitate shelter spaces and enhance larger neighborhood environments. Staff in several programs emphasized that the presence of the gardens and the activities it took to create them had helped to boost morale, create a stronger shelter community, and build stronger ties to the surrounding neighborhood.

An Oakland-area shelter transformed a previously stark asphalt and concrete urban churchyard that had been used for a children's play area into a lush environment with raised beds (wheelchair accessible and just wide enough for the children's reach) containing vegetables, flowers, and

Figure 3.4
Gardens rehabilitate bleak shelter spaces, creating more peaceful environments (photo by Susan Stuart).

citrus trees. A San Diego program completely changed the area around the family resource center by reclaiming a barren vacant lot for a community garden project. They removed debris and several large eucalyptus trees, amended the soil, installed irrigation lines and raised beds, and eventually created a beautiful, productive 42- by 65-foot garden area with a wide variety of fruits, vegetables, and flowers. The community participation in the resource center's activities increased because people were drawn to the center by the gardening activities: "Our community has taken ownership and feel protective of the project."

Staff at another San Diego–area agency referred to their shelter courtyard as "desolate" prior to the garden program. Over the course of the pilot project, this space (which was shared by their emergency shelter and transitional housing program) was transformed to a flower and vegetable garden. It contained a variety of tomatoes; green, red, and purple peppers; cucumbers; jalapeños; and zucchini and other types of squash. Herbs and flowers were planted in window boxes on the apartments of the transitional program, and each apartment received a container citrus tree of the resident's choice. One client stated, "It looks and smells so much better around here that I feel like I have moved," and another said, "It livened it up a lot more. I can't remember what it looked like before." An 11-year-old girl said, "Everything looks so much prettier."

Even the agency director said that the creation of the garden had been a source of relaxation and job satisfaction:

"Mine is a very stressful job. Responsibilities are immense. During the start-up phase it was so wonderful [creating the garden]. Good for me. I increased my involvement with the shelter to daily involvement. I used to go there once or twice a week."

A Los Angeles–area program altered the shelter environment by completely renovating a small 620-square-foot front yard. Along the way, staff had to contend with an extremely expensive coastal real estate market, toxic soil, zoning regulations, security concerns, and many other hurdles. Eventually, they created a low-maintenance garden that included fragrant herbs and other visually appealing plants (emphasizing sage and olive green colors) that were usable for cooking and crafts, Japanese maples, a picket fence, a drip irrigation system, a new front porch, and a coat of paint for the shelter. These changes, which softened and improved the shelter environment, took well over a year to develop.

Sometimes administrators were excited about the programs, but staff had to be convinced that the garden was not just another duty. Some were concerned that the garden would take up space used for other purposes or would be incompatible with children's play areas. Several staff members reported that these concerns were gradually replaced by enthusiastic support after they saw the aesthetic changes that the gardens made to the shelter environment:

"I was a doubting Thomas at first. I believe now."

"Turned out to be more than expected. . . . Made the sites more homey."

"Dirt and a few scattered plants became . . . attractive and productive."

Although some did not particularly enjoy the actual garden work, they still enjoyed having a garden in their environment. One 22-year-old staff member in a shelter in Orange County who preferred other aspects of GROW, particularly the farmers' market where shelter residents shopped, bartered orchard gleanings, and worked in a booth selling lemon and avocado crops, said:

"I'm allergic to sun and bugs. . . . But I think it's cool, watching onions, sunflowers grow. . . . I wish we would plant at night. I see the women coming and really getting into it. . . . I love going to the farmers' market. . . . I love interacting with farmers. The oranges are the best oranges I've ever had, so juicy. It reminds me of the *tianguis* [markets] in Mexico where I grew up. Farmers' market is the whole community thing. Farmers give us tips on the garden. . . . The garden has helped me get into nature and enjoy the shade. Really, I'm a city girl."

A number of staff members said that gardening provided a special way to relate to their clients. One executive director spoke of it as "dispensing with the hierarchy . . . when people gardened together." Others said that "gardening brought out a lot of history sharing between clients and staff" and was "a different way to communicate [with the clients] in a way that I hadn't before."

Across the pilot projects, staff and program graduates talked about the new gardens they installed in their own homes because of what they had seen in the shelter gardens:

"Can grow my own garden and now I have my own hobby."

"Have my garden at home now because of the shelter gardening classes. I spend a lot of time just sitting out there."

"It has inspired me to do my garden. . . . I never ate chard before. Now, I eat chard once a week with rice, and I eat more greens."

Some staff reported that gardening was not always seen as therapeutic or interesting to all women residents. They noted that the competing demands and stresses that women faced made it hard to focus on new activities, particularly in short-term shelters. This was sometimes frustrating for staff who were avid gardeners. Interestingly, the least successful garden programs were in rural areas. Staff and administrators in these programs attributed this to low program censuses, inhospitable climates, personnel shortages, and lack of client response. Rural areas also typically lack the plethora of gardening experts and resources that exist in larger urban areas, making it harder to sustain gardening programs. It is also possible that poor people in rural California are less likely to see horticultural activities as therapeutic or beneficial in other ways because of greater exposure to industrial agriculture and heavy field labor.

Although the rural programs continued to do a small amount of gardening activities, they refocused their projects early on to emphasize food security and nutrition activities. One program administrator said that they were going to explore the possibility of animal therapy, which they thought might fit well with their low census and rural clientele.

Shared Culture, Gardening, and Comfort Food

In California urban areas, shelters are often a little United Nations, with people from many different cultures speaking multiple languages. Both clients and staff said that gardening helped to serve as a cultural unifier within shelters by bringing people from diverse traditions together and helping to diminish cultural misunderstandings or simple problems with communication that sometimes added to the stress of the environment.

One German immigrant said, "Because we come from so many backgrounds we don't know what to talk about so we talk about domestic violence, which isn't good. This [gardening] gives us something else to talk about." One Latina said, "I liked hearing stories about other people's gardens." Some women also told us that they had begun to share the foods of other cultural groups. A Vietnamese woman said, "I see Mexican people grow cilantro and use it. So I learn about it." One Anglo woman who wanted to plant more cilantro, chiles, and small green lemons said, "It's a Latino thing. You know." And in another shelter a woman said, "We cook a lot of Mexican foods. I didn't used to like hot stuff. I eat it now. Love homemade salsa."

It has long been recognized that familiar foods bring enormous comfort in times of stress. Being able to grow customary cultural foods appeared to be especially important to first- and second-generation immigrants from Latin America and Asia who were accustomed to diets that included fresh produce. This aligns with research that has shown that traditional Asian and Latino dietary patterns and foods of recent immigrants tend to be more healthful (and contain more fruits and vegetables) than the acculturated diets of their white, nonimmigrant counterparts, except for higher fat consumption (Townsend, Gong, and Prehm 1999).

An Asian American woman who was able to list all the vegetables she had grown in her own garden years earlier talked about the importance of being able to get fresh food: "We get fresh vegetables. Otherwise, we have to eat frozen since these are the only fresh vegetables that the shelter gets." A young Belizean immigrant said, "What I like best is the fact that you can pick fresh *vegi* and herbs out of the garden to cook. And it teaches a lot about nature. What you can grow in certain seasons and what you can't."

At one shelter, the presence of a garden that was not very productive seemed to raise expectations and produce cultural friction among a number of residents who were being offered nutrition classes. One Mexican immigrant spoke of the frustration in not being able to regularly eat the foods that she and her children preferred: "We like fresh things. There are no vegetables to cook a stew or soup. . . . There is no fresh fruit, not even salad."

Another immigrant complained, "Many things we use are canned. I want fresh." At the same time, one Mexican American in the same program who was less used to eating fresh fruits and vegetables and did not have experience cooking Mexican recipes said that the garden had helped her connect to her roots: "I never used green tomatillos. Now I use them. The little ones like to pick tomatoes. . . . I feel more like a Mexican. All Mexican girls like chiles. We all share salsa."

Conclusion

Because domestic violence programs can be such trying places physically and psychologically, gardens have a great potential, especially in urban areas, for beautifying and humanizing shelter environments. They have a potential for relieving stress, providing recreation, helping women and children reconnect to family backgrounds, strengthening children's programs, and building bonds across cultural divides. Gardens in shelter settings can also motivate staff and residents to create gardens in their own homes. Besides the benefits of providing a fresh source of food, increased food security, and a supplement to nutrition education, gardens can help to build shelter community, soften and enliven shelter spaces, beautify and strengthen neighborhoods, and increase staff job satisfaction. Garden programs can also link domestic violence agencies to new sources of funding and community support.

Issues such as program emphasis and requirements, lengths of stay, and the difficulty of producing a regular abundance of food or sustaining an educational gardening program on a year-round basis no doubt affected people's feelings about the relative benefits of the Project GROW gardening programs. Even when these factors are taken into account, the testimonies from Project GROW remain a compelling case for the recreational and restorative powers of gardens for the traumatized victims of domestic violence.

Acknowledgments

I thank Robert Gottlieb, Marilyn Prehm, and Margaret Haase for their support and assistance.

Notes

1. Barnicle and Midden (2003), Dunnett and Qasim (2000), Fjeld (2000), Goodwin et al. (1994), Kaplan, Talbot, and Kaplan (1988), Kohlleppel, Bradley, and Jacob (2002), Kuo et al. (1998), Lohr and Pearson-Mims (1996), McGuinn and Relf (2001), Parsons et al. (1998), Taylor, Kuo, and Sullivan (2001, 2002), Ulrich (1984), and Whitehouse et al. (2001).

2. Boys over the age of 12 are not officially served by most shelters.

3. Colleagues who helped to produce the original study and report (Stuart et al. 2002) were Robert Gottlieb, Marilyn Prehm, Michelle Mascarenhas, and Kate Stafford. For a more complete look at other aspects of Project GROW and individual case studies, access the project report at: www.departments.oxy.edu/uepi/cfj/resources/ Project_GROW_Final_Report.pdf.

Children under 12 were interviewed at two sites using a shorter version of the cross-site gardening tool. Eight of 60 women were surveyed in Spanish.

4. The two programs located in small, remote rural communities did not administer surveys.

5. Twelve of 22 (or 55 percent) women who were interviewed (not asked on surveys) said that they had never gardened before. A number of in-house questionnaires also revealed that about half of the women had some previous experience with houseplants or gardening.

References

Barnicle, Tom, and Karen Stoelzle Midden. 2003. The Effects of a Horticultural Activity Program on the Psychological Well-Being of Older People in a Long-Term Care Facility. *HortTechnology* 13(1):81–85.

Blair, Dorothy, Carol C. Giesecke, and Sandra Sherman. 1991. A Dietary, Social and Economic Evaluation of the Philadelphia Urban Gardening Project. *Journal of Nutrition Education* 23(4):161–167.

Coulter, Anne H. 1999. Healing Gardens: When Nature Is the Therapy. *Alternative and Complementary Therapies* April:64–73.

Dotter, John. 1994. Cultivating People-Plant Relationships in Community and Cultural Heritage Gardens, San Jose California (1977–1992). In *People-Plant Relationships: Setting Research Priorities*. Joel Flagler and Paymond P. Poincelot, eds. Pp. 153–170. Binghamton, N.Y.: Food Products Press.

Dunnett, Nigel, and Muhammad Qasim. 2000. Perceived Benefits to Human Well-Being of Urban Gardens. *HortTechnology* 10(1):40–45.

Feenstra, Gail, Sharyl McGrem, and David Campbell. 1999. *Entrepreneurial Community Gardens: Growing Food, Skills, and Communities*. Oakland: University of California Agriculture and Natural Resources Publication 21587.

Fjeld, Tove. 2000. The Effect of Interior Planting on Health and Discomfort among Workers and School Children. *HortTechnology* 10(1):46–52.

Gerlach-Spriggs, Nancy, Richard E. Kaufman, and Sam Bass Warner, Jr. 1998. *Restorative Gardens: The Healing Landscape*. New Haven, Conn.: Yale University Press.

Goodwin, Georgia K., Caroline H. Pearson-Mims, and Virginia I. Lohr. 1994. The Impact of Adding Interior Plants to a Stressful Setting. In *The Healing Dimensions of People-Plant Relations*. Mark Francis, Patricia Lindsey, and Jay Stone Rice, eds. Pp. 353–362. Davis: University of California, Center for Design Research.

Kaplan, Rachel, and Stephen Kaplan. 2002. Adolescents and the Natural Environment: A Time Out? In *Children and Nature*, Peter H. Kahn and Stephen R. Kellert, eds. Pp. 227–258. Cambridge, Mass.: MIT Press.

Kaplan, Stephen, Janet F. Talbot, and Rachel Kaplan. 1988. *Coping with Daily Hassles: The Impact of Nearby Nature on the Work Environment*. Project Report, U.S. Forest Service, North Central Forest Experiment Station, Urban Forestry Unit Cooperative Agreement 23–85–08.

Kohlleppel, Tammy, Jennifer Campbell Bradley, and Steve Jacob. 2002. A Walk through the Garden: Can a Visit to a Botanic Garden Reduce Stress? *HortTechnology* 12(3):489–492.

Kuo, Francis E., and William C. Sullivan. 2001. Environment and Crime in the Inner City: Does Vegetation Reduce Crime? *Environment and Behavior* 33(3):343–376.

Kuo, Francis E., William C. Sullivan, Rebekah L. Coley, and Liesette Brunson. 1998. Fertile Ground for Community: Inner-City Neighborhood Common Spaces. *American Journal of Community Psychology* 26:823–851.

Kweon, Byoung-Suk, William C. Sullivan, and Angela R. Riley. 1998. Green Common Spaces and the Social Integration of Inner-City Older Adults. *Environmental Behavior* 30(1):832–858.

Lee, Sinang H. 2002. Community Gardening Benefits as Perceived among American-Born and Immigrant Gardeners in San Jose, California. www.istsocrates.berkeley.edu/~es196/projects/2002final/Lee.S.pdf. Accessed Nov. 10, 2003.

Lewis, Charles. 1994. People-Plant Relations Past and Future. In *The Healing Dimensions of People-Plant Relations*. Mark Francis, Patricia Lindsey, and Jay Stone Rice, eds. Pp. 13–25. Davis: University of California, Center for Design Research.

Lohr, Virginia I., and Paula D. Relf. 2000. An Overview of the Current State of Human Issues in Horticulture in the United States. *HortTechnology* 10(1):27–33.

Lohr, Virginia I., and Caroline H. Pearson-Mims. 2000. Physical Discomfort May Be Reduced in the Presence of Interior Plants. *HortTechnology* 10(1): 53–58.

McGuinn, Catherine, and Patricia D. Relf. 2001. A Profile of Juvenile Offenders in a Vocational Horticulture Curriculum. *HortTechnology* 11(3):427–433.

Mohr, Hope. 1998. *Gardens for Survivors: A Feasibility Analysis for Developing Healing and Food Security Strategies for Survivors of Domestic Violence*. Los Angeles: The Community Food Security Project, Occidental College.

Parsons, Russ, Louis G. Tassinary, Roger S. Ulrich, Michelle R. Hebl, and Michelle Grossman-Alexander. 1998. The View from the Road: Implications for Stress Recovery and Immunization. *Journal of Environmental Psychology* 18:113–140.

Patel, I. C. 1991. Gardening's Socioeconomic Impacts: Community Gardening in an Urban Setting. *Journal of Extension* 29(4). http://www.joe.org. Accessed Nov. 10, 2003.

Relf, Diane, and Virginia Lohr. 2003. Human Issues in Horticulture. *HortScience* 38(5):984–993.

Schmelzkopf, Karen. 1995. Urban Community Gardens as Contested Space. *Geographical Review* 85(3):364–381.

Stuart, Susan, Robert Gottlieb, Marilyn Prehm, Michelle Mascarenhas, and Kate Stafford. 2002. *Growing Food, Healing Lives: Linking Community Food Security and Domestic Violence*. Los Angeles: Center for Food and Justice, Urban and Environmental Policy Institute.

Sullivan, W. C., and Francis E. Kuo. 1996. *Do Trees Strengthen Urban Communities, Reduce Domestic Violence?* Forest Report R8-FR 55, Technical Bulletin No. 4. Athens, Ga.: USDA Forest Service Southern Region.

Taylor, Andrea F., Francis E. Kuo, and William C. Sullivan. 2001. Coping with ADD: The Surprising Connection to Green Play Settings. *Environment and Behavior* 33(1):54–77.

Taylor, Andrea F., Francis E. Kuo, and William C. Sullivan. 2002. Views of Nature and Self-Discipline: Evidence from Inner City Children. *Journal of Environmental Psychology* 22:49–63.

Townsend, Marilyn S., Elizabeth J. Gong, and Marilyn S. Prehm. 1999. *Food Practices of Nine Cultural Groups in California*. Davis, Calif.: University of California Cooperative Extension and Nutrition Department.

Ulrich, Roger. 1984. View through a Window May Influence Recovery from Surgery. *Science* 224(1):420–421.

Whitehouse, Sandra, James W. Varni, Michael Seid, Clare Cooper-Marcus, Mary Jane Ensberg, Jennifer R. Jacobs, and Robyn S. Mehlenbeck. 2001.

Evaluating a Children's Hospital Garden Environment: Utilization and Consumer Satisfaction. *Journal of Environmental Psychology* 21:301–314.

Elaborating New Forms of Connection

4

Community Gardens in New York City: Place, Community, and Individuality

Malve von Hassell

How do you rally people to fight back? You start a garden.
—Charles Lott, Baptist Minister

At the corner of Houston Street and the Bowery in New York City's Lower East Side is a community garden.[1] The Liz Christy Garden is one of the oldest community gardens in New York City, in existence since 1974. Once the site had accommodated a tenement building, and later it was a desolate garbage-strewn lot. Squeezed into a narrow space, the garden literally clings to the walls of adjoining buildings with tenacious tendrils of Boston ivy and pungent St. Joseph's Coat roses. Only a sidewalk separates the constant rush of traffic on this main thoroughfare of Lower Manhattan from the peaceful serenity inside the garden. It contains a garden shed with a composting area, various sitting areas, a lily pond, and diverse miniature landscapes created by different members. The survivor of heated battles with the city administration and developers, a genuine community enterprise with individual member plots and common areas, and a horticultural jewel in the heart of the city, the Liz Christy Garden has been one of the flagships of the vibrant community garden movement in New York City.

The Liz Christy Garden concretizes the notion of claiming a place and reengaging with the natural world. Like other community gardens in New York City, the garden is at once intensely personal and political, intensely local and increasingly globalized in its struggle to survive, intensely engaged with the natural world and actively using all the means of modernity at its disposal to facilitate such an engagement. Starting in the early 1970s, community gardeners and activists in New York City have appropriated the concept of empowerment and allied it with themes of political, economic, social, and cultural resistance; notions of an endangered environment at local, national, and global levels; and alternative visions of community, society, and urban life. The struggle on behalf of community gardens straddles grassroots community activism, urban agriculture, environmental activism, and a more individualized search for meaning, spirituality, and community.

Naomi Klein speaks about the process of becoming globalized as a form of becoming empowered and thus regaining control of the local (Klein 2002). This process is apparent in New York City's community gardens and in activism on their behalf. Identification with place, a specific locality, and an individual plot intersects with identification with the entire garden, the neighborhood, the city, other localities, and other countries. The intersection of private-personal realms and public-political realms is reflected in the existence of individual member plots next to common or shared areas within gardens, the production of food for private consumption and for soup kitchens, neighborhood giveaways and markets, the use of gardens for family and community activities, and the nature of activism by individual gardens and the wider community of gardens.

Community gardens represent far more than green space. Gardens represent settings for the experience of growth and decay and active participation in such processes. Gardens are places where life occurs. They are sites for urban renewal far beyond notions of beautifying a neighborhood. To name some of the tangible and intangible benefits of gardens, one might consider opportunities for community life, food production, engagement with nature, psychological and physical benefits to health, education, and political action. For the people involved in these initiatives, the social, cultural, and economic connections are immediate and compelling. In the language of activists, the struggle on behalf of community gardens represents a battle on all fronts, a fight for an entire way of life. This struggle involves the right to design one's own individual garden plot, one's garden, or one's community—but to do so within parameters that do not infringe on others or the sustainability of the environment. These parameters are continually redefined, but recurring themes are resistance to standards imposed by governmental agencies and administrations and to domination by the market economy at various levels of existence, and the need to create spaces for community life, however defined, within the urban maelstrom.

The struggle on behalf of community gardens has been the context for ongoing renegotiations of concepts of community and individuality, linked to a self-conscious examination of how community gardens are perceived and can represent themselves in the public eye. The strategies used over the past decades include legal and legislative efforts, public outreach and media campaigns, and direct action. In order to ensure continued access to and opportunities for creating spaces for nature that partially recapture possibilities for spontaneity and unmediated experiences, community gardeners and activists have been engaged in a process of careful construction, staging, and framing.

In this chapter, I focus on community gardens of the Lower East Side of New York City and more specifically on garden pageants as part and parcel of the struggle on behalf of the gardens.[2] A focus on developments on the Lower East Side helps to illuminate the history of community gardens in New York City as well as the inherent contradictions and conflicting agendas.

I offer some historical background on the community garden movement and outline the philosophical antecedents that have been inspiring gardeners and garden activists. This is the basis for examining garden pageants on the Lower East Side, which epitomize the process of defining individuality and community in relation to each other. This process is central to the nature of activism on behalf of the gardens and the creation of a vision for sustainable human communities that emerged over the last decades of the twentieth century.

Historical Background on the Community Garden Movement

On September 17, 2002, the City of New York and Attorney General Eliot Spitzer settled a lawsuit filed by Spitzer in May 1999 on behalf of community gardens. For three years, this lawsuit and a resulting temporary restraining order had prevented bulldozing of community gardens. Between 1984 and 2002, 91 gardens had been destroyed in New York City; 13 of these were on the Lower East Side. The settlement provided for the preservation of 200 gardens in addition to those already granted permanent status. Thirty-eight gardens were to be released for immediate development and another 198 to be considered for possible preservation. According to activists, at least 50 gardens have been bull-dozed since the settlement. Approximately 2,000 units of housing were to be built on those garden sites released for immediate development. According to GreenThumb, the municipal community gardening orga-nization, in 2004 there were approximately 600 community gardens in New York City altogether; at least 100 of those are still subject to a review process.

The settlement represented a victory of sorts. It brought the total number of gardens that may become permanent to 500 in all boroughs of the city and ensured that all gardens considered for development must undergo due process before being bulldozed. Nevertheless, working community gardens have been bulldozed since the settlement (and will continue to be), while there are approximately 10,000 or more vacant lots and an estimated 20,000 abandoned buildings in New York City potentially available for development (Neighborhood Open Space Coali-tion 2000). Some garden activists question whether the new housing to be constructed will serve the people in the respective neighborhoods, suggesting that it might in effect exacerbate processes of gentrification, resulting in their ultimate displacement from the neighborhood.[3] Others argue that a disproportionate number of gardens still threatened are in poor and low-income communities where the majority of the population are people of color. Furthermore, the preservation stipulation is contin-gent on other developments and can potentially be rescinded. The garden community has been divided as to the ultimate import of the settlement and the next steps to be taken. Since the settlement, only a few garden organizations have maintained the same level of active involvement in fighting for gardens that are threatened.

This is another phase in a long drawn-out struggle that began decades ago. It illustrates that community gardens in America today are unlike urban gardens anywhere else or in any other time.[4] In the United States, the predecessors of today's community gardens date back to the late nineteenth century.

Figure 4.1
Community gardener and child at La Plaza Cultural, Ninth Street and Avenue
C, New York City, 2001 (photo by Malve von Hassell).

Historical Time Line

Bassett identified seven distinct periods, in some instances overlapping,
in the history of urban gardening in the United States (1979). He
describes the Potato Patch Gardens (1894–1917), School Gardens
(1900–1920), Garden City Plots (1905–1920), Liberty Gardens (1917–
1920), Relief Gardens (1930–1939), Victory Gardens (1941–1945), and
Community Gardens (1970–present).

These various periods in the history of urban gardens can be divided
into two major categories: gardens initiated by federal and local governments (1894–1945) and gardens emerging as a result of local grassroots initiatives (1970–present). In the first category, several themes are
replicated over and over again. Urban gardening was to provide poor
relief, improve soul and body, provide moral uplift, encourage self-
reliance and hard work, enhance food supply with home-grown and
fresh produce, beautify neighborhoods, and help dispel social tensions
and curb disorder (Bassett 1979). In addition, during the two world

wars, community gardening was encouraged and presented as making a direct contribution to the war effort. Beginning in the 1970s, there was a shift from a theme of orchestration of gardening from above initiated by federal, state, and municipal governments and institutions for the benefit of gardeners and society as a whole to a theme of empowerment at the local level, with attendant conflicts between gardeners and owners of the respective sites and city administrations.

After almost three decades of little to no urban gardening activities across the United States, the community garden movement took off in the 1970s (von Hassell 2002:47–50). Gardens began to appear in inner-city neighborhoods in different parts of the country. Using buckets, shovels, and bare hands, people cleared vacant lots filled with debris and garbage and turned them into vibrant green spaces.

Various local and citywide gardening coalitions and associations, greening organizations, and nationwide alliances were founded in the 1970s and 1980s. These organizations have focused on community gardens, urban ecology, notions of public ownership of land, waste management, and community revitalization. They include the Green Guerillas, the Neighborhood Open Space Coalition, the Council on the Environment of New York City, the Cornell Cooperative Extension Urban Horticultural Program, and the Trust for Public Land. In the various boroughs, numerous community garden coalitions have emerged, among these the Greening of Harlem Coalition, the Brownsville Garden Coalition in Brooklyn, Bronx United Gardeners (BUG), and the Lower East Side Garden Preservation Coalition, to name just a few. In 1996, these coalitions formed an umbrella organization, the New York City Coalition for the Preservation of Gardens, to advocate better for the gardens.

The municipal organization Operation Green Thumb, now called GreenThumb, has played a critical role. It was formed in 1978 without a budget and with one part-time staff person. By the mid-1990s, funded by federal Community Development Block Grants and under the engaged leadership of Jane Weissman, it had become the largest munic-ipally run community gardening program in the United States. Yet its efforts have always been hampered by its precarious position as a fed-erally funded entity under the auspices of the municipal government. For instance, in 1998 Mayor Rudolph Guiliani transferred gardens administered by GreenThumb to the Department of Housing Preservation and Development, thus eroding GreenThumb's ability to advocate for those gardens.

In the United States, the community garden movement has grown steadily over recent decades. By 1994 there were more than 80 American cities with community gardening programs (Gallup Organization 1994). According to a national survey in 1996, to which a total of 38 cities responded, there were 6,018 gardens (American Community Gardening Association 1998).[5] The most prominent type was the neighborhood or community garden, which accounted for 67.4 percent of the total.

The community garden movement in the United States in the last three decades of the twentieth century was (and continues to be) subject to four interlocking sets of dynamics: the politics of space in the context of urbanization and land scarcity; the transformation of the relationship between processes of food production and food supply in urban environments; conflicting agendas framed around aesthetics and urban beautification, on the one hand, and functionality and urban agriculture, on the other; and the clashes between administrative policies and ideologies and grassroots initiatives.

Politics of Space

Site permanency was and continues to be an issue for most gardens. In 1996 only 92 of approximately 6,000 gardens were in permanent ownership or a land trust (American Community Gardening Association 1998). Only 15 cities reported significant open space initiatives such as spending of funds for garden development or maintenance, formation of coalitions with other groups for advocacy of open space and garden preservation, and inclusion of community gardens in a city's overall plan. In New York City, the community garden movement thrived due to the particular nature of the politics of space and a unique combination of historical developments, including the history of in- and out-migration in different neighborhoods, a complex housing market, and large-scale housing abandonment and neighborhood disinvestment during the late 1960s and 1970s. At the same time, the political struggle with the city administration has been more intense than in other cities in the United States, culminating in the 2002 lawsuit settlement.

The politics of space with respect to community gardens in New York City and other cities in the United States is inseparable from the history of economic fluctuations, changing labor markets, immigration, and the transformation from industrial cities to services-based cities. These developments are reflected in processes of increasing disenfranchisement of large portions of the population, inner-city deterioration, housing abandonment, poverty, and gentrification. The real estate market is the decisive factor in the fate of contested public spaces. Community gardens for the most part are situated on city-owned land with insecure tenure at best. Complicating the status of these garden sites, urban gardening programs in various cities have reported a tendency on the part of developers to consider garden sites as more preferable for development than other urban sites that have not yet been cleaned up (Brown 1980:11). Accordingly, one might argue that gardens, laboriously created out of urban waste sites by predominantly poor and low-income people, represent a step toward gentrification of a neighborhood by making that neighborhood more attractive. Gardens have been and continue to be subject to the forces of the market as much as to shifting political and ideological pressures.

Food Production and Supply in Urban Environments

The extremely rapid transformation of the relationship between production and cities over the past two centuries has proven to be a powerful, emotionally galvanizing factor in today's community gardening movement. In consideration of the historical background of late twentieth-century urban community gardens, urban agriculture and community-based open space management are both relevant dimensions. If one thinks of community gardening as urban agriculture, it is a concept that goes back to the very beginning of cities and their provisioning. Societies in the Western Hemisphere have been transformed from societies where food production was an essential component of the psychological base of existence to societies in which a majority of the population is largely alienated from any processes associated with food production and where production is essentially something that happens elsewhere, even in other countries. The community gardening movement, meanwhile, is increasingly allied with diverse organizations involved in restructuring food production and food supply in urban areas in the United States and elsewhere. The language employed in efforts to promote and protect community gardens from encroaching city administrations and development interests reflects efforts to emphasize relevance in terms of notions of concrete, even marketable "productiveness" such as food production and environmental considerations, along with unquantifiable social, cultural, and aesthetic benefits.

Economic and other benefits of community gardens are hard to quantify, yet there is increasing evidence for such tangible benefits (von Hassell 2002). Community gardens on the Lower East Side are involved in an astounding number of projects and programs—among them, food cooperatives and community-supported agriculture programs, education, art, music, theater, dance, environmental activism, recycling, composting, creation of wildlife habitats, food production, job training, counseling, and senior citizen programs. On a given day in summer on the Lower East Side, one might encounter children gathered around a beekeeper and his hive in rapt attention; garden members hosting a cookout with vegetables from their plots; an old man holding forth on the healing properties of comfrey, chamomile, and mint; or people at tables shaded by grape vines playing a game of dominoes. Community gardeners have accomplished all this in the face of a largely unsupportive, if not hostile, city administration.

Conflicting Agendas

The conflicting agendas surrounding conceptualizations of the purpose of community gardens can be traced back to the nineteenth century, In the mid-nineteenth century, the Schrebergärten movement in Germany and Austria resulted in the creation of allotment gardens that in principle were modeled on earlier Armengärten (gardens for the poor).[6] In contrast to previous urban agriculture efforts, the Schrebergärten movement emphasized another conceptual element: the notion of the healthfulness of gardening allied with notions of aesthetic and moral improvement. The Schrebergärten movement and its later incarnations reflect a shift in the conceptualization of the activity of gardening.[7] Initially conceived as

Figure 4.2
Child about to enter Tranquilidad Garden, Fourth Street and Avenue C, New York City, 2001 (photo by Malve von Hassell).

an activity suitable and beneficial for members of the working class, providing access to subsistence farming and kitchen garden produce, the emphasis shifted to notions of beautification, of both the soul and its environment, combined with healthfulness as bulwarks in a stressful industrial city. Gardening for food production was no longer the sole or principal goal.

In urban garden initiatives in the United States over the last decades of the twentieth century, the emphasis shifted back to a renewed concern with food, paralleled by a growing concern with organic production and the perceived need to reinject the experience of food production into daily lives. This is supported by nationwide associations that are seeking to develop sustainable communities and establish food security in urban areas. In the current community garden movement, utilitarian concerns and aesthetic concerns are most closely allied in the environmental movement, where food production, in particular organic food production, sustainability, and greening or beautification of the environment are part and parcel of the same effort. Together, such concerns also lend impetus to initiatives of social reconstruction of neighborhoods.

The community garden movement in New York City and in the United States as a whole does not represent a single homogeneous entity with a single agenda. Instead, it has been characterized by heterogeneity, diversity, and a great variety in the types of initiatives that have emerged: school gardens, senior gardens, gardens with a focus on horticulture, gardens strongly vested in urban agriculture, and gardens as settings for community organization and events. These initiatives include individual gardens with their respective histories and marked by internal diversity and fragmentation; neighborhood, citywide, and national coalitions that cut across these microcommunities; diverse greening and food security organizations; and individual activists, lawyers, and other supporters. The community garden movement with its eclectic set of agendas cuts across economic and noneconomic interests. Community gardeners come from a range of backgrounds, with the majority low-income and poor people of color. The diversity of race, class, and cultural backgrounds is evident within and between individual gardens and in garden coalitions, and it is inherent in an ongoing process of renegotiation of issues and conflicts on an almost daily basis in the gardens and in the struggle on their behalf.

Throughout, the community garden movement has retained much of its ad hoc character. The generally flexible organizational patterns within gardens mirror the organizational patterns of coalitions. The tenuous nature of relationships among community gardeners, bound by nothing other than individual commitment—that is, the very frailty of these microcommunities—has proven to be a strength. The nature of the praxis of gardening, particularly within the confines of an urban community garden, involves a continuous reworking and revitalization of activism on the ground. Each garden consists of a complex web of interpersonal dynamics that involve issues of race, class, and gender. Each garden community confronts the ongoing challenge of balancing individual interests and needs and interests of the group. Gardens offer a training ground for democracy in practice. The resulting flexibility and resilience have contributed to the vitality of garden coalitions, repeatedly overcoming fragmentation and conflicting agendas.

Ideological Dynamics, Economic and Political Developments, and Local Initiatives

Ideological dynamics, reflective of and in tandem with economic and political developments, have subjected urban community garden initiatives to the push and pull effects of alternating paternalism, manipulation, suppression, and benign neglect. Beginning in the late nineteenth century as a form of paternalistic charity and moral and physical improvement of the poor and working class imposed by federal, state, and municipal authorities, community gardening initiatives have evolved into vibrant, locally based grassroots movements that are increasingly allying themselves with nationwide and global concerns.

The 1960s and 1970s provided much of the ideological impetus behind the community garden movement in the latter part of the twentieth century. The civil rights movement spawned a generation of pioneer community organizers. From civil rights, the focus turned to poverty, housing, labor, and the environment. The multilevel approach to community revitalization that emerged in the 1980s can be traced back to these years. At the grassroots level, the growing awareness of a threatened environment gave rise to a multitude of efforts that ranged from organic gardening to back-to-nature initiatives. These efforts were informed by idealized concepts of Mother Earth, a perception of human beings as destructive—proverbial snakes in paradise—and a notion of a biotic community in which human beings had to relearn to find their proper place.

In the 1980s and 1990s, a growing realization of the effects of a global market economy resulted in various kinds of retrenchment and siege mentalities across the United States, from utopian communities to gated communities. At the level of community activism, it was reflected in a focus on the microcontext; locally based efforts presented themselves as a form of concrete resistance and action in the face of an overwhelming, alienating, and opaque global economy in both real and symbolic terms.

Community gardens in New York City and on the Lower East Side have emerged in the context of housing abandonment and gentrification. Contradictory trends and dynamics of urban history are played out in these spaces. The Lower East Side has been the setting for a series of spectacular conflicts between community gardeners, developers, and the city administration. In this context, various garden groups and coalitions emerged in this neighborhood that have embraced the struggle for community gardens in all of New York City. Like other urban neighborhoods, the Lower East Side is subject to shifting populations and patterns of in- and out-migration. Community gardens flourish in the place of buildings demolished in the 1970s, 1980s, and 1990s. Many residents in those buildings were displaced from the neighborhood. Community gardens include both old-time residents of the neighborhood and newcomers who moved in during successive waves of gentrification. The gardens emerged as the result of initiatives to resist precisely these efforts at gentrification as much as initiatives to improve the neighborhood, thus reinforcing the process of gentrification.

Community gardens represent microhistories of urban life in America, revealing not only the shifting forces of the market but also histories of different population groups as active agents. Community gardens become repositories of various ideological strains and historical perceptions and thus have been the locus of and transformative agent for a new urban politics.

Philosophical Antecedents

Community gardeners point to various writers whom they consider seminal to their ideas about community gardening. Among them are Simone Weil, Iris Murdoch, Ronald Ableman, and Wendell Berry. These writers are concerned with the contradictions of the demands of the group versus the needs of the individual within a fragile, even damaged environment, seeking to find a constructive and dynamic middle ground between untrammeled individualism and stifling communal rules. Simone Weil argues that the individual needs to escape the collective frenzy and that such an escape is possible only through progressive decentralization of social life in conjunction with a place-based focus for individual existence (Weil 1977:62). Like Weil, Iris Murdoch looks at advances in the sciences and technology over the past centuries as a double-edged sword, partially responsible for the growing malaise and sense of life as self-enclosed and purposeless (Murdoch 1970:79). According to Murdoch, a way out of this despair of the modern individual locked in on self is to look outside self—for instance, at nature. This experience can open the soul and become the basis for one's ability to live in the world and with others in a constructive and non-destructive fashion. In the work of Paul Ableman (1993) and Wendell Berry (1985), these philosophical positions are transmuted into a poetic language of concrete experience: the love for the soil, creation, growth and decay, and the cycle of life and death.

These philosophers, poets, and writers address the questions associated with the challenge of negotiating a meaningful and fulfilled individual life in the context of modern society, with its trappings of consumerism, anomie, alienation, and environmental degradation. The concern with these questions reappears in community gardens, in the manner in which gardeners speak about the gardens and their fight for the gardens, and in actions and events associated with the gardens.

Gardeners, environmentalists, and activists selectively embrace an amorphous set of beliefs and values. Described as ecospirituality and ecofeminism in some of the literature on environmentalism (Milton 1993, 1996), it is appropriated from a political, philosophical, religious, and mythological smorgasbord. Certain basic tenets can be discerned:

• A rejection of aspects of the modern materialistic culture
• A partial embrace of alternative notions of property ownership and cooperative management
• A profound concern with the future of the environment
• A vision of a community that is self-consciously multiracial and multi-ethnic, extends across age and gender divisions as well as across class lines, and extends beyond the borders of the local site or area to include the block, the neighborhood, and the entire city
• An identification with the struggle of people in other parts of the country, such as other community gardeners and regional farmers
• An embrace of the notion of sustainability
• A conceptual linkage with comparable and related struggles at a global level

The Rites of Spring pageant on the Lower East Side transforms these philosophical tenets into a day-long ceremony that expresses both individuality and community in the context of a compelling vision for sustainable urban communities of the future.

Garden Pageants as Performance of Community and Individuality

The annual Rites of Spring pageant is a 10-hour procession through the Lower East Side in May. Formally referred to as a Procession to Save Our Gardens, the pageant is a cross of a political demonstration, a ritualized invocation, and a community celebration. The result of a process of construction on many levels, the pageant incorporates diverse religious themes and myths from India, Africa, and ancient Greece. The pageant was originally composed as an entity by Felicia Young, the founder of the organization Earth Celebrations, in 1991; since then it has been appropriated by gardeners and other neighborhood residents.

Artists, actors, and others from all over the city volunteer in the pageant every year. It is the product of creativity on part of both

Figure 4.3
Rites of Spring pageant: (L to R) Gaia on a float, Wind (in white), Water, and Fire, with map of gardens to be visited (carried behind), May 1996 (photo by Malve von Hassell).

"outsiders" and "residents" of the neighborhood, rather than something "indigenously" developed. I qualify these terms in that they are entirely subjective and open to interpretation. On the Lower East Side, the community garden population essentially reflects the population of the neighborhood; approximately 70 percent of the gardeners are Puerto Rican and the remainder white, African American, and Asian. The ratio of people of color versus white people participating in the pageant is roughly the reverse of the ratio in the gardens. The pageant attracts participants from all boroughs as well as from outside New York City. The majority of participants in the procession are white, while the members in the various gardens visited reflect the population distribution of those gardens. This factor is part of the constructed image of the pageant as local, rooted in place. The pageant is constructed on the fault lines of these contradictions, just as the tenements of the Lower East Side are situated precariously on top of swamp land, underground streams, and landfill. Thus, the pageant expresses and is defined by the destructiveness and fluidity of an urban environment and constructed images of a community.

More than five hundred people are involved in the production of the Rites of Spring pageant. The central cast of characters includes Gaia, the four seasons, the elements, the Earth, Compost, Rainbow, and the Green Man. There are flowers, garden insects, and other beings associated with gardens and nature. The costumes, made by hand by the volunteers and involving a minimum of purchased materials, are stunning in their beauty and creativity. Some individuals identify with particular characters in the procession and craft their own costumes every year. Summer wears a full-length wide skirt woven with grass that swishes softly along with every step and a broad-rimmed hat with grass growing out of it. The Vegetable Goddess wears a crown of carrots and a necklace made of giant radishes, looking a bit wilted at the end of the day. Herbena represents the world of herbs; she wears a fragrant costume decorated with bunches of fresh and dried herbs, cinnamon sticks, cloves, and nutmeg. Cultures from all over the world inspire the creation of characters in the procession, including the Mud People, derived from characters in theatrical performances among New Guinea peoples. They are coated in pale white mud and wear oversized wobbly full-head masks that only hint at eyes and

Figure 4.4
Rites of Spring pageant. The Mud People followed by Primavera puppet on a float, May 1996 (photo by Malve von Hassell).

mouths. They are not assigned to a specific position in the procession, but rather weave in and out of the line up and move freely among the spectators, acting as tricksters of sorts.

The procession moves from one garden to the next on the Lower East Side and conducts blessing ceremonies at each garden visited. Each garden develops its own welcoming ceremony. In some, gardeners read poetry or perform a piece of music. Some gardens offer food and drink. In one garden, the beautifully attired garden mistress of ceremonies stands next to a table set with a tablecloth, a vase, candles, and a tray with a teapot. Gaia, the Earth Mother, a white-clad figure made of wire, papier-maché, and lacy fabric on a float under a bower of roses, is carried into the garden, while the mournful sound of conch shells fills the air. Inside the garden, the mistress of ceremonies takes a tulip bulb out of Gaia's belly and gravely hands it to the gardener in charge of ceremonies at that particular garden. A bowl of clay is "constructed" throughout the day; in each garden visited, a garden representative receives a piece of clay from the mistress of ceremonies and attaches it to the rim of the bowl, also placing a leaf or fruit from the garden into the bowl. The "work in progress" is carried along as the procession makes its way from one garden to the next. At the end of the day, the "communal salad bowl," as it is called in the script, is completely formed and is filled with an accumulation of diverse greens from all the gardens.

The procession visits the locations of various gardens that have been eliminated over the years, staking out claims to a landscape of place memories, current sites of struggle, and visions for the future. For instance, commemorative stops are made at the sites of the former Garden of Eden (bulldozed in 1986); the Jardín de la 10th Street, also known as "Little Puerto Rico" (bulldozed in 1997); and the Jardín de Esperanza (bulldozed 2000). These gardens are referred to as "martyrs."

As the procession makes its way through the Lower East Side, it enacts a drama of birth, marriage, struggle, and successful emergence from struggle. The procession tells the story of the birth of Gaia, the Earth Mother, emerging from a giant pink birth canal, her marriage to the Green Man, and her abduction by developers in black business suits. In these scenes a participant plays the role of Gaia. The developers drag Gaia away and place her on a pickup truck. Throughout the rest of the day at certain intersections, one can see the truck roll by with Gaia screaming vociferously from the back of the truck. Eventually, in a dramatic battle with the developers, the gardeners, supported by earth and garden spirits, emerge victorious. The developers flee, their business suits in disarray, and the developer spirits, represented by robot-like figures, fall to the ground lifeless, disintegrating into their various components. In the closing ceremony, children release butterflies into the spring air.

The physical character of the procession is unique in its fragility and impermanence. For months, adults and children work on the giant puppets, floats, and costumes for the procession. Most of this work takes place in a room in the community center on East Sixth Street, which also houses most of the costumes and makings for the floats throughout the remainder of the year. Flower wreaths carried by garden spirits and helpers are prepared the night before the pageant. Volunteers make everything out of inexpensive materials—cardboard, glitter paints, beads, dried herbs, chains of nuts, and seashells. They lovingly remake and repatch collages and constructs used in the pageant every year. The pageant's inventiveness and creativity proudly proclaim its character as an evanescent, handmade product of a labor of love in affinity with the thriving and equally evanescent gardens.

Analysis

The dynamic tension between conceptualizations of community and individuality is a central element in the Rites of Spring pageant. Visions of community are as diverse as community gardeners themselves; this diversity inspires the process of production, the script of the pageant, and its enactment. The pageant with its rituals of unity celebrates the inherent contradictions of such a notion of community as a tension-filled, amorphous entity. It is contingent on a conceptualization of individuality that reflects existence in the late twentieth century. Only fragments of the whole are visible to the observer and to the self; individual actions are only partially communicable and partially perceived. Creativity at times approaches the nature of an individual vision quest, the portent of which cannot be fully communicated. Collaboration in the pageant and at the neighborhood or citywide level on behalf of community gardens is a fragile balancing act, characterized by an idiosyncratic mix of spontaneity and carefully constructed displays, individual creativity, and diverse visions of community.

Conceptualizations of Individuality and Community

Participants in the pageant are self-consciously aware of the fragmentary nature of modern existence and in fact celebrate this as a central part of individual experience. A conversation with gardeners and participants on the eve of a pageant provides a window for thinking about this concept. I had gone to the Community Center on Sixth Street, where people were preparing for the pageant on the following day. Some were sewing costumes; some were making flower wreaths; others were folding brochures that were to be handed out during the procession. I sat on the tar roof and helped to fold brochures. It was hot, and the conversation ranged freely; we talked about jobs, personal lives, the struggle for the gardens, the mayor, and practical matters regarding the pageant.

At some point, someone raised the question of communicability of elements in the pageant. This woman, not a gardener but a volunteer assisting with the pageant, argued that no person perhaps other than the original founder, Felicia Young, had a complete understanding of what the various figures and compositions and choreographed scenes were supposed to symbolize. Each of the figures or spirits had his or her own ideas of what they were to represent, and these individual images could not really be communicated or explicated to others, least of all to people in the audience. A gardener and activist, who earlier had argued that the pageant has an educative component, now qualified that statement. He said that in some respects, the pageant is just for those participating in the procession throughout the long day until the closing ceremony at night, further adding that the principal element was not necessarily about communicating. This statement points to the concept of individuality and the idea of what community gardening means to the individuals involved in it. Participants acknowledge experience as a solitary activity and at the same time as a vital component of a larger entity. Individuality is not submerged; it is the defining element, while fragile links of meaning between individuals are reaffirmed and renewed repeatedly in ritualized fashion. The pageant affirms and expresses moments of union, whether through the ritual of blessing ceremonies in every garden or in the opening and closing ceremonies.

Initially the result of one individual's creative effort and still driven by this individual's commitment, the pageant has become a collaborative effort. This particular history echoes the history of many community gardens. Many gardens were started by a few individuals and quickly expanded to turn into a project involving an entire community. In a mirror image of gardens, the pageants link individuality, communicability, and community in a dynamic relationship. Pageants, gardens, and individual member plots are creations of internal visions and an aesthetic of hope; thus, they are only partially communicable. Gardens and pageants allow space for individual creativity, while offering points of intersection with others. They provide a framework for experiential learning about nature and the individual's place in it, contingent on recognition of needs of the community. In community gardens, ideas for alternative forms of existence in an urban environment are made concrete; pageants transform these same ideas into a stylized celebration that acquires a life of its own in the process.

Individuality, Community, and Activism

Activism on behalf of community gardens is subject to the tensions between individual and community interests and agendas. Self-display and affirmation of the local, sustained by identification with citywide and even national and global struggles, become part and parcel of the theater of resistance. Community-based organizations, garden coalitions, individual garden groups, and individuals act both spontaneously and as self-conscious, directed players in a script, alternating between roles as victims and as empowered agents. Concepts of community, history, and memory are both the themes of and props for the script. They inspire individual gardens' self-representation in brochures, statements, public displays, and stories told about individual gardens' histories and creation. These concepts also play a central role in the scripts for different forms of activism by diverse garden coalitions. The themes are carefully constructed and displayed. The press is invited to protests, commemorative garden events, and pageants. Photographers and film-makers record the pageant, which in itself represents a construct of spontaneity and a carefully planned and directed performance.

The observed is involved in the construction of his or her own image, staging events and preparing appropriate backgrounds. In turn, the observer plays a part. In the construction of community in the context of initiatives on behalf of community gardens, the gaze of the observer— both concrete by looking into the semiprivate gardens from the outside and conceptual through the media—helps to create and shape the internalized image of community.

In their language, themes, organizational patterns, and forms of action, individual gardens, pageants, and garden activism are urban collages in which the very precariousness of the constructs becomes a central element in their self-display and appeal—a part of the dialectical process of identity creation. The contradiction between creativity for its own sake and for display and effect reflects creative efforts in an urban context—in the artistic sense as much as in the sense of political action. Disparate and contradictory elements are joined to create a whole and to make a statement. Visions for community gardens and for urban communities of the future are based on rejection and simultaneous embrace and transformation of urban environments. Like other forms of activism on behalf of community gardens, pageants weave eclectically assembled images of the past into ideas for the future in a language of struggle that is derived equally from the community housing initiatives and the environmental justice movement in the second half of the twentieth century.

Efforts on behalf of community gardens are fraught with conflict at many levels, beginning with individual gardens' internal politics and continuing to different visions for the community. Poised on the edge of an ideological sword in their contradictory roles in political, economic, and social changes and in their diverse class and cultural compositions, community gardens are both expressions of and the embodiment of resistance to processes of gentrification of neighborhoods.[8] Garden coalitions, organizations, individual garden groups, and activists are engaged in an at times acrimonious sparring about which gardens will be "chosen" to survive, the nature of the process of selection, the precise parameters for the maintenance of existing community gardens and the creation of future ones, and vehicles for the long-term preservation of such spaces. This divisiveness reflects the same kind of fragmentation along social class, cultural, and ethnic/racial lines that has plagued the struggle all along. Yet these efforts represent a remarkable instance of locally based initiatives, supported by highly idiosyncratic and diverse groups, that have grown to include the entire city. In fact, they draw on this expanded base as a source of strength and have brought about a rethinking of policies and attitudes at local and state administrative levels. This is reflected most notably in the 2002 settlement. Community garden activism in effect succeeded in forcing the city administration to the bargaining table and in obtaining the sustained support of numerous high-ranking government officials at both municipal and state levels.

Conclusion

The brochure for the Winter Candle Lantern pageant, an annual event on the Lower East Side, invites people to join in "the Odyssey of the Earth." By definition, an odyssey involves pain and suffering as well as the discovery of beauty. Participants make a conceptual linkage between a spiritual odyssey, the struggle for the gardens, and the notion of the environment as a place for a spiritual odyssey; accordingly, nature can explain the nature of suffering and ultimately the meaning of life by providing an experiential setting for coming to terms with the existence of pain.[9] Modern society, with a landscape dominated by urban sprawl, suburban strip malls, and factory farming, is perceived as failing to provide such a setting.

One might argue that in this self-conscious embrace of nature, joined with a perception of modern society as devoid of such a power, community gardeners seek to return to an idealized concept of community in a symbiotic relationship with nature. The various ideological strains involved, however, indicate that the ideas behind community gardening are not reducible to a simplistic utopian, back-to-nature enterprise. Community gardeners select aspects from different sets of beliefs and ideologies and combine these with a skillful manipulation of all the means of contemporary society at their disposal to achieve their goal. The goal and the strategies to achieve it are multifaceted, reflecting the diversity of groups involved. This army does not march in lockstep and does not have a clearly discernible organizational structure or chain of command. Sometimes described in the press as a motley crew, the individuals involved in the community garden movement are characterized by diversity and stubborn individualism. They confront bulldozers and the powers of the market with weapons fashioned out of informed utilization of all forms of media, carnivals of reversal, recycled soda cans turned into candles, seed bombs, and flowers. The fight for community gardens is a struggle for a way of life that is by no means a return to a simpler existence, but rather a creation of something new on the basis of existing elements.

Notes

1. Charles Lott, Baptist minister at the community garden on Glenmore Avenue and Barbed Street in East New York, one of New York City's oldest gardens (Hickey 1994:49).

2. See also my ethnography on community gardens in New York City (von Hassell 2002). The bulk of the research was conducted between 1995 and 2001.

While I was familiar with many of the approximately 45 gardens and also visited gardens in other neighborhoods, I focused on 10 gardens for more in-depth observation in addition to research about activism on behalf of the gardens on the Lower East Side as well as citywide.

3. According to the Department of Housing Preservation and Development in New York City, the new homes to be built on garden sites slated for development are intended for buyers with incomes of $35,000 to $75,000 a year, and people in the respective neighborhoods are to be given preference. This may be of little comfort to the people whose gardens in Brownsville have been bulldozed. The U.S. Census shows that Brownsville had a median household income of $19,722 in 2000.

4. Other urban gardens involve comparable elements but are nevertheless profoundly different in terms of historical, organizational, cultural, and political dynamics. One might consider dachas in Kiev, Ukraine, Schrebergärten in Berlin, Germany, or even the so-called Victory Gardens and Liberty Gardens in the United States during the two world wars. Russian and Ukrainian dachas, originally country cottages, offer privacy away from the eye of the state, a sense of control over one dimension of life as well as produce, albeit often grown on polluted soil, social life, and an exposure to nature of sorts. Schrebergärten, originating in the nineteenth century in Austria and Germany, now reflect two dominant ideological strains—one intensely conservative and the other countercultural, both reflecting notions of gardens as status symbols. The first involves members of the urban middle class striving to reengage with nature. The second strain is linked to efforts by a disenfranchised working-class community, in particular in the former German Democratic Republic and now the so-called new states, to obtain control over some aspects of their lives in a framework that offers at least the illusion of privacy from the eye of the state and opportunities for community life. The Victory Gardens and Liberty Gardens of World Wars I and II, respectively—individual kitchen gardens and large areas in and along the margins of urban centers—were organized and encouraged by local and federal administrations in support of the war effort and were linked to poor relief as well as to various forms of social control; they involved little to no independent input by local communities or participating gardeners.

5. As of this writing there has been no new nationwide survey of community gardens. However, ongoing publications such as the *Community Greening Review* published by the American Community Gardening Association and Web sites set up by organizations and associations that support urban community gardens attest to the vibrancy of community garden initiatives all over the country, as well as in New York City. This is particularly remarkable in the light of the state of the economy over the past few years, social and political pressures, and funding cutbacks across the board that leave little margin for "nonessentials" such as community gardens.

6. The term *allotment gardening* refers to a process where municipal, state, or federal administrations assigned or made plots of land to individual

families for growing food. In Germany and Austria, this was the basis for the so-called Schrebergärten. In the United States, allotment gardening played a role most notably during the two world wars and in the 1930s as a form of poor relief.

7. The originator of the Schrebergärten movement was Daniel Gottlieb Moritz Schreber, a doctor from Leipzig. For Schreber, the activity of gardening and the associated physical exercise represented one of the routes toward creating healthy minds and bodies and, by implication, a healthier society, hence strengthening the German people and enabling them to gain ascendancy over other nations. This nationalistic ideal was taken to its extreme by Nazi ideology. It is difficult in retrospect to consider the Schrebergärten movement in Germany today as something separate and distinct from this ideology. It is important to acknowledge this set of ideological strains underlying the back-to-nature notions in community gardening. At the same time, it is equally important to refrain from reducing all these strains to its later reincarnation as part of an ultranationalist and racial agenda. Rather, one must recognize the equally powerful and compelling elements of communitarian thought and notions of sustainable communities, allied to a fundamental critique of society, which have been inspiring community gardening initiatives in the latter half of the twentieth century and the early twenty-first century.

8. Also see Martinez for a discussion of the dynamics of class on the Lower East Side (Martinez 2001).

9. Also see Stanley Diamond for a discussion of the role of art and ritual in modern society, in particular, what he describes as "the integrated arts of the crisis rite that reunites man, woman, nature, and society and resolves its ambivalence while defending and defining the liberty and potential of the person" (Diamond 1982:877).

References

Ableman, Paul. 1993. *From the Good Earth: A Celebration of Growing Food around the World*. New York: Abrams.

American Community Gardening Association. 1998. *National Community Gardening Survey*. New York: City of New York, Department of General Services, Operation GreenThumb.

Bassett, T. J. 1979. Vacant Land Cultivation—Community Gardening in America 1893–1978. Master's thesis, University of California at Berkeley.

Berry, Wendell. 1985. *Collected Poems, 1957–1982*. San Francisco: North Point Press.

Brown, Allison. 1980. *Extension Urban Gardening: The 16 Cities Experience*. Washington, D.C.: U.S. Department of Agriculture.

Diamond, Stanley. 1982. Subversive Art. *Social Research* 49 (4):854–877.

Gallup Organization. 1994. *National Gardening Survey*. Princeton, N.J.: Gallup Organization.

Hickey, Mary Frances. 1994. Greening the Mean Streets. *New York*, Oct. 17:47–53.

Klein, Naomi. 2002. *Fences and Windows: Dispatches from the Front Lines of the Globalization Debate*. New York: Picador USA.

Martinez, Miranda. 2001. Constructing Community: The Community Gardens of the Lower East Side. Ph.D. dissertation, New York University.

Milton, Kay, ed. 1993. *Environmentalism: The View from Anthropology*. London: Routledge.

Milton, Kay, ed. 1996. *Environmentalism and Cultural Theory: Exploring the Role of Anthropology in Environmental Discourse*. New York: Routledge.

Murdoch, Iris. 1970. *The Sovereignty of Good*. London: Routledge.

Neighborhood Open Space Coalition. 2000. *Urban Outdoors Review*. New York: Spring.

von Hassell, Malve. 2002. *The Struggle for Eden: Community Gardens in New York City*. Westport, Conn.: Bergin and Garvey.

Weil, Simone. 1977. *The Simone Weil Reader*, ed. George Panichas. New York: David McKay Company, Inc.

5

Urban Connections to Locally Grown Produce

Susan L. Andreatta

Whether in the form of countermovements to globalization or urbanites acting on issues of personal or environmental health, awareness in Europe and the United States is growing that industrialized agriculture needs to change. Agriculture, direct marketing, and support for organic and sustainable agriculture practices offer evidence that consumers and farmers are changing their interaction in the agriculture and food system. As food production and consumption become more consciously entwined, urban populations become more closely linked to natural environments and the local economy, reducing the distance from field to plate.

In this chapter, I examine the agriculture and food system (which from here on will be referred to as the agrofood system) and the emergence of alternatives that challenge the industrialized food system. I briefly explore globalization of agriculture, the slow food movement, and direct marketing for small-scale farmers and urban consumers through local farmers markets and community-supported agriculture arrangements. I also identify some alternative connections emerging in urban agriculture movements. As an applied anthropologist who has examined small-scale food production internationally and domestically, I report from my current research in North Carolina to identify various trends that illustrate growing connections to place throughout the United States.

Globalization of Agriculture

For the past century, a large sector of the agrofood industry has been moving toward industrialization, concentration, and globalization.[1]

Technological advances in food storage, transportation, and processing have moved our agrofood system from the local and regional to the global scope. More specifically, the transformations of food regimes from Fordism (1943–1973) to the post-Fordist era (1973 to the present) have seen a gradual increase in monoculture crop specialization and a reliance on transportation and other technologies aimed for profit.[2]

Some scholars are less sympathetic to the concept of globalization of the agrofood sector, suggesting that it adds nothing new to the debate, for trade and contact on a global scale have been around more than a few centuries (Goodman and Watts 1994; Mintz 1985, 1996). Such scholars tend to emphasize a shift in the use of rural space to understand the transformations occurring in the agrofood sector on a global scale (Andreatta 1998; Andreatta and Wickcliffe 2002). As Spector points out,

We have created a profound cultural divide between farmers and the rest of society. No longer do we see small diversified farmers scattered across the land-scape. No longer do the majority of farmers maintain farming as their only occu-pation. As we have lost farmers to this "efficiency" in agriculture, we have also lost farm land—nearly a million acres in this past decade. And we have lost our connection to our food source and to the land (Spector 2000:289).

Mass production of commodities through industrializing the agri-culture and food system has turned agri-"culture" into agri-"business." These strategies are not completely original acts or new phenomena. Major transnational corporations (TNCs) such as Cargill, Con Agra, Geest, Tate and Lyle, United Fruit, and Uniroyal have long histories of obtaining raw materials globally (consider rubber, petroleum, cotton, and sugar). What is changing among TNCs, however, are their multiple interests. Corporations such as Con Agra, Cargill, and Monsanto, which once specialized in agricultural trading and manufacture, have diversi-fied their assets and activities to include the production of steel and cement and investments in construction, real estate, and insurance. As a result, TNCs are involved in a number of international activities and multiple enterprises that enable them to source globally and easily relo-cate to maintain their operations (McMichael 1994). The global indus-trialized agrofood system has therefore put a greater distance between rural food producers and the consuming public. In fact, "consumers have lost contact with those who grow their food and sadly farmers have lost contact with those who eat their food" (Corum, Rosenzeig, and Gibson 2001:viii).

Today a considerable amount of food is being produced overseas for big business. To grow and process food requires land, labor, and capital. Although capital moves freely between TNCs and across borders, land and labor are less mobile. Food production has therefore gone to where land and labor are cheapest. The current agrofood system is devoid of geographical dependencies, seasonality, and, some might add, taste. Moreover, the World Bank, among other organizations, encourages wealthier nations to consume from the soils of the less wealthy nations as part of structural adjustment strategies for indebted countries. They urge poor nations to use their best lands to produce not staple foods such as rice, beans, and corn for local consumption, but strawberries, red peppers, broccoli, flowers, and other exportable crops to reduce their foreign debt. They often push production of staples for local consumption onto less productive and more fragile lands, whose misuse can lead to a number of other environmental problems, such as erosion, famine, pollution, and potable water shortage. "Consuming the products of others' soil makes us ignorant of the limits of our own dependence on the natural world" (Baum 2002:24).

Globalization of the agrofood system has transformed many people's access to the production of agricultural products and to food. Donna Gabaccia, in her book entitled *We Are What We Eat* (1998), examines the history of ethnic foods and the making of the American food system. She presents a historical account of the cooking customs of Native Americans and immigrant populations in America and the transformation from authenticity to the homogenization of canned food, TV dinners, microwaved meals, and eating out. This mass production of food, spearheaded by a number of TNCs involved in the agrofood industry, has made it easier for family members to be "liberated" from the kitchen. Freedom from the kitchen, from growing and cooking one's own meals, has affected society, culture, and the use of rural space. A vast number of eaters now rely on convenience foods for their daily food intake, food that is grown many miles away from where it is prepared and consumed. Food items travel an average of 1,300 miles before they reach the consumer's plate (Schlosser 2001). Not only have global processes been translated into a greater distance between field and plate, there have also been losses in control of production, marketing, and consumption, in biodiversity and cultural knowledge of agricultural practices in the production, preservation and consumption of food.

As a response to these transformations, urban groups are organizing formally and informally to protect their local agrofood system (see chapter 6). A local agrofood system comprises all the individuals and processes involved in getting food from local farms to local tables. Emphasized and celebrated in this process is the "taste of localness." By reducing the number of hands and miles involved in moving a product from the field to the table and bringing the table closer to the field, a local agrofood system not only saves energy, but also supports local communities and, often, small-scale producers (Andreatta and Wickliffe 2002). Negative environmental impacts are also reduced, and consumers come to see their food purchases as part of a more sustainable food system. Alternatives addressed in this chapter illustrate the urban public's support for local agriculture and their growing reconnection with nearby farms and farmland.

I turn now to several movements that are contributing to an alternative agrofood system.

Alternatives to Globalization: Slow Food International

One reaction to homogenizing the food system and to the increasing dependence on fast food chains (the so-called McDonaldization of food as a consequence of the globalized industrial agro-food system) was the creation of the slow food movement. In 1986, Carlo Petrini reacted to the opening of a McDonald's hamburger restaurant in Rome's famous Piazza di Spagna by organizing Slow Food International to protest eating fast, eating without consciousness, eating without recognizing taste, and eating without reverence for local cuisine (Petrini 1997). The group of protesters along with Petrini "proclaimed it was time to get back to the two-hour lunch and the four-hour dinner" (Kummer 2002). "Formally founded at a Paris gathering in 1989, the *Agricola* Slow Food Movement has become an international rallying point for the inevitable backlash against societal velocity and homogenized, industrial grub" (Ecoglobe

News 1999:1). Slow Food concentrated its efforts on valuing time, the "slow" life philosophy, bringing back the kitchen and table as centers of pleasure, culture, community, and conviviality—of sharing an appreciation of great food and wine among friends and family. The organization adopted the snail, a creature both slow and edible, as its symbol to illustrate its opposition to fast life and fast food. There are offices in Paris (1989), Switzerland (1995), Germany (1998), and New York (2000). Members are also organized in Brazil, Japan, Singapore, Venezuela, and many other countries.

By the 1990s, Slow Food convivia members increasingly became advocates for the protection of the environment as well as for the enjoyment and appreciation of fine food and drink. "Convivium comes from the word conviviality, which means to share, not be stagnant promoting not just sharing of food but the sharing of the human experience with people from different backgrounds and food cultures, including consumers and producers" (Binder 2001:1). Slow Food members reject homogeneity of the agrofood system by supporting and preserving local, authentic cuisine and the artisan food makers. Petrini contends, "A hundred years ago, people ate between 100 and 120 different species of food. Now our diet is made up of at most ten or twelve species" (Stille 2001:1). To protect such food sources and foods, the movement created the Slow Food Ark of Taste, inspired by Noah's Ark, that seeks to identify and publicize the endangered foods and drinks (Slow Food 2004b). Some of the endangered items in the United States include the Delaware Bay oyster, the Bourbon Red turkey, and naturally grown wild rice from the lake regions of Minnesota and Wisconsin. These products are economically and ecologically fragile, yet they are an important part of local economies and culture (Slow Food USA 2004b). It is believed that if market demand increases, supply will increase for these culinary delights. Slow Food hopes to keep alive a culture that values a locally grown, vine-ripened tomato, as opposed to a picked-green artificially reddened supermarket tomato.[3]

The Piedmont market town of Bra located in the foothills of the Italian Alps is the headquarters of Slow Food International. Since 1995, the Slow Food organization has grown from 25,000 to 80,000 members in 100 countries organized into 560 local convivia (in Italy known as *condotte*) (Slow Food 2004a). The Slow Food movement is expanding in North America, with more than 10,000 members, loosely organized into 85 convivia (Martins 2002). Members include farmers, chefs, and consumers/eaters who are combining their efforts to promote a lifestyle alternative. As Axelrod extols, "Believing that efficiency, biotechnology and other global forces erode our abilities to savor not only our food, but also our lives, Slow Food suggests our defense should begin at the table. Let us rediscover the flavors and savors of regional cooking and banish the degrading effects of Fast Food" (Axelrod 2001:1).

Eco-gastronomy seeks to preserve diverse and endangered traditional and regional food sources, support farmers and rural traditions, and address issues of equity and hunger. As such, Slow Food members support sustainable agricultural practices and oppose unnecessary chemical and technical treatment of food. At the heart of Slow Food is support for quality and diversity over convenience and regularity (such as standardization of size, color, and availabilities). Slow Food works toward bringing food and food cultures together. Members of the movement teach an appreciation for where food comes from and create excitement for members to teach their own children, friends, and family about the values of food from their local communities.

Members of Slow Food share in a number of guiding values. These values focus on sustainability, cultural diversity, pleasure, and quality in everyday life, inclusiveness, authenticity, and integrity. According to Petrini,

I want Slow Food not to be merely a gastronomical organization but deal with problems of the environment and world hunger without renouncing the right to pleasure. The American gastronomical community simply contemplates its own navel and has no political consciousness, while the American environmental movement has tended to have a self-denying, ascetic component that regards eating anything other than tofu as hopelessly selfish and decadent. By now even the Food and Agriculture Organization has recognized that you can't talk about hunger without talking about pleasure. At the same time, you can't deal with pleasure without being aware of hunger. In fact, many of the foods that Slow Food is protecting, although treated as delicacies today, were peasant foods that were brilliant strategies to stave off hunger and contain worlds of knowledge about intelligent use of the environment. Their preservation and development may mean more than a few good meals. (Petrini in Stille 2001:6)

Food movements that emphasize equitable access to fresh food play a vital role in altering Americans' approach to food today. Once consumers become discriminating eaters and critical of how food tastes, they can have a hand in affecting how food is produced and consumed. Support in the United States for the organic food movement and the growth in microbreweries, wineries, and artisan cheese and bread makers illustrates this trend. Once limited to Miller, Anheuser Busch, and other major breweries, our choice of domestic beer now includes 1,600 microbreweries nationally. Organic agricultural food products have now become an industry generating close to $10.8 billion a year in both foods and nonfood products (Organic Trade Association 2004). U.S. organic food sales have grown between 17 and 21 percent each year since 1997, to nearly triple in sales (Organic Trade Association 2004).

Direct Marketing: Urban Connections to Locally Grown Produce

Whether we speak of globalization, industrialization, centralization, or vertical integration of the agrofood system, the end result is similar: food production and consumption have lost their interconnectedness with nature, ensuring the health of humans and the environment. Consumers can be disconnected from agricultural realities. A dairy goat farmer who also is a homestead cheesemaker in North Carolina tells the story of a cheese customer in his forties who asked the farmer at market one day, "Do you have to kill the goat to get the cheese?" A second example is from a dairy farmer who welcomed a public school class to see cows and sheep in the pasture and eat freshly made ice cream. The farmer recounts, "After the children got off the bus, the teacher pointed out to the pasture that contained both cattle and sheep grazing, and exclaimed with great enthusiasm, 'Look children, this is where cotton comes from.'"

Several efforts have made an impact in restoring the urban connection to agriculture. Direct marketing of fresh farm products is one of the most important, and it involves farmers selling directly to the public through roadside stands, pick-your-own, as well as through farmers markets and community-supported agriculture arrangements. Eliminating the middle people in the agrofood system facilitates the interconnectedness of community and agriculture networks and puts more of each dollar in the farmer's pocket. As Deborah Madison writes in her foreword to *Slow Food*, "America's farmers markets look a lot like Slow Food, it is a way of life. . . . Knowing that our food system is grown nearby and not in some unknown places give us shoppers a sense of security and connection. I have come to believe that true pleasure at the table comes from intimately knowing the source of our food" (2001:x). Direct marketing therefore offers the public an opportunity to connect with someone who produces what they consume.

A long-standing tradition, farmers markets allow farmers to sell directly to consumers. In fact, markets contributed to the rise of civilization. In part, cities evolved from where people congregated to market, so markets have been a part of great cities and small towns for millennia (Corum et al. 2001). According to Corum et al., "Democracy and economic freedom are connected to the encouragement of markets by government in certain times. When markets were banned and destroyed during the Roman Era and the Mercantile Era in Europe, the result was monopoly, inefficiency, loss of quality, and a decline in the quality of life" (p. ix). The ebb and flow of the marketplace and its importance in urban people's access to fresh farm products or handcrafted items presents a sharp contrast to our dependence on mass production for similar products. Corum et al. contend, "America has changed from a substantially small, local business culture to a corporate chain culture. Most economic activity ends up in the hands of a few thousand, even a few hundred major retailers. We have largely lost our regional cultures in favor of a homogenized experience wherever we go" (p. ix). Nevertheless, farmers markets have been continually present, bringing the farm gate to the city. For example, a farmers market in Halifax, Nova Scotia, has existed within the city's limits for over 250 years (Kilcup 1998).

The 1990s saw a renewed interest in farmers markets in the United States, with a 79 percent increase from 1994 until 2002, and in 2002 there were 3,137 farmers markets reported nationwide. Roadside stands and small tailgate markets are not included in these statistics; thus, the number of direct marketing outlets for both farmers and consumers is actually higher (U.S. Department of Agriculture 2004).

A great deal can happen with a continuous farmers market connection (that is, a weekly one). As customers come to know their local

Figure 5.1
Roosters Farmers Market, Greensboro, North Carolina, 2002 (photo by Susan Andreatta).

Figure 5.2
Chefs buy local produce at market (photo by Susan Andreatta).

farmers, they begin to place the farm in a personal (local) landscape. As they become regular visitors to both a farmers market and a particular farmer's stand, familiar information is exchanged—favorite recipes, birth and death of animals, farm conditions, how table guests enjoyed a meal prepared with fresh farm products, and so on. After they visit and possibly work on the farm, customers develop a deeper appreciation for farming and life on the farm. As a result, the landscape of food takes on a new meaning: a farmscape is to be cared for, protected, and shared. The romanticism of farming may be shattered, pragmatism may take over, and a new relationship may be forged. This interdependence between food producer (and direct marketer) and the consuming public (a farmers market shopper) plays a central role in small and midsize farm survivability. Direct marketing outlets provide urban consumers (and the chefs who feed them) the opportunity to assist farmers in sustaining a livelihood, contribute to a living food heritage, and enjoy the benefits of sustainability, cultural diversity, and authenticity (Madison 2001).

Community-Supported Agriculture Arrangements

A less well-known direct marketing approach is community-supported agriculture (CSA), a production and distribution arrangement in which consumers (known as shareholders or subscribers) prepay for produce in the off-season and receive fresh produce weekly during the harvest season at predetermined pickup locations.[4] This "arrangement" provides a direct link between nonfarmers and farmers and is founded on the idea of building community among those who share in the harvest. The goal of these relationships is to provide solutions to the problems of small farm survival, food quality, nutrition, sustainability, and quality of life. In the process, consumers become linked to one particular food producer, his or her soils, and food quality.

CSA arrangements are based on a contractual agreement between a farmer and a consumer, although each arrangement operates differently and may adopt any of a variety of forms. The concept is that the consumer, often described as a shareholder, purchases a "share" or "membership" prior to the growing season. Preselling the harvest not only provides the farmer with capital with which to begin the planting season, but also ensures a guaranteed market. Most important, members are paying close to 100 percent of the cost of the produce—their share of the harvest—directly to a farmer in advance of the planting season. In turn, they receive fresh, local produce once a week throughout the growing season. As shareholders in the farm business, they share the risks with the farmer. In this way, the risks are spread throughout the whole membership rather than falling solely on the farmer.

An objective of some CSA arrangements is to get shareholders involved in the production of their food by establishing core groups that take on responsibilities for helping with the harvest labor, writing newsletters, and making major field or farm repairs. Some farmers may work out agreements with shareholders that reduce the cost of a share in exchange for labor, while others require labor during the season. Workdays, open house days, or picnics on the farm encourage members to see how their food is grown and how the farm operates.

Community-supported agriculture originated in Japan in the 1960s where it was known as *teikie*, literally meaning face-to-face, which became extended to put a face on food. The concept reached Europe in the 1970s and came to the United States in the 1980s. In her book *Sharing the Harvest*, Elizabeth Henderson (1999) provides an overview of the history of CSAs and their origins in the sustainable agriculture movement that has taken hold in New England and other parts of the United States. According to Spector, "CSAs range from small gardens with 5 to 20 members to large farms serving nearly 1,000 families" (Spector 2000:292). As with farmers markets, the number of CSAs in the United States has increased in the past decade. CSA arrangements were estimated to be 50 in 1990 and have since grown to over a thousand (Spector 2000).

For households with limited financial resources, a traditional CSA arrangement is completely inaccessible. The likelihood of a low-income household having $300 to $600 to prepay a farmer in January or February to receive a share of a farmer's harvest in May is remote. To experiment with making a CSA a more equitable partnership, Project Green Leaf, created at The University of North Carolina at Greensboro to support the local agrofood system, began a pilot CSA project (Andreatta and Dery 2003).[5] This project provided support for local small-scale farmers in the Piedmont region of North Carolina who are challenged by market prices, weather, economy of scale, and community dependence on a local agrofood system. It was designed to provide low-income households access to quality, fresh farm products. A goal set for this project was that shareholders incorporate fresh farm products into their food routines.

This particular project was specifically designed to provide North Carolinians who may not otherwise have the opportunity to access fresh farm products with the chance to meet a farmer and visit a farm or a farmers market. Financial assistance from the North Carolina Department of Agriculture Food Policy Council enabled us to purchase 44 shares from ten local farmers. Each of the 44 households qualified for federal or state assistance programs such as the Food Stamp Program (FSP) and the Special Supplemental Nutrition Program for Women, Infants, and Children (WIC), and the National School Lunch Program, all designed to provide nutritious foods to households meeting certain eligibility requirements.[6]

When we initiated this CSA project, we knew little about how to implement such a complex arrangement with low-income households. We developed a modified approach, in part, as a step toward creating a more equitable food access system for low-income households (Andreatta and Dery 2003). We worked with community members in distributing the CSA shares to those shareholders without a means to the distribution site or farm. Approximately 41 percent of the shareholders met their farmers at farmers markets or the designated drop-off sites weekly. For those who were unable to pick up their own bags, volunteers from several Sunday school classes served as the CSA share distributors and made home deliveries. These volunteers were also able to report back to farmers directly as to how things were going over the course of the summer weeks.

A number of positive outcomes from this pilot CSA project have been reported by shareholders and farmers. Community-supported agriculture benefited farmers by providing them an early income with the presale of their harvest. Farmers commented they were pleased to be part of the project. As a farmer stated, "We loved it! It was great to help needy people. I would rather give my food to someone who needs it than someone who can roll in there and pay for it. Thankful shareholders made us feel good."

Shareholders also benefited by receiving fresh produce and the opportunity to make a connection with their food provider—the farmer—for the entire 2003 growing season, from spring through fall. Shareholders speak of "family members cooking," learning "what those red things are" (radishes), and making requests for additional food items such as basil and onions. Other shareholders commented on the new meals they became expert in cooking, such as a stir fry. Overall, shareholders commented that the items in their share bags were fresher and tasted better. In fact, one shareholder exclaimed, "Fresh greens [collards] are so much better than canned greens"(Rhyne, Andreatta, and Dery 2004).

Through this project, embryonic connections to place were made by participants. In some instances, the connection was made at the farm from the weekly share pickups or when attending farm workdays or on-farm potluck dinners, while others were made at farmers markets where weekly share pickups were made. Undoubtedly, the true success of this project will be seen if the shareholders, independent of Project Green Leaf's assistance, rekindle their connections with "their" farmer or seek out local farmers markets as their source for fresh produce.

A Farmers Market in North Carolina

North Carolina has a long history of agricultural production, and agriculture remains the state's primary revenue generator. A growing interest in farmers markets on the part of both farmers and consumers provided the opportunity for a research program to examine the reasons that consumers shop at farmers markets and the characteristics of those markets that makes them successful. One study (Andreatta and Wickliffe 2002) collected data from 463 consumers shopping at a state-operated farmers market (the market sample). A second study (Andreatta, unpublished) involved an independent sample of 334 people (the community sample) in a variety of other venues away from any farmers markets (such as YMCAs, YWCAs, health clubs, libraries). Some of the community sample reported that they shop regularly at a farmers market or at other direct market outlets, such as roadside stands or pick-your-own farms. We used questionnaires to assess various aspects of the participants' behavior and motivations.

Data from the market sample were collected at a state-operated farmers market located in Colfax, Guilford County, close to three major urban areas in central North Carolina (Greensboro, Winston-Salem, and High Point) with a combined population of more than 500,000. This farmers market, established in 1995, is open seven days a week, although the great majority of visitors attend on Saturdays, when we collected our data. As many as ten thousand people attend the market each Saturday from May through August; attendance is much lower during the week. Each participant was interviewed only once, using an opportunistic sampling procedure.

Our results showed that people shop at farmers markets for a variety of reasons, several of which reflect a connection to place. Of the market sample, 88 percent said they came because the produce is fresh and 64 percent came to buy local products (participants could select more than one reason for shopping at the market). Only 16 percent came to buy inexpensive food, suggesting that financial savings are not as important a factor in the decision to shop at the market as a commitment to the local food system. Indeed, the modal purchase amount in our sample was $16 to $20 per trip, much more than the $6 per trip reported by Lloyd, Nelson, and Tilley (1987; $6 in 1987 adjusted for inflation is $9.35 in 2004 dollars) for Oklahoma. Further, when participants were asked how much they would be willing to spend at the market to buy a food item costing $1 in a supermarket, 80 percent said they would pay the same amount or more, and only 4 percent expected to buy it for 50 cents or less. Nor was convenience a significant factor: 86 percent traveled 6 miles or more to reach the market and, of those, 15 percent traveled over 20 miles. Despite the distance they traveled to reach the market, most people shopped there regularly. During the summer (May through August), 34 percent came every Saturday, and another 22 percent came at least twice a month. Although participants came to the market primarily to buy fresh local food, the atmosphere of the market, the opportunity to meet the farmer who grew the food, and a desire to support the local economy were also mentioned as reasons.

The nonfarmers market community sample included a number of people (36 percent) who also shop at this market regularly (more than twice per month) and another 43 percent who buy fresh produce from other local sources rather than supermarkets. When they do visit a farmers market, the median distance they travel is 10 miles. This sample also reported little interest in buying cheap food at a farmers market, with 69 percent saying they would be willing to pay a 50 percent premium for fresh, local produce. It is estimated that between 10 and 12 percent of local residents shop at farmers markets at least once year. Taken together, these data strongly suggest that North Carolina consumers are willing to go out of their way to patronize a local farmers market on a regular basis and that most of them do so not to save money but to buy fresh, local food in a setting that connects them with the person who grew it. Clearly, farmers markets are a successful way to bring consumers in contact with the grower and support the idea of a changing urban culture of food.

Connecting the Public to Local Food Providers: Examples from North Carolina

North Carolina has a long agricultural history of producing tobacco, cotton, peanuts, and grains. The loss in government support through agricultural commodity programs, coupled with the loss in revenues from low market prices, have influenced the public imagination to create a new relationship to the land. Identifying alternative crops and niche markets has been an active pursuit for all those involved in sustaining local agriculture. A number of food movements are occurring in the Piedmont region of North Carolina, several of which illustrate how the urban public is reconnecting to farmscapes and their food providers. Although there are many more than those noted here, these few serve to illustrate a cultural shift for urban residents and institutions.

The University of North Carolina at Greensboro's Project Green Leaf (PGL) is an example of university support for increased urban ties to surrounding rural areas.[7] The project's mission is to promote and support a local agrofood system by strengthening community between farmers and consumers. PGL staff give presentations to the farming and eating public on topics such as "Save the Farm," "Organic Farms and Foods," "Direct Marketing," and "Community-Supported Agriculture." Education and outreach about alternative agriculture are combined with efforts to encourage urban food production.

In 2002, Project Green Leaf secured a lease of nearly 2 acres of unoccupied city land to develop an urban community farm. The farm was for local residents interested in growing vegetables for market and coordinated with the city's plan to establish another farmers market in the heart of the downtown area. PGL staff helped to prepare the lands, installed the irrigation system, and provided hand tools, transplants, and seeds. Some of the participants also brought their own tools, familiar seeds, and transplants. Thirty-five residents were involved with the first growing season (2003) and over a hundred residents were involved in year two (2004).

Motivated by a desire to create a multicultural farm and farmers market experience, PGL staff reached out to refugee communities in Greensboro that had agrarian roots. The farm was supported mainly by Montagnard farmers and African American neighborhood residents. Produce was grown for home consumption and to sell at the new market (Shoaf 2003). The overall experience with both farm and market enabled the participants to increase consumption of fresh foods, provide a small profit from sales, and create new opportunities to make connections with community residents. A key spokesperson from within the Montagnard refugee community commented, "The city residents now recognize the Montagnards as good immigrants. They accept our culture because they bought our food and our weavings." Discussions with both the elders and younger participants indicate that they are looking forward to another growing and marketing season (Shoaf 2003).

Project Green Leaf staff are involved in a number of other activities that connect community to place. Staff organized another small, weekly farmers market in a supermarket plaza across the street from a residential neighborhood in Greensboro. This market, similar to others in the surrounding area, is not limited to middle-income marketers, but attracts people from all economic levels. In addition, participating farmers established an advisory board and put together a list of guidelines for those who could sell there and how they were to conduct their business. One

Figure 5.3
Montagnard farmers in community garden (photo by Susan Andreatta).

of the key rules agreed on was that farmers could sell only what they grew or made (such as bread) and they had to sell their own products; no middlemen were allowed to sell, and no resale of products was permitted. For its first year, the market was a success; those frequenting the market contributed an additional $2,000 to $5,000 into each of the farmer's pockets.

A new community event illustrates the growing satisfaction among consumers with their new food habits and new connections to local producers. PGL staff were instrumental in sponsoring a local Farmer Appreciation Day. The day was coordinated by a mother of two young children who was first introduced to her local farmers market by way of a WIC coupon earmarked for use only at farmers markets accepting the coupons. This mother visits the market weekly with her children and has learned to can fresh vegetables, bake bread, make cheese, and eat food in season. To show her appreciation to the farmers, together with the

Figure 5.4
Montagnard elder with Asian "yard-long" beans (photo by Susan Andreatta).

PGL staff, she spent the better part of a year gathering donations and contributions for the Farmer Appreciation Day. First celebrated in September 2002, festivities began with a breakfast made from locally grown ground grits, sausage, and biscuits. Four local bluegrass bands provided entertainment, and a number of nonprofits and universities set up displays on food, nutrition, and the environment. Drawing from the diversity in the community, male and female volunteers ranging in age from 18 to 76 served the meal to all those who visited the market that day. Farmers indeed felt honored: "No one has ever done this before for us." A second "annual" Farmer Appreciation Day was held in 2003, with even more community groups setting up displays on healthy living and healthy eating. A fall ritual for urban market shoppers is emerging in which they collectively show their appreciation directly to their local food providers while making a connection to a local place—a farmers market.

Conclusion: From Alienation to Relationship

Project Green Leaf staff's involvement in creating urban connections to local food producers is an example of a national trend. It endeavors to bring urban consumers back to awareness of the natural world through taste and local experiences. Numerous city gardens, community gardens, farmers markets, children's garden projects and local farm-to-school projects are emerging around the country. Eliot Coleman (1995), a successful Maine farmer who manages to farm 12 months of the year, suggests that much of our food need not travel farther than 25 miles from field to plate. In many parts of the United States and elsewhere around the world, communities' commitment to their agrofood system is needed to protect farmscapes, urban agriculture, community gardens, and regional foodsheds.

As farmers also change production and marketing practices and recognize the importance of connecting with all eaters, a significant event is taking place: a reduction in the gap between farmers and the public. Modifying the agrofood system has built new relationships, and a more integrated agrofood system is emerging. Hence, "through the new connections of fully integrated food systems we are healing our farm communities, the earth and ourselves" (Spector 2000:294).

Acknowledgments

I thank the farmers of North Carolina who provide fresh farm products to their communities. I also thank PGL staff who give their time and share their enthusiasm in assisting farmers and the public in making fresh farm products accessible to everyone. Finally, our research and outreach activities could not have been conducted without the support from The University of North Carolina at Greensboro, U.S. Department of Agriculture, the Sustainable Agriculture Research and Education program of USDA, North Carolina Department of Agriculture, North Carolina Cooperative Extension—Guilford County Center, North Carolina State University, North Carolina Agricultural and Technological State University, the Hillsdale Foundation, the Z. Smith Reynolds Foundation, the

Community Foundation of Greater Greensboro, and Greensboro's Redevelopment Commission.

Notes

1. For further reading in the area of industrialization, concentration, and globalization of agriculture, see Adams (1994), Andreatta (1997), Barlett (1993), Bonanno (1994), Doyal (1985), Friedland (1994), Friedmann (1993), Goldschmidt (1978), Goody (1997), Grey (2000a, 2000b), Heffernan and Constance (1994), McMichael (1994), and Schlosser (2001).

2. Fordism refers to the system of industrialized mass production based on the development and sale of standardized commodities to undifferentiated national markets (post–World War II to 1973). Fordism takes its name from the assembly production of strategies based on standardized products for a mass market, using largely unskilled workers on a semiautomatic assembly line (Gartman 1991 in Lawrence and Vanclay 1994). Post-Fordism refers to a system of flexible specialization and global sourcing empowered by transnational corporations to sell to niche markets—specialized production for privileged markets (1973 to the present) (Lawrence and Vanclay 1994).

3. While I was at a farmers market one Saturday, a farmer recounted a story to me of when she was giving out samples of her tomatoes to the public at the market. She said a little boy tasted her tomato and spat it out, exclaiming, "It's wet."

4. For additional reading on CSA farms, see Andreatta (2000), DeLind and Harmen Fackler (1999), Henderson (1999), Goland (2002), Kane (1997), and Ostrom (1997).

5. Susan Andreatta (director), Nicole Dery, and Misty Rhyne worked on this project together (January 2003–March 2004). This research was supported by the University of North Carolina at Greensboro under Project Green Leaf, the North Carolina Department of Agriculture, and the Society for St. Andrews, a second harvest gleaning ministry.

6. According to the new WIC guidelines effective July 2003 through June 2004, a family of four is eligible if its gross income is less than $655 a week (U.S. Department of Agriculture 2003b). Unlike food stamps, WIC coupons are made out for specific items; milk, eggs, cheese, fruit juice, cereal and formula are the only items that can be purchased with these coupons. WIC also offers a Farmers Market Nutrition Program designed to provide fresh, locally grown fruits and vegetables to WIC recipients while helping improve awareness of, use and sales of farmers markets (U.S. Department of Agriculture 2003a).

7. Since August 2001, Project Green Leaf (PGL) has operated out of The University of North Carolina at Greensboro. It provides assistance to North Carolina farmers and the public. PGL has as its mission to provide support for a local agro-food system. Staff include Susan Andreatta, director; Nicole Dery,

Misty Rhyne, and Stacy Shoaf, research assistants; and Graham Pettigrew and Miranda Roberts, co–farm managers.

References

Adams, Jane. 1994. *The Transformation of Rural Life Southern Illinois, 1890–1990*. Chapel Hill: University of North Carolina Press.

Andreatta, Susan. 1997. Bananas, Are They the Quintessential Health Food? A Global/Local Perspective. *Human Organization* 57(4):437–449.

Andreatta, Susan. 1998. Transformation of the Agro-Food Sector: Lessons from the Caribbean. *Human Organization* 57(4):414–429.

Andreatta, Susan. 2000. Marketing Strategies and Challenges of Small-Scale Organic Producers in Central North Carolina. *Culture and Agriculture* 22(3):40–50.

Andreatta, Susan, and Nicole Dery. 2003. A Pilot Project for Community Supported Agriculture Arrangements: CSA Farmers to Limited Resource Households. Paper presented at the Annual Meeting of the American Anthropological Association, Chicago, Nov. 19–23.

Andreatta, Susan, and William Wickliffe II. 2002. Managing Farmer and Consumer Expectations: A Study of a North Carolina Farmers Market. *Human Organization* 60(2):167–176.

Axelrod, Lauryn. 2001. Don't Eat So Fast! The Slow Food Movement Wants Us to Savor Our Food and Cultures. http://www.gonomad.com/features/0105/ axelrod_slowfood.html. Accessed July 15, 2004.

Barlett, Peggy. 1993. *American Dreams, Rural Realities: Family Farms in Crisis*. Chapel Hill: University of North Carolina Press.

Baum, Hilary. 2002. The Incompatibility of Food and Capitalism. *The Snail* 2/3:22–25.

Binder, Jae. 2001. The Pleasure of Eating Slow. http://www.gaiam.com/retail/ gai_content/learn Article Print.asp?article_id=1700. Accessed Jan. 7, 2005.

Bonnano, Alessandro, ed. 1993. *From Columbus to Con Agra: The Globalization of Agriculture and Food*. Lawrence: University Press of Kansas.

Coleman, Eliot. 1995. *The New Organic Grower: A Master's Manual of Tools and Techniques for the Home and Market Gardener*. White River Junction, Vt.: Chelsea Green Publishing Company.

Corum, Vance, Marcie Rosenzeig, and Eric Gibson. 2001. *The New Farmers' Market*. Auburn, Calif.: New World Publishing.

DeLind, Laura, and Holly Harmen Fackler. 1999. *CSA: Patterns, Problems and Possibilities: The Many Faces of Community Supported Agriculture (CSA): A Guide to Community Supported Agriculture in Indiana, Michigan and Ohio*. Hartland, Mich.: Michigan State Press.

Doyal, Jack. 1985. *Altered Harvest: Agriculture, Genetics and the Fate of the World's Food Supply.* New York: Viking Penguin Books.

Ecoglobe News. 1999. Slow Food Movement—Opposed to Fast Food, Eat What Is in Season, Maintain Cultural and Agricultural Diversity. Nov. 19. http://www.ecoglobe.org/nz/news1999/n199news.htm. Accessed July 15, 2004.

Friedland, William. 1994. The Global Fresh Fruit and Vegetable System: An Industrial Organization Analysis. In *The Global Restructuring of Agro-Food Systems.* Philip McMichael, ed. Pp. 173–189. Ithaca, N.Y.: Cornell University Press.

Friedmann, Harriet. 1993. Distance and Durability: Shaky Foundations of the World Food Economy. In *The Global Restructuring of Agro-Food Systems.* Philip McMichael, ed. Pp. 258–276. Ithaca, N.Y.: Cornell University Press.

Gabaccia, Donna. 1998. *We Are What We Eat: Ethnic Food and the Making of Americans.* Cambridge, Mass.: Harvard University Press.

Goland, Carol. 2002. Community Supported Agriculture, Food Consumption Patterns, and Member Commitment. *Culture and Agriculture* 24(1):14–25.

Goldschmidt, Walter R. 1978. *As You Sow: Three Studies in the Social Consequences of Agribusiness.* Montclair, N.J.: Allanheld, Osmun & Co.

Goodman, David, and Michael Watts. 1994. Reconfiguring the Rural or Fording the Divide? Capitalist Restructuring and the Global Agro-Food System. *Journal of Peasant Studies* 22(1):1–49.

Goody, Jack. 1997. Towards the Development of a World Cuisine. In *Food and Culture: A Reader.* Carole Counihan and Penny Van Esterik, eds. Pp. 338–356. New York: Routledge.

Grey, Mark. 2000a. Industrial Food Stream and Its Alternatives in the United States: An Introduction. *Human Organization* 59(2):143–150.

Grey, Mark. 2000b. Those Bastards Can Go to Hell! Small Farmer Resistance to Vertical Integration and Concentration in the Pork Industry. *Human Organization* 59(2):169–176.

Heffernan, William D., and Douglas H. Constance. 1994. From Columbus to ConAgra. In *The Globalization of Agriculture and Food.* Alessandro Bonanno et al., eds. Pp. 29–51. Lawrence: University of Kansas Press.

Henderson, Elizabeth. 1999. *Sharing the Harvest: A Guide to Community-Supported Agriculture.* White River Junction, Vt.: Chelsea Green Publishing Company.

Kane, Deborah. 1997. Maximizing Shareholder Retention in Southern CSAs. *OFRF Information Bulletin* 5(Summer):8–9.

Kilcup, Fred. 1998. *Halifax Farmers Market: Chasing the Dawn, Recipes and Recollections from Canada's Oldest Farmers Market.* Halifax: Nova Scotia Press.

Kummer, Corby. 2002. *The Pleasures of Slow Food: Celebrating Authentic Traditions, Flavors and Recipes.* San Francisco: Chronicle Books.

Lawrence, Geoffry, and Frank Vanclay. 1994. Agricultural Change in the Semi-periphery: Australia. In *The Global Restructuring of Agro-Food Systems*. Philip McMichael, ed. Pp 76–104. Ithaca, N.Y.: Cornell University Press.

Lloyd, Renee, James R. Nelson, and Daniel S. Tilley. 1987. Should I Grow Fruits and Vegetables? *Oklahoma State University Extension Facts* 185:1–4.

Madison, Deborah. 2001. Foreword. In *Slow Food: Collected Thoughts on Taste, Tradition, and the Honest Pleasures of Food*. Carlo Petrini, ed. Pp. ix–xi. White River Junction, Vt.: Chelsea Green Publishing Company.

Martins, Patrick. 2002. A Letter from the National Office. *The Snail: Slow Food USA Newsletter* 4/5:3.

McMichael, Philip, ed. 1994. *Global Restructuring of Agro-Food Systems*. Ithaca, N.Y.: Cornell University Press.

Mintz, Sidney. 1985. *Sweetness and Power*. New York: Viking Penguin.

Mintz, Sidney. 1996. *Tasting Food, Tasting Freedom: Excursions into Eating, Culture and the Past*. Boston: Beacon Press.

Ostrom, Marcia Ruth. 1997. Toward a Community Supported Agriculture: A Case Study of Resistance and Change in the Modern Food System. Ph.D. dissertation, University of Wisconsin.

Organic Gardening. 2001. The Organic Barometer Random Facts to Ponder. *Organic Gardening* 48(3):13.

Organic Trade Association. 2004. 2004 Manufacturer Survey: Organic Product Sales Show Strong Growth. http://www.ota.com/news/press/141.html. Accessed July 15, 2004.

Petrini, Carlo. 1997. *Slow Food: Collected Thoughts on Taste, Tradition and the Honest Pleasures of Food*. White River Junction, Vt.: Chelsea Green Publishing Company.

Rhyne, Misty, Susan Andreatta, and Nicole Dery. 2004. Lessons Learned from Advocating CSAs for Food Challenged Households. Paper presented at the Society for Applied Anthropology Annual Meeting, Dallas, Mar. 31–Apr. 4.

Schlosser, Eric. 2001. *Fast Food Nation*. Boston: Houghton Mifflin.

Shoaf, Stacy. 2003. The Balance of Identity and Place in a Montagnard Refugee Community. Master's thesis, University of North Carolina at Greensboro.

Slow Food. 2004a. Slow Food. http://slowfood.com/ Accessed July 15, 2004.

Slow Food. 2004b. The Slow Food Foundation for Biodiversity. http://www.slowfoodfoundation.com/welcome_en.lasso. Accessed July 15, 2004.

Slow Food USA. 2004c. The Ark USA. Saving Cherished Slow Foods, One Product at a Time. http://www.slowfoodusa.org/ark/index.html. Accessed Jan. 7, 2005.

Spector, Rebecca. 1997. Fully Integrated Food Systems: Regaining Connections between Farmers and Consumers. In *The Fatal Harvest Reader: The Tragedy of Industrial Agriculture*. Andrew Kimball, ed. Pp. 289–294. Washington, D.C.: Island Press.

Stille, Alexander. 2001. The Global Slow Food Movement. *The Nation*. Aug. 20, 2001. http://www.thenation.com/mhtml/?i=200108208s=stille. Accessed July 15, 2004.

U.S. Department of Agriculture. 2003a. Food Stamp Program. http://www.fns.usda.gov/fsp/. Accessed July 15, 2004.

U.S. Department of Agriculture. 2003b. WIC Program. http://www.fns.usda.gov/wic/. Accessed July 15, 2004.

U.S. Department of Agriculture. 2004. AMS USDA Farmers Market Growth. http://www.ams.usda.gov/farmersmarkets/FarmersMarketGrowth.htm. Accessed July 15, 2004.

6

The Missouri Regional Cuisines Project: Connecting to Place in the Restaurant

Elizabeth Barham, David Lind, and Lewis Jett

For all our human history, we have been shaped by nature, while shaping it in return. But in our industrial age, we are losing the stories, memories and language about land and nature. These disconnections matter, for the way we think about nature and wildernesses fundamentally affects what we do in our agricultural and food systems.

—Jules Pretty, *Agri-Culture* (2002)

Food provides one of our most intimate daily connections with nature, but only rarely does it seem to remind us of this fact. Physical distance separates most of us from agricultural land because the majority of the world's population lives in urban areas, a trend toward human concentration in cities that is expected to continue globally for the foreseeable future. A revolution in transportation and communications since World War II, coupled with increased levels of technological control and mechanical manipulation, have enabled the development in the industrialized countries of a food system that is in many ways quite detached from the soil (Bonanno et al. 1994; Kneen 1993). Agro-industrial producers, wholesalers, and retail outlets seek foods that can travel great distances, store well, and have a long shelf life so that they can make the most of market opportunities. This is so much the case that Harriet Friedmann (1993) has identified distance and durability as the dominant principles of the industrialized food sector.

We are gradually impoverished by this trend. We are slowly losing the stories, memories, and language that link our meals to an appreciation of natural cycles, weather, and cultural practices suited to particular environments. We cannot continue to care about something we do not understand and to which we feel no connection. Indeed, this lack of understanding and concern is already reflected in the weakness of our public policy response to urban sprawl, rural decline, the loss of fertile topsoil from our farms, and the ground and water pollution resulting from industrial production methods.[1] Furthermore, estrangement from the land has negative long-term effects on how we value and relate to people in rural areas.[2] It is as though our physical disconnectedness from the land is paralleled by an increasing social indifference toward the farmers, farm workers, and laborers who grow and process our food. If we have lost much of our sense of connection to nature and season, we have also lost touch with the more intangible, socially constructed aspects of a sense of place that food once conveyed.

Recent surveys, however, reveal signs of growing rejection of modernist agriculture (Hartman Group 1999; Stevens and Raja 2001; Wimberley et al. 2002). Consumers are organizing for change, and their expectations are shifting (Doherty and Etzioni 2003; Lockeretz 2003; Ray and Anderson 2000). They are demanding to know much more about what they purchase than simply whether it is safe to eat. They want details on the packaging, the preparation and production methods, the inputs, and the farmers themselves. They want to know if certain values that they hold as consumers, such as fair working conditions for labor and humane treatment of animals, are also being respected along the entire food chain (Barham 2002).

One phenomenon related to the consumer shift in attitudes that taps most directly into the loss of a sense of place is the pronounced rise in demand for local food (Food Processing Center 2001; Food Routes Network 2003; Harris, Burress, and Eicher 2000; Pirog and Tyndal 1999; Pirog and Schuty 2003; Stephenson and Lev 1998). Vague yet obviously appealing to many, it seems to gather together several strands of the different values consumers are seeking (Pirog 2003). And these consumers are not just the remnants of 1960s American counterculture, as several studies have noted. An alternative beef producer was recently quoted as saying in relation to consumers' demand for more information, particularly in the form of new food labels, "When we started 18 years ago, our customers ranged from hippies to urban gourmets. . . . But now mainstream urbanites want to know where their food is coming from. It's not just about nuts and twigs any more" (Murphy 2004:28).

This growing trend toward demand for local food is the frame for the discussion that follows. The first section reviews several approaches to defining local food, evaluating how they contribute to a reunification of urban consumers with the natural and social bases of their food supply. This provides a context for the second section describing a particular local food experiment based on ecoregions: the Missouri Regional Cuisines Project. Drawing on institutional examples from Europe and elsewhere, the project makes an explicit attempt to link food products more tightly to the particularities of place, including the know-how of local inhabitants. The third section shares the results of research undertaken in the planning stages for the Missouri Regional Cuisines Project with chefs in the city of St. Louis. It revealed both the extent of their interest in local food and the difficulties they had defining it, a gap that will have to be overcome if the ecoregional approach to local food proposed by the project is to take hold.

Local Food: Visions and Goals

The upswing in consumer interest in local food derives from several sources. Material impacts of the industrialization of the food system on our eating habits and on the environment are clearly part of the dynamic. Academics have voiced the importance of relocalizing our food sources along with public actors such as government agencies. They have been joined by nonprofit entities such as churches, foundations, and nongovernmental organizations working on particular causes and thousands of less formal community-based activities such as school and community garden programs. All of these efforts have merit. Collectively, they sensitize us to the promise and difficulty of reorienting the values embedded in our current food system.

Academic Arguments for Local Food

Within academic literature, local food systems are typically defined in contrast to the global food system and the conventional or industrial model of agricultural production (see chapter 5). The conventional system combines capital-intensive agricultural production with increasingly international commodity markets to bring mass-produced foods to consumers around the globe. It focuses on reducing human labor and land in favor of mechanization, synthetic inputs, and large-scale commodity production (Barham 1999; Beus and Dunlap 1990; Meares 1997). Early work in the sociology of agriculture, in particular, focused on the consequences of this industrial production model on rural society. Researchers were concerned with the loss of an agrarian way of life and the associated economic security, democratic values, and normative principles symbolized by independent family farmers and their rural communities (Goldschmidt 1978; Rodefeld et al. 1978).

As the model of conventional modernist agriculture matured over the last half of the twentieth century, researchers became increasingly focused on the internationalization of this form of production agriculture and the development of international complexes or "regimes" of agricultural production and distribution (Bonanno et al. 1994; Friedman and McMichael 1989). The entrepreneurial model of agricultural production impinged on the family farm model (Barlett 1993), both nationally and around the globe, and researchers began to shift their focus to food and food politics, which had previously been a peripheral concern (see McMichael 1995). Work by Arce and Marsden (1993), Friedmann (1995), Kloppenburg, Hendrickson, and Stevenson (1996), and McMichael (2000) brought food squarely to the forefront of the discussion and contributed to what is referred to as the consumer turn.[3]

In part, the conceptual shift to a focus on food and consumption is strategic. While agricultural policy and corporate interests center on market criteria, efficiency, and economies of scale, a concern with food broadens the framework to address issues of hunger, quality, employment, community relations, and ecological sustainability. Friedmann argues that "food, not agriculture, is the appropriate unifying principle," because food allows us to link "what is produced, how, and by whom to socially desirable employment, just access to quality diets, and sustainable, socially beneficial land uses" (1995:29–30). Local food systems are thought to produce these desirable outcomes because they reembed the food system into the needs and capacities of local communities and regions.

The Views of Academic Activists

A large and growing number of academics have contributed to food-centered research as well as to organizing efforts on behalf of local food initiatives. Among them are Kloppenburg, Hendrickson, and Stevenson, authors of "Coming in to the Foodshed" (1996), which provides perhaps the best summary statement of the spirit behind local food efforts. In their formulation, the term *foodshed* conjures mental pictures of food flowing into a particular place, like water flowing through a watershed.[4] The term thus combines the sociocultural and natural worlds into one image. It is a "unifying and organizing metaphor for conceptual development that starts from a premise of the unity of place and people, of nature and society" (p. 34).

In this vision, a foodshed is "not a determinate thing," with fixed boundaries, but rather is "constituted by the concrete activities of those who seek to learn about the food system in order to change it" (p. 40). The concept is intended to form a bridge "from thinking to doing, from theory to action" (p. 34), providing a tool to guide critical thought and transformative intervention. To begin, we need to know where our food is coming from, how, and why. But we also need to recognize that the scale of action resulting from that analysis will sometimes be "regional, national and even global" (p. 40). In the end, the hope that animates the concept is that a "multiplicity of local foodsheds" (p. 34) will flower and combine to form a mosaic vision of an alternative food future to replace the present virtual, global economy of food and the destructive corporate-fed consumerism that drives it.

There is no simple map to take us directly to this alternative foodshed future. But Kloppenburg, Hendrickson, and Stevenson recognize five guiding principles that they believe will lead us in the right direction:

1. The search for a *moral economy* that reembeds food in human needs and is not dominated by market imperatives (such as ability to pay) (see Polanyi 1957; Barham 2002). Such an economy builds "non- or extra-market relations" (p. 36) that are "conditioned by such things as pleasure, friendship, aesthetics, affection, loyalty, justice and reciprocity" (p. 37).

2. The rebuilding of a *"commensal community"* that will "encompass sustainable relationships both between people (those who eat together)

and between people and the land (obtaining food without damage) (p. 37).

3. *Self-protection, secession, and succession.* These involve carving out "insulated spaces" to "maintain or create alternatives that will eventually bring substantive change" (p. 37), working through these spaces to "secede" from the dominant system and pursue a strategy of "slowly hollowing out (Orr 1992:73) the structures of the global food system" (p. 38), and strengthening these efforts by conscious "succession," or "the transfer of resources and human commitments from old food-associated relationships and forms to new ones" (p. 37).

4. *Proximity (locality and regionality).* The authors are confident that emphasizing relations of proximity as a general principle will encourage a stronger sense of responsibility and caring toward one another and the land. They do not take a position on the desirable size of a foodshed, preferring to leave the boundary setting to those who engage in food-shed activism. For some, the very local may be the most appropriate scale, while others will work at a broader regional level.

5. *Nature as the measure* uses the local ecosystem as a guide in choosing appropriate practices and, in particular, the use of agricultural technology. Nature sets the limits for developing "regional palates," attuned to what is available locally and seasonally (p. 39; see also Jackson 1996).

A number of other authors have promoted the foodshed concept, using it to encourage a range of efforts from the very proximate (grow your own food to the extent possible), to the highly global (eliminate food dumping in international markets), and everything in between.[5] Anticipated benefits include revitalization of community, creation of viable economic opportunities for growers, provisioning of better tasting and more nutritious food to eaters, the encouragement of more ecologically sustainable production and distribution practices, the enhancement of social equity and democracy for all members of the community, and the achievement of a more fair and just international food trading system.[6]

These claims are provocative, but local food theorizing can also have a utopian cast. We need more empirically grounded research exploring how local food systems actually operate to avoid an overly nostalgic view of how real communities work. Hinrichs (2000), for example, recognizes that realizing the goals and values promised in the local food literature will require that we not confuse geographical proximity of producers and consumers with the creation of equitable and sustainable communities. Buying or distributing local food needs to be situated in the various settings of a person's life to explore how it is or is not constituted relationally to different realms of value. Only then can we begin to understand the ways in which it may prefigure broader processes of social change.

Local Food Projects in Action

As all community development specialists know, making change on the ground is quite different from theorizing it from the proverbial ivory tower. While academic activists make an important contribution to local food movements in both thought and action, in the end communities and activist groups working within them have to take up the challenge themselves of finding new ways of doing things and making them work. Here we summarize some of the practical efforts to create local food systems carried out by what Kloppenburg et al. (2000) have called "ordinary, competent people." These attempts are loosely grouped into categories to point out the types of values and goals they seem to stress. They are also arranged roughly in order of scale, from the very local to the regional. Concrete or comprehensive attempts at actually linking local food projects together at a global scale are lacking for the time being, but some important organizations working in this direction are mentioned in the final category.

Besides growing your own garden, the most direct or face-to-face possibilities for engagement in local food action include community gardens and community-supported agriculture (CSA) groups, described in this volume by Andreatta (chapter 5), Lynch and Brusi (chapter 8), and von Hassell (chapter 4). Other forms of direct purchasing opportunities that involve farmers include pick-your-own farms, farmers markets, roadside stands, individual street vending, local food delivery routes, direct purchasing by advance order, and farm-to-school programs that feature meetings between students and farmers. Promoters of these arrangements stress the importance of relationship, community building, the quality of local food (freshness, seasonality, taste, frequently organic or sustainably produced), and values such as humane animal treatment or a sense of "doing right" by the environment because they believe "their" farmer will exercise certain ethics of care.

For consumers, achieving their goals depends in large measure on the trust they can have that farmers share their values and are enacting them in their farming practice. These local food arrangements are in general the least regulated of any and can usually sustain themselves with little or no support from the state. Cone and Myhre, however, have questioned the long-term sustainability of CSAs, "given the lifestyle and needs of the farmers in tension with the constraints and competing values of shareholders" (2000:187). Nonetheless, current efforts around the country make the goals of *moral economy; commensal community; self-protection, secession, and succession* seem attainable under the right circumstances.

A new breed of specialty stores and restaurants featuring mostly, or only, local food (variously defined) has also begun springing up across the country. They make accessing food from nearby sources more possible for consumers who do not or cannot participate in direct-local schemes. In addition, some larger-scale purchasers, such as grocery chains, government facilities, hospitals, marketing cooperatives, and regional marketing centers, are beginning to move more local food within easier reach of urban consumers. These situations can provide a sense of localness to consumers, but they do not provide the same level of community building as direct-local options

Before moving to programs with a wider reach, we should mention the work of Food Policy Councils, which usually begin as urban-based efforts but sometimes expand to encompass entire states.[7] They are typically established with a focus on eliminating hunger and achieving greater social justice related to food access. The work of Food Policy Councils has streamed into the collected energy of the national Community Food Security Coalition (CFSC), which has over 250 member organizations and is dedicated to "building strong, sustainable, local and regional food systems that ensure access to affordable, nutritious, and culturally appropriate food for all people at all times."[8] Whether the laudable projects collected under the CFSC umbrella will indeed change the course of hunger nationally remains to be seen. Dowler and Caraher (2003) have been critical of local food projects in the United Kingdom as "the New Philanthropy," accusing them of providing short-term solutions rather than challenging entrenched economic structures with radical policy change. Such criticism may be warranted in the United States as well. But there is no question that food security proponents are faced with deeply rooted issues of class, race, and gender discrimination that are endemic to the conventional food system, issues that the groups promoting local food systems under a sustainable agriculture banner do not always take up (Allen and Sachs 1993).

The next level of local food projects to be considered are those that could more properly be described as regional in scope. We might consider well-known state-based promotions for conventional agricultural products here, such as "Taste of Iowa" and "Pride of New York." But these have little connection to the values typically sought by local food systems advocates aside from presumably promoting farm viability and economic development in rural areas. More challenging to the status quo, but primarily on an environmental basis, is the concept of "Food Miles" as a gauge for the local. Pioneered by the Leopold Center at Iowa State University (Pirog et al. 2001), this approach is appealing because "most consumers understand the concept . . . and information needed to estimate food miles for fresh foods such as produce is available" (Pirog and Schuh 2003:69). Thus, it shares the virtue of transparency, much as state-based programs do, and like them it holds the potential to engage state agencies. But it does little to organize producers, unlike some local food projects, and it is unclear how motivating it may be to consumers in the long run.

More ambitious regional schemes have emerged in the United States as well. The Food Circles model developed by the Food Circles Networking Project at the University of Missouri developed an urban-rural linkage around the Kansas City area that promoted "the consumption of safe, regionally-grown food that will encourage sustainable agriculture and help to maintain farmers, who will sustain rural areas."[9] And the "Buy Fresh, Buy Local" campaign of the FoodRoutes Network based in Millheim, Pennsylvania, has extended to states across the country via its Web site, which allows farms, markets, restaurants, food co-ops, or other food-related businesses to register free and have their location displayed on an interactive map for consumers.[10]

One regional program, the Food Alliance, has gone further toward implementing the goals implicit in a foodshed than most others. Based in Portland, Oregon, it issues a seal of approval to farmers who meet their criteria of limiting chemical use, conserving soil and water, providing safe and fair working conditions for farm laborers, and humane treatment of farm animals.[11] It attempts to educate consumers about the benefits of buying from Food Alliance–approved farmers so they will seek out and pay more for products bearing the seal. Operating in Oregon and Washington since 1994, Food Alliance has expanded into the Midwest. Several features of this program extend its potential. It fosters a certification process with strict standards and verification,[12] includes labor and animal welfare goals, and has demonstrated its potential to structure a broader alternative to the conventional system by reaching more than one large region of the country. The Food Alliance also attempts to make products available to urban consumers through local grocery stores (Kane and Ennis 2003).

The final category of local food programs are those that operate in the global arena. Slow Food International, discussed by Andreatta (chapter 5) focuses on preserving and celebrating traditional, authentic foods and recipes from around the world.[13] While accused by some of being elitist (its publications frequently feature advertisements for luxury items), Slow Food leaders point out that most of the dishes and products they defend were originally peasant foods, tied to regional cultures and ecologies. With over 80,000 members in over 100 countries, their approach to valuing typical regional products, the people who produce them, and the time to enjoy them with friends and loved ones has found strong resonance with overworked, overstressed people around the world who are seeking an alternative to a fast food, fast life culture.

The International Society for Ecology and Culture (ISEC) takes a somewhat more politicized stance toward local food, using it as a tool to protect biological and cultural diversity in a number of Third World locations.[14] The organization attacks the health risks, environmental damage, economic costs, and threats to food security caused by the global industrial food system. Its activism on the ground includes supporting farmers markets and CSA farming, but it also produces reports and conducts workshops to educate the public about the benefits of shortening the distance between producers and consumers as a way of counteracting the negative effects of globalization. It helps disseminate its anticorporate, antiglobalization message through lectures, seminars, and interviews with ISEC director Helena Norberg-Hodge.

Finally, a new international group, ORIGIN (Organization for an International Geographical Indications Network), has formed of over 100 producers of traditional and typical products from 24 countries.[15] These producers are uniting to gain a more forceful voice in international negotiations governing the intellectual property status of their products as "geographical indications" (an international treaty term for labels of origin). One of the most salient features of globalization is the rapid extension and strengthening of intellectual property rights over creative invention and expression. The signing in 1994 of the Agreement on Trade-Related Aspects of Intellectual Property Rights (TRIPS), which took place at the conclusion of the negotiating rounds that led to the creation of the World Trade Organization (WTO), was a turning point in global policymaking on many fronts. While space will not allow us to go into detail on its ramifications in the world of food alone, of particular note for those wishing to promote local food are the provisions related to geographical indications, which protect traditional and typical regional products in the market from fraudulent abuse. Supporters of the kinds of products celebrated by Slow Food International would do well to follow and encourage the aims of ORIGIN, which in the long run will have worldwide ramifications for foods that are closely linked to their region of origin and the small-scale producers that make them. ORIGIN is poised to become a key local food player, acting at the most global of levels.

Taken together, these different approaches to promoting local food intersect and overlap in complex ways that are not always apparent. They all recall the triad of economic, social, and ecological goals typically associated with sustainability, but they emphasize different aspects and pursue them with different strategies. Perhaps this reflects the fact that food plays a particular role in orienting the person in terms of self (identity), place (community, region, country), and politics (local and global), thus cutting across and complicating issues of sustainability.

The next section introduces a version of local food that we are developing (with help from many others): the Missouri Regional Cuisines Project. The project encourages the development of new specialty products based on inputs from particular ecoregions, the retrieval of dishes and foodways that have been lost or obscured, and the celebration of cuisines tightly linked to the givens of a particular environmental place and the know-how of its inhabitants. It borrows a little from each of the categories discussed here, including the last, because in the end it aims to develop a label-of-origin system in Missouri along the lines of European models. It falls within the ambit of foodshed projects but retrieves a role for the state that is more pronounced than in the approaches reviewed thus far. It proposes at once a more ecologically bounded view of the local and a more resolute engagement with its articulation to the global. It is not a panacea for all that ails the current industrial food system. But it can provide one powerful tool for reconnecting people to nature through their food, a tool that can potentially be replicated in rural areas across the United States.

The Missouri Regional Cuisines Project: Local Food and Regional Identity

For the past five years, the lead author of this chapter, Elizabeth Barham, has been researching the rural development impacts of label-of-origin systems in other countries. Such labels have proven to be economically beneficial to many rural regions in Europe because they help local traditional and high-quality products gain recognition in the market and command a higher price. Research in France, Spain, and Portugal, where such systems are well established, and in Quebec, where the first North American label of origin of the European type is being pursued, illuminate successful examples of how nonmarket values can be translated into product labels that enter the market to change it (Barham 2002, 2006). In this context, labels of origin are considered alongside other values-based labels, such as fair trade or labels indicating humane treatment of animals. The practical purpose of the research is to apply insights from abroad to help American rural regions and producers adapt a label-of-origin system to their own needs.

Putting a New Concept on the Ground

Beginning in 2002, the University of Missouri-Columbia, in association with the Missouri Department of Agriculture's Grape and Wine Program and with funding from a Federal-State Market Improvement Grant (USDA-AMS), launched a project in Missouri to lay the groundwork for a labeling system. Wine was considered the natural lead product because labeling systems in Europe originally emerged to protect wine, and the tie of wine to the land that it comes from is rarely questioned. A survey was undertaken to assess the economic impact of the wine industry on the state of Missouri and the winery quality control measures already in use, and to evaluate the degree of ongoing cooperation and intersectoral coordination within specific regions of the state (Barham 2003b). The project also aims to increase opportunities to market existing and new local items such as sausages, cheeses, fruits, and vegetables, both fresh and transformed (e.g., jams), and other specialty products. Missouri is famous for its cured hams, as well as for a particular type of pecan that is native to parts of the state, but these products have not been marketed on a regionally specific basis in the past. Within the framework of this project, producers will be encouraged to differentiate their products on a more local basis. They will then be marketed in wine tasting rooms, restaurants in the region and nearby cities, and regional stores that feature local products. Producers with sufficient volume of production and technical capacity may choose to pursue marketing products over the Internet.

Early research into values-based food labeling efforts led us to the conviction that because the element of place specificity is missing in most approaches, they remain incomplete and not as effectual as they might be. Place is the link that brings together the abstract rigor of principles being developed for "virtual" or placeless labels (such as organic, which stipulates practices but not origin) with the historical, cultural, and ecological specificities of real places. Tying the goals of values-based virtual labels to the needs and possibilities of actual places provides an opportunity to address the goals of sustainability in a more accountable fashion. Unless we specify the boundaries of the place of concern, we have no clear way of collecting before and after data to evaluate the impact of our efforts to effect change in the overall system. A label-of-origin system requires that boundaries be defined and so lends itself to bringing place and other value criteria together.

Given the need to define relevant territories or regions for labels of origin in Missouri that would include a critical mass of wineries, we began work with the Missouri Ecological Classification Project's geographic information systems (GIS) data.[15] We mapped the state's wineries and then, using the GIS, delineated three regions that form eco-logically coherent landscapes—meaning that if a person were in the region and crossed out of it, a change in the landscape would be appar-ent. Within the delineated regions themselves, several ecological factors such as soils, land cover, species mix, and types of elevation are relatively consistent. A map of the three regions selected is shown in figure 6.1. Regions protected by labels of origin in Europe are usually drawn based on the historical presence of a product that exists in a location because that is where it *could* be produced. The label boundaries tend to reflect the natural variations of ecosystems. In the Missouri project, we tried to compensate for less product history with more ecological science and data.

In actuality, a label-of-origin system of the kind known in Europe is a complex mixture of components including ecological, social, cultural, legal and political (Barham 2003a). With the ecological piece in place, we still need to build the social and political organization that backs a labeling system. Socially, producers must be organized within the region to set standards for products that will bear the label. At the political level, the state or some certification organization must establish offices to certify the production methods required for the label. Having this par-ticipation by the state is a key advantage for small family producers under such systems. Once the label is in the market and gains recogni-tion, it will also presumably gain value. In the event of usurpation or fraud, the state, not the producers themselves, pursues legal redress.

The Missouri effort falls within the realm of foodshed projects because it calls on concepts of bioregionalism, as do Kloppenburg et al. (1996) and many other authors promoting local food. It is based on proximity

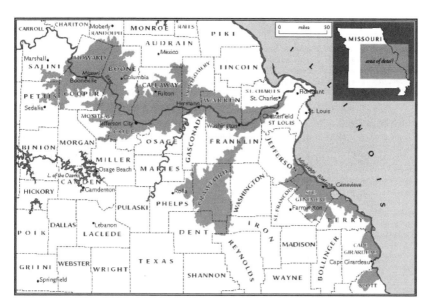

Figure 6.1
Ecoregion delineations for Missouri based on data from the Missouri Ecological Classifications Project. (Map by Tim Nigh, Missouri Department of Conservation, and Andy Dolan, Department of Geography, University of Missouri–Columbia).

(as regionality) and encourages face-to-face trust relations of moral economy. But while we plan to work within the region to build a stronger sense of moral economy and cooperation, the project does not begin with issues such as food security and labor practices in the forefront. We hope to address these issues in the future, but only after a period of relationship building and development of organizational capacity in the region.

The Missouri Regional Cuisines Project certainly follows the principle of nature as measure. But despite being based on ecological data, the project does not set out with a call to environmental protection. While this may come, what has been observed in the European situation is that as producers become aware of the link in consumers' minds between their product and their environment, protecting the latter becomes in part a business decision, taken to maintain the reputation and market value of the label. What scientists involved in the project can do is make certain that producers and other residents in the region are fully aware of the ecological value of what they have within their region; its patterns, needs, and vulnerabilities; and how to maintain it in good health.

The foodshed concept emphasizes studying how food flows into an area, as into a watershed. But the focus of the Missouri project focuses on the ability of regions to assert the value and distinctiveness of their particular place as a source of food with an identity attached as its products move outward in an otherwise homogeneous global marketplace. The Missouri project does draw heavily on commensality because it sets out explicitly to integrate all aspects of locally produced food into a distinctive regional cuisine over time. Kloppenburg et al. (1996) raised the point that a key problem with the global food system is that we are not able to know about the processes behind the products that we buy. The Missouri project attempts to rectify this by tying production processes to ability to use the label of origin to gain market value-added. Consumers who are familiar with the label should be able to purchase confidently the products it covers anywhere, assuming they approve of the standards behind the label itself. These labels would therefore function somewhat like fair trade labels that can travel long distances carrying their message, relating one place in the world to the values of consumers elsewhere.

Of course, this puts a burden on producers to meet consumer demands for added value in the broadest sense, not simply in the immediate sense of taste, texture, and quantity. But it allows producers in a region to join the global trading system more squarely on their own terms, taking varying geographies into account and perhaps coming closer to the original meaning of the concept of comparative advantage. Producers in regions would still compete, but collectively with other regions based on their own distinctiveness, not based on whether they can make a product more cheaply than another region at the cost of their own people or their environment. Such a system could potentially empower local people not through secession, but by gaining a new form of local control over how they connect to the world market.

An overarching goal of the Missouri project is to reconnect the food chain from nature through production to consumption in a material sense, but also in the imagination of consumers (Goodman and Du Puis 2002). With this in mind, one thread of research has looked at the interest of chefs in the St. Louis area in featuring local food products. Chefs can play an important role in relocalizing the food system because they have the ability to reconnect the highly urbanized population of the United States to its rural agricultural base in new ways. Furthermore, rural regions are not likely to thrive agriculturally without ties to urban markets. This is particularly true of the type of regional labeling efforts described here. The final section of this chapter shares the early results of research with chefs in St. Louis for the insight it provides into urban demand for local food and how that demand might be met to the advantage of nearby regions.

Connecting to Place in the Restaurant

Very early in the Missouri Regional Cuisines Project, we realized the importance of chefs to overall goals we wished to pursue. They are a source of information for assessing the urban interest in local food, but they are also leaders of food tastes in their own right and can have an influence on the choices of urban consumers. Therefore, while work was ongoing to delineate ecological regions, we began a survey of chefs in St. Louis who choose and purchase their own food and plan their own menus.

Using the Yellow Pages and on-line resources, we identified an initial list of 523 restaurants that did not appear to be national restaurant chains or franchises. We wanted to meet with approximately 50 chefs, so to narrow the list we contacted St. Louis food critics and writers Joe and Ann Lemons Pollack who have over twenty years of experience in the area (Pollack and Pollack 2001). We asked them to help us identify restaurants they felt would be most interested in purchasing local food. They selected 66 from our initial list and added 9 others we had not discovered. Two trained interviewers visited the extremely busy chefs in these restaurants and were able to collect data to complete 46 surveys.

The survey, entitled "Cooking Local: Urban Cuisine from Local Farmers," asked chefs to gauge the most important reasons restaurants might want to buy from local farmers. Figure 6.2 reflects their responses. Freshness was identified as the most important aspect, followed by their customers' concerns for food safety, implying greater trust in local producers than in the globally sourced system even when restaurants act as

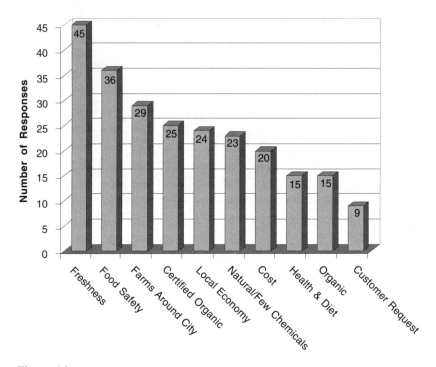

Figure 6.2
Most important reasons chefs report for buying local food products.

intermediaries. Both of these attributes are related to personal interests, but keeping local farms around the city and having a positive impact on the local economy were ranked third and fifth in importance, respectively. Purchasing organically grown food ranked fourth and can be considered to serve both personal and larger environmental interests.

Only nine respondents indicated customer request was a factor in buying local, the lowest number of responses to this aspect of the survey. This tells us that the project cannot rely on patron demand in the short term and will need to make other kinds of connections for chefs to promote local foods. Perhaps consumer interest in local food is not translated into direct requests when dining out, although restaurants with their own chef are in the best position to satisfy such a request. Further research can explore whether patrons seek local foods to an extent not appreciated by chefs.

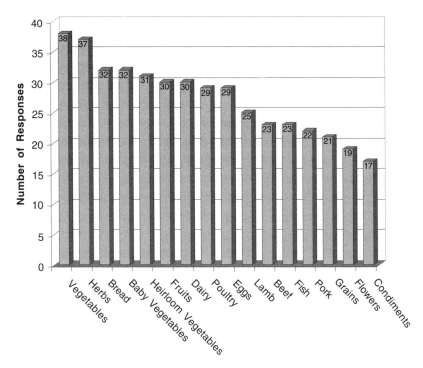

Figure 6.3
Local products chefs are most interested in purchasing.

We also asked the chefs to indicate their degree of interest in a number of products that are produced near St. Louis that could be purchased locally. Figure 6.3 reflects which products were of most interest to them, with fresh vegetables and fruits holding five of the top six positions (local breads were ranked third). These included baby and heirloom vegetables, both popular restaurant fare. Dairy ranked seventh in demand, followed closely by poultry and eggs.

We then asked the chefs to indicate, using a provided list, those products they already purchase from local producers. Figure 6.4 indicates their responses. We were somewhat surprised at the number of chefs already buying local products, which illustrates that the interest in local foods has emerged with substantial force. Space was provided to indicate products they were buying that were not listed. They included mushrooms, herbs, spinach, and squashes, items we had overlooked in preparing our list.

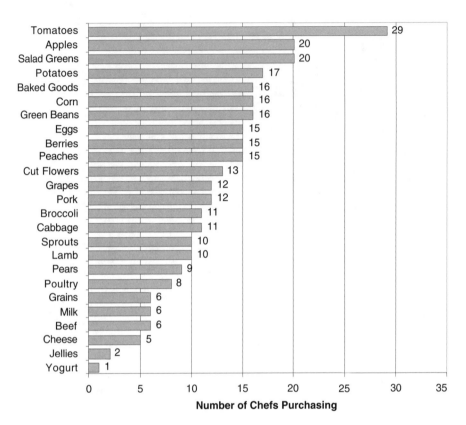

Figure 6.4
Local products chefs are already purchasing.

We asked the chefs how much they would be willing to pay above market price for three types of specialty products: out of season, organic, and local. They indicated that on average, they would be willing to pay 11 percent above market for both out of season and organic but only 9 percent above market for local products. At the time of the survey, we were not discussing the possibility of origin-labeled products with the chefs. In reality, in the European case many origin-labeled products are also organic, and so the combination of the factors local and organic might have pushed the willingness to pay even higher. In addition, one of the authors, Lewis Jett, is currently working with vegetable producers on the use of protective hoop structures for early- and late-season produce. This means potentially all three of the criteria we tested could be combined, almost certainly boosting the value-added potential.

Finally, we asked the chefs what their preferred distribution strategies would be for receiving local products, should they wish to buy them. Thirty-two chefs preferred direct delivery by a farmer, 19 would prefer a fax-based system, 16 preferred a distributor, 15 might use the Web, and 9 would buy directly from the farmer at the farm. Only 5 indicated that they might buy local products at a farmers market, a rather surprising result for an urban area, and 1 indicated a preference to buy local products at a supermarket. A fax system linking chefs and farmers has been successfully piloted in Kansas City. Although this particular effort is no longer operating, it was successful enough that it will probably be folded into a new initiative to be undertaken by the state's Department of Agriculture that will include more cities, such as St. Louis. In the Kansas City situation, weekly lists of available fresh produce and monthly lists of meats and wines were compiled and sent to interested chefs. The chefs ordered directly from producers and received their orders from them. In addition, meetings were held bringing chefs and farmers together to share their needs and tailor the system, which evaluators considered one of the most valuable aspects of the effort.

Taken together, these results present a generally optimistic picture for marketing local food to chefs, but they also indicate some important challenges. Market garden farming clearly holds the edge, particularly for farmers willing to make extra efforts for specialty items (baby or heirloom vegetables, early- and late-season produce). These types of products are among the most labor intensive and require special handling to arrive in good condition for restaurant presentation. The category of dairy products could be further explored, as this one category could possibly be split out to more products to get a clearer picture (fresh milk, cream, butter). However, there does appear to be room for poultry and egg sales from local sources to be increased.

While a 9 percent price premium seemed rather low for local products, we also realize that the only descriptor given in this survey ("local") is vague. We could hope that with additional information on quality-certified regional products, a higher value-added could be reached. But delivery will remain an issue for the project, as most producers will not be able to make regular trips to the city to deliver in person, which most chefs would prefer. One possible benefit to organizing the producers locally by sector would be a collective approach to delivery, either by rotation or with certain farmers acting as representatives for the others in making delivery and receiving a larger percentage of the profit in return.

After we conducted the survey, we interviewed some of the chefs who had participated to find out more about the meanings they attached to local food. We wanted to know the relative importance for them of geographical, social, and economic factors, and how they understood the notion of quality. The chefs whom we talked to defined the geographical boundaries of local very broadly, focusing more on social, economic, and quality concerns.

"I buy produce 'locally' which is defined for me by the low-tech distribution system of small growers. . . . In a way, part of the definition of local is face-to-face dealing with the grower."

"I don't define it in terms of geographic boundaries. I associate it with independent growers."

In the end, social concerns related to keeping small farmers in business appeared to be one of the most important dimensions of the chefs' preference for face-to-face relations with producers.

"Definitely, I associate it with supporting local farmers."

"A good part of the appeal to me is political. I think there should be more small farms closer to St. Louis instead of fewer and fewer, further and further away. The only way to achieve that goal is to buy their stuff. Buying locally is a statement of support for small scale agriculture over factory farming, for the local economy, for knowing how the products were raised and treated and for quality."

However, social concern often comes at a cost. Despite the fact that the sample was taken from relatively high-end restaurants, a number of the chefs mentioned that management imposed price controls that limited the degree to which they could favor local food:

"Well, you don't save any money buying local. The cruel fact is that when spinach is in season here it is at its season lowest price point from

California, too. The economies of scale usually make the factory farm product less expensive despite the cost of transportation."

"The issue isn't really that it is more expensive but the restaurant I work at sets certain price parameters. My feeling is that a potato dug out of the ground yesterday is always better, but I have to deal with price parameters."

Nonetheless, chefs were quick to balance out the equation by making reference to the issue of quality, particularly freshness, pointing out that price is not always the central issue:

"It could be high or low priced. It's more a question of quality."

"I never miss a chance to [list in the] menu 'fresh raspberries picked THIS MORNING.'"

"[Local food] is definitely higher quality. Well, they are closer. Something that just got picked yesterday is always going to be better."

"Frequently small local growers are able to grow more delicate varieties because they sell more quickly and, for instance, hand harvesting is much easier on the product than machine harvesting."

Other dimensions of quality touched on the environmental practices of small-scale local farmers. Most chefs were not strictly seeking organic products but were concerned with lower chemical inputs. This was related to a sense of trust in the relationships cultivated with local farmers:

"I do not deal exclusively with organic producers, but even the local farmers who do use chemical inputs use them as little as possible as a function of their cost and are able to do so because their smaller scale makes 'routine' spraying, for instance, less necessary."

"It is usually higher quality but not 100 percent of the time. But local food is usually guaranteed a bit more. I guess you could encapsulate that by saying, a lot better service."

One chef pointed out that his customers associate his inclusion of the names of growers and some background on the foods he uses in his restaurants as a sign of his commitment to provide high-quality foods:

"I believe that regardless of their personal level of commitment to the concept, almost all of my customers identify my commitment to local growers as a positive sign of the care with which we buy and the pride with which we serve."

One question for us is whether these positive associations can be successfully transferred to an ecoregional definition of local that would include a number of quality controls. We found it encouraging that quality dimensions of local tended to open up the concept. For example, although the chefs we interviewed currently purchase most of their local products from Missouri counties, when pressed, they did not seem strongly attached to the state as a defining feature of local. Instead, they tended to blur notions of local with handmade or craft products that are strongly local to particular places.

"I don't sell it as 'local,' but I buy certain artisanal products from much further afield. For the same reasons of quality that I buy St. Louis County tomatoes, I get andouille sausage air freight from New Orleans, blue cheese from an Amish coop in Wisconsin."

"I don't know if it falls in the bailiwick of your study, although it should. I market the local provenance of prosciutto that I buy from John Volpi on the Hill in St. Louis [a well-known Italian neighborhood] and the sausages from G&W Meats on South Kingshighway."

Conclusion

In the Missouri Regional Cuisines Project, we will continue to focus with chefs on this liaison between a simultaneous sense of local and quality, attempting to transfer the association to an ecoregional scale. Chefs occupy a special place in our culture as tastemakers, go-betweens, and "translators" of food as it comes from nature to the plate of the consumer. By featuring local and regional foods and educating their customers about their qualities and origins, they can help overcome the distance and estrangement many city dwellers feel toward the rural regions that surround their city.

Through menu descriptions, informal conversation with customers, and the cuisine itself, chefs can also help restore some of the knowledge and language we need to reengage with American agriculture on a new footing. The Chef's Collaborative, cofounded in 1993 by Alice Waters (owner and executive chef of Chez Panisse Restaurant and Café in Berkeley, California), provides an excellent example of blending an appreciation of food as art with a desire to fight hunger, preserve farmland, and secure sustainable agriculture.[17] These goals are in reality mutually reinforcing. Although not everyone may enjoy specialties prepared by a chef on a daily basis, the simple pleasures of eating fresh, healthy food that reconnects us to our bodies and nature is a fundamental human need that we should strive to secure for everyone.

As this book has stressed, many efforts are already underway to redirect our food system, making it more just, sustainable, and humane. Bringing about this kind of positive change can seem overwhelming, but ordinary individuals have begun to act and are working together to reweave the connection between themselves and nature through their food. We are more in need of that connection than perhaps ever before in human history. A key characteristic of our modern age is the fragmentation of our experience of reality (Featherstone 1995). A regained sense of place can be one of the most powerful antidotes to counteract the anomie that this can induce in our lives (Amit 2002).

Food can be a powerful constructor of a sense of place. It is interwined with our sense of a place's meaning and identity (Bell and Valentine 1997; Brown and Mussell 1985). Memories of food that are strongly associated with a place can cause even casual visitors to take away some sense of it (Sutton 2001). In all probability, they will remember not just the people and food, but the nature and landscape that make it up, as well. We have an essential need to hold such memories, even of places that we do not inhabit every day but visit over our lifetime (Simpson 2002). They speak directly to us of our dependence on the earth (Bailey 2002; McGinnis 1999).

Farming landscapes in particular, both inhabited and remembered, are the basis and testing ground for our possibilities of blending nature and the human on a positive basis (Jackson and Jackson 2002). To make them sustainable will take dedication and new policy measures (Dirlik 2001; Honadle 1999; Lockeretz 1997). And we have no time to waste, because industrial agriculture is spreading rapidly to the poorest regions in the world, places with much less capacity than the West to resist its destruction or reflect on its checkered history (Fitzgerald 2003). If we can still regain the connection we have lost to the land through conscious choices concerning our food and help others do so, we may yet be able to reshape the values that guide Western agriculture, and with them its products and the lifestyles and landscapes they sustain.

Notes

1. See Berry (1977), Goodman and Redclift (1991), Kimbrell (2002), Olson and Lyson (1999), and Youngberg, Schaller, and Merrigan (1993) for discussion of these trends and the weakness of public policy response.

2. Fitchen (1991), Gouveia and Juska (2002), Lyson and Falk (1993), and Stull, Broadway, and Griffith (1995) have explored various aspects of the social impacts of industrial agriculture.

3. A number of articles reflecting renewed consideration of consumption and its linkages to production can be found in special issues of *Sociologia Ruralis* 42(4) (2002) and *Journal of Rural Studies* 19(1) (2003), both edited by David Goodman.

4. Kloppenburg et al. (1996) identify Hedden (1929) as the originator of the term, but credit Getz (1991) with introducing them to it.

5. Local food is often promoted by academic authors with practical how-to guides or publications. Some are in print form (Green and Hilchey 2002; Valen 2001), and others are downloadable from the Web (see Dahlberg et al. 2002 at http://homepages.wmich.edu/ ~dahlberg/ResourceGuide.html and the Northeast Regional Food Guide information sources at http://www.nutrition.cornell.edu/foodguide/cfs2_lead.html).

6. Several authors have developed arguments for these anticipated benefits. See Feenstra (1997), Garrett and Feenstra (1999), Halweil (2002), Nabhan (2002), and Thayer (2003).

7. Two of the best-known examples are the Toronto Food Policy Council (http://www.city.toronto.on.ca/health/tfpc_index.htm) and the Connecticut Food Policy Council (http://www.foodpc.state.ct.us/).

8. Quoted from their Web site at http://www.foodsecurity.org/.

9. From their Web site at http://www.foodcircles.missouri.edu/.

10. See http://www.foodroutes.org/ for the FoodRoutes campaign.

11. More detail on their program is available at http://www.thefoodalliance.org/, and information on their Midwest partners can be found at http://www.thefoodalliance.org/ midwest.html.

12. The Food Alliance seal is a form of ecolabel. The Consumers Union site at www.ecolabels.org provides consumer-friendly access to an assessment of many of the ecolabels now on the market.

13. See the international site for Slow Food International at http://www.slowfood.com/, and its U.S. incarnation at http://www.slowfoodusa.org/.

14. The ISEC Web site is found at http://www.isec.org.uk/.

15. Their Web site can be found at http://www.origin-gi.com/.

16. More information on this project is available at http://www.cerc.cr.usgs.gov/morap/.

17. See their Web site at http://www.chefscollaborative.org/.

References

Allen, Patricia, and Carolyn Sachs. 1993. Sustainable Agriculture in the United States: Engagements, Silences, and Possibilities for Transformation. In *Food for the Future: Conditions and Contradictions of Sustainability*. Patricia Allen, ed. Pp. 139–167. New York: Wiley.

Amit, Vered, ed. 2002. *Realizing Community: Concepts, Social Relationships and Sentiments*. New York: Routledge.

Arce, A., and T. K. Marsden. 1993. The Social Construction of International Food: A New Research Agenda. *Economic Geography* 69(3):293–311.

Bailey, Robert G. 2002. *Ecoregion-Based Design for Sustainability*. New York: Springer.

Barham, Elizabeth. 1999. Sustainable Agriculture in the United States and France: A Polanyian Perspective. Ph.D. dissertation, Cornell University.

Barham, Elizabeth. 2002. Towards a Theory of Values-Based Labeling. *Agriculture and Human Values* 19(4):349–360.

Barham, Elizabeth. 2003a. Translating Terroir: The Global Challenge of French AOC Labeling. *Journal of Rural Studies* (19)1:127–138.

Barham, Elizabeth. 2003b. *Missouri Wineries: Present Status and Future Scenarios*. Columbia, MO: University of Missouri. http://www.ruralsociology.missouri.edu/RuralSoc/ FacultyF.html.

Barham, Elizabeth. 2006. The Lamb That Roared: Origin Labeled Products as Place Making Strategy in Charlevoix, Quebec. In *Remaking the North American Food System*. Claire Hinrichs and Thomas Lyson, eds. Lincoln, Neb.: University of Nebraska Press.

Barlett, Peggy F. 1993. *American Dreams, Rural Realities: Family Farms in Crisis*. Chapel Hill: University of North Carolina Press.

Bell, David, and Gill Valentine, eds. 1997. *Consuming Geographies: We Are Where We Eat*. New York: Routledge.

Berry, Wendell. 1977. *The Unsettling of America: Culture and Agriculture.* New York: Avon.

Beus, Curtis E., and Riley E. Dunlap. 1990. Conventional Versus Alternative Agriculture: The Paradigmatic Roots of the Debate. *Rural Sociology* 55(4):590–616.

Bonanno, Alessandro, et al., eds. 1994. *From Columbus to ConAgra: The Globalization of Agriculture and Food.* Lawrence: University Press of Kansas.

Brown, Linda Keller, and Kay Mussell, eds. 1985. *Ethnic and Regional Foodways in the United States: The Performance of Group Identity.* Knoxville: University of Tennessee Press.

Cone, Cynthia Abbott, and Andrea Myhre. 2000. Community-Supported Agriculture: A Sustainable Alternative to Industrial Agriculture? *Human Organization* 59(2):187–197.

Dahlberg, Kenneth A., Kate Clancy, Robert L. Wilson, and Jan O'Donnell. 2002. Strategies, Policy Approaches, and Resources for Local Food System Planning and Organizing. http://homepages.wmich.edu/~dahlberg/ResourceGuide.html. Accessed Jan. 14, 2005.

Dirlik, Arif. 2001. Place-Based Imagination: Globalism and the Politics of Place. In *Places and Politics in an Age of Globalization.* R. Prazniak and Arif Dirlik, eds. Pp. 15–51. New York: Rowman & Littlefield.

Doherty, Daniel, and Amitai Etzioni, eds. 2003. *Voluntary Simplicity: Responding to Consumer Culture.* Lanham, Md.: Rowman & Littlefield.

Dowler, Elizabeth, and Martin Caraher. 2003. Local Food Projects: The New Philanthropy? *Political Quarterly* 74(1):57–65.

Featherstone, Mike. 1995. *Undoing Culture: Globalization, Postmodernism and Identity.* Thousand Oaks, Calif.: Sage.

Feenstra, Gail W. 1997. Local Food Systems and Sustainable Communities. *American Journal of Alternative Agriculture* 12(1):28–36.

Fitchen, Janet M. 1991. *Endangered Spaces, Enduring Places: Change, Identity and Survival in Rural America.* Boulder, Colo.: Westview Press.

Fitzgerald, Deborah. 2003. *Every Farm a Factory: The Industrial Ideal in American Agriculture.* New Haven, Conn.: Yale University Press.

Friedmann, Harriet. 1993. After Midas' Feast: Alternative Food Regimes for the Future. In *Food for the Future: Conditions and Contradictions of Sustainability.* P. Allen, ed. Pp. 213–233. New York: Wiley.

Friedmann, Harriet. 1995. Food Politics: New Dangers, New Possibilities. In *Food and Agrarian Orders in the World-Economy.* Phillip McMichael, ed. Pp. 15–34. New York: Praeger.

Friedmann, Harriet, and Philip McMichael. 1989. Agriculture and the State System: The Rise and Decline of National Agricultures, 1870 to the Present. *Sociologia Ruralis* 29(2):93–119.

Food Processing Center, Institute of Agriculture and Natural Resources, University of Nebraska–Lincoln. 2001. Attracting Consumers with Locally Grown Products. Lincoln: University of Nebraska. http://www.farmprofitability. org/local.htm. Accessed Jan. 14, 2005.

Food Routes Network. 2003. *Where Does Your Food Come From? Recipes for Communicating Effectively about American Agriculture*. Millheim, Pa.: Food Routes Network. www.foodroutes.org. Accessed Jan. 14, 2005.

Garrett, Steven, and Gail Feenstra. 1999. *Growing a Community Food System*. Pullman: Washington State University.

Getz, Arthur. 1991. Urban Foodsheds. *Permaculture Activist* 7(3):26–27.

Goldschmidt, Walter. 1978 (1947). *As You Sow: Three Studies in the Social Consequences of Agribusiness*. Montclair, N.J.: Allanheld, Osmun.

Goodman, David, and Melanie E. DuPuis. 2002. Knowing Food and Growing Food: Beyond the Production-Consumption Debate in the Sociology of Agriculture. *Sociologia Ruralis* 42(1):5–22.

Goodman, David, and Michael Redclift. 1991. *Refashioning Nature: Food, Ecology, and Culture*. New York: Routledge.

Gouveia, Lourdes, and Arunas Juska. 2002. Taming Nature, Taming Workers: Constructing the Separation between Meat Consumption and Meat Production in the U.S. *Sociologia Ruralis* 42(4):370–390.

Green, Joanna, and Duncan Hilchey, eds. 2002. *Growing Home: A Guide to Reconnecting Agriculture, Food and Communities*. Ithaca, N.Y.: Community, Food and Agriculture Program, Department of Rural Sociology, Cornell University.

Hedden, Walter P. 1929. *How Great Cities Are Fed*. Boston: Heath.

Halweil, Brian. 2002. *Home Grown: The Case for Local Food in a Global Market*. Washington, D.C.: WorldWatch Institute.

Harris, Brian, David Burress, and Sharon Eicher. 2000. Demands for Local and Organic Produce: A Brief Review of the Literature. Lawrence, Kans.: Institute for Public Policy and Business Research. http://www.ku.edu/pri/resrep/ pdf/m254A.pdf. Accessed Jan. 14, 2005.

Hartman Group. 1999. *The Hartman Report: Food and the Environment: A Consumer's Perspective: Phases I, II and III*. Bellevue, Wash.: Hartman Group. http://www.hartman-group.com/ products/reports.html. Accessed Jan. 14, 2005.

Hinrichs, C. Clare. 2000. Embeddness and Local Food Systems: Notes on Two Types of Direct Agriculture Market. *Journal of Rural Studies* 16:295–303.

Honadle, George. 1999. *How Context Matters: Linking Environmental Policy to People and Place*. West Hartford, Conn.: Kumarian Press.

Jackson, Dana L., and Laura L. Jackson, eds. 2002. *The Farm as Natural Habitat: Reconnecting Food Systems with Ecosystems*. Washington, D.C.: Island Press.

Jackson, Wes. 1996. *Becoming Native to This Place*. Washington, D.C.: Counterpoint.

Kane, Deborah, and James F. Ennis. 2003. Food Alliance: Transforming a Regional Success Story into a National Network. In *Ecolabels and the Greening of the Food Market*. William Lockeretz, ed. Boston: Friedman School of Nutrition Science and Policy, Tufts University.

Kimbrell, Andrew, ed. 2002. *Fatal Harvest: The Tragedy of Industrial Agriculture*. Washington, D.C.: Island Press.

Kloppenburg, Jr., Jack, et al. 2000. Tasting Food, Tasting Sustainability: Defining the Attributes of an Alternative Food System with Competent, Ordinary People. *Human Organization* 59(2):177–186.

Kloppenburg, Jr., Jack, John Hendrickson, and G. W. Stevenson. 1996. Coming in to the Foodshed. *Agriculture and Human Values* 13(3):33–42.

Kneen, Brewster. 1993. *From Land to Mouth: Understanding the Food System*. Toronto: NC Press Limited.

Lockeretz, William, ed. 1997. *Visions of American Agriculture*. Ames: Iowa State University Press.

Lockeretz, William, ed. 2003. *Ecolabels and the Greening of the Food Market*. Boston: Friedman School of Nutrition Science and Policy, Tufts University. http://nutrition.tufts.edu/conferences/ecolabels/order.html. Accessed Jan. 14, 2005.

Lyson, Thomas A., and William W. Falk, eds. 1993. *Forgotten Places: Uneven Development in Rural America*. Lawrence: University of Kansas Press.

McGinnis, Michael Vincent, ed. 1999. *Bioregionalism*. New York: Routledge.

McMichael, Philip, ed. 1995. *Food and Agrarian Orders in the World-Economy*. Westport, Conn.: Praeger.

McMichael, Philip. 2000. The Power of Food. *Agriculture and Human Values* 17(1):21–33.

Meares, Alison C. 1997. Making the Transition from Conventional to Sustainable Agriculture: Gender, Social Movement Participation and Quality of Life on the Family Farm. *Rural Sociology* 62(1):21–47.

Murphy, Richard McGill. 2004. Truth or Scare: What Food Producers Need to Know about American Demands for Details on What They Buy to Eat. *American Demographics*, Mar. 1:26–32.

Nabhan, Gary Paul. 2002. *Coming Home to Eat: The Pleasures and Politics of Local Foods*. New York: Norton.

Olson, Richard H., and Thomas A. Lyson. 1999 *Under the Blade: The Conversion of Agricultural Landscapes*. Boulder, Colo.: Westview Press.

Orr, David. 1992. *Ecological Literacy: Education and the Transition to a Postmodern World*. Albany: State University of New York Press.

Pirog, Rich, ed. 2003. *Ecolabel Value Assessment: Consumer and Food Business Perceptions of Local Foods.* Ames: Leopold Center and the Iowa State University Business Analysis Laboratory. http://www.leopold.iastate.edu/pubinfo/papersspeeches/ecolabels/ecolabels.html. Accessed Jan. 14, 2005.

Pirog, Rich, and Pat Schuh. 2003. The Load Less Traveled: Examining the Potential of Using Food Miles and CO_2 Emissions in Ecolabels. In *Ecolabels and the Greening of the Food Market.* William Lockeretz, ed. Boston: Friedman School of Nutrition Science and Policy, Tufts University.

Pirog, Rich, and John Tyndall. 1999. Comparing Apples to Apples: An Iowa Perspective on Apples and Local Food Systems. Ames: Leopold Center for Sustainable Agriculture, Iowa State University. http://www.leopold.iastate.edu/pubinfo/papersspeeches/apples/apple.html. Accessed Jan. 14, 2005.

Pirog, Rich, et al. 2001. Food, Fuel, and Freeways: An Iowa Perspective on How Far Food Travels, Fuel Usage, and Greenhouse Gas Emissions. Ames: Leopold Center for Sustainable Agriculture. Available at: http://www.leopold/iastate.edu. Accessed Jan. 14, 2005.

Polanyi, Karl. 1957 [1944]. *The Great Transformation: The Political and Economic Origins of Our Time.* Boston: Beacon Press.

Pollack, Joe, and Ann Lemons Pollack. 2001. *Beyond Gooey Butter Cake: Further Adventures in St. Louis Dining.* St. Louis, Mo.: Virginia Publishing.

Pretty, Jules. 2002. *Agri-Culture: Reconnecting People, Land and Nature.* London: Earthscan.

Ray, Paul H., and Sherry Ruth Anderson. 2000. *The Cultural Creatives: How 50 Million People Are Changing the World.* New York: Harmony Books.

Rodefeld, Richard D., et al. 1978. *Change in Rural America: Causes, Consequences, and Alternatives.* Saint Louis, Mo.: C. V. Mosby.

Simpson, John Warfield. 2002. *Yearning for the Land: A Search for the Importance of Place.* New York: Pantheon Books.

Stephenson, Garry, and Larry Lev. 1998. *Common Support for Local Agriculture in Two Contrasting Oregon Cities.* Eugene: Oregon State University Extension Service. http://smallfarms.oregonstate.edu/marketing/publications.php. Accessed Jan. 14, 2005.

Stevens, Mark R., and Samina Raja. 2001. What's Eating You about What You Eat? Madison Food System Project Working Paper Series MFA-WPS-05. Madison, Wis. http://www.wisc.edu/ urpl/mfsp/pubs/wps5.pdf. Accessed Jan. 14, 2005.

Stull, Donald D., Michael J. Broadway, and David Griffith. 1995. *Any Way You Cut It: Meat Processing and Small-Town America.* Lawrence: University of Kansas Press.

Sutton, David E. 2001. *Remembrance of Repasts: An Anthropology of Food and Memory.* New York: Berg.

Thayer, Robert L., Jr. 2003. *LifePlace: Bioregional Thought and Practice.* Berkeley: University of California Press.

Valen, Gary. 2001. *Local Food Project: A How-to Manual.* Washington, D.C.: Humane Society of the United States.

Wimberley, Ronald C., Craig K. Harris, Joseph J. Molnar, and Terry J. Tomazic eds. 2002. *The Social Risks of Agriculture: Americans Speak Out on Food, Farming, and the Environment.* Westport, Conn.: Praeger.

Youngberg, Garth, Neill Schaller, and Kathleen Merrigan. 1993. The Sustainable Agriculture Policy Agenda in the United States: Politics and Prospects. In *Food for the Future: Conditions and Contradictions of Sustainability.* Patricia Allen, ed. Pp. 295–318. New York: Wiley.

7

Urban Volunteers and the Environment: Forest and Prairie Restoration

Robert L. Ryan and Robert E. Grese

Restoration of forests, prairies, and watersheds has become a major movement involving thousands of volunteers from all walks of life. Studies of these volunteers reveal the impact of the experience and illuminate another avenue by which people are reconnecting with urban nature. Ecological restoration is an activity that centers on restoring, managing, and maintaining native ecosystems, including removing invasive exotic plant species, assisting with prescribed burns, and collecting and planting native seeds, shrubs, and trees. William Jordan (2003:24), a leader in ecological restoration, likens the movement to gardening in that it involves an active relationship between people and their natural environment. Restoration builds on many activities typically associated with gardening—harvesting seed, propagating plants, tilling, planting, weeding, cultivating—and uses many of the same tools. However, Jordan also notes some important distinctions: gardening is a creative act, while ecological restoration is specifically noncreative and strives to copy nature. It is this restorative or healing aspect of ecological restoration that makes it especially appealing to many environmentalists and has expanded the environmental movement beyond its traditional pursuits of land protection, environmental education, and political organizing.

Urban forests and streams need the help of local residents to nurture these valuable resources. Urban forests are essential for providing habitat for wildlife, recreation areas for people, cleaning polluted air, buffering urban streams and rivers, and moderating the climate extremes in the city (Hough 1995). In fact, urban natural areas are often treasure troves of biodiversity. The highest concentration of endangered species in Illinois occurs within the Chicago metropolitan region (Chicago

Regional Biodiversity Council 1996). Unfortunately, urban natural areas are threatened by development if they are not legally protected land. Even once protected, urban wildlands are threatened by pollution, soil erosion and compaction, vandalism, and neglect (Botkin and Keller 1995:543). Invasive nonnative plant species can overwhelm native urban forests, prairies, and wetlands, degrading the habitat for native plants and animals. Urban streams and rivers are also threatened by nonpoint source pollution, altered hydrology, and invasive species.

Ecological restoration efforts are underway in many urban areas to restore degraded natural areas and streams. Urban parks departments facing declining budgets have turned to volunteer programs to undertake ecological restoration projects and other related efforts. In New York City, over 70,000 volunteers donated an estimated 1 million hours in service to the city parks in 2001 (Benepe 2002). The goal of this chapter is to understand how ecological restoration work in urban forests and watersheds affects the environmental attitudes and outlook of volunteers. Most accounts focus on the way volunteers have transformed thousands of acres of urban natural areas into ecologically healthier environments, a worthy effort with many benefits to the city. But how have these volunteers, in turn, been transformed by their volunteer efforts? How does restoration work reconnect urban residents to the natural world? This chapter focuses on restoration studies in the Midwest, where there is a long history of ecological restoration.

In order to understand the attitudes of ecological restorationists, it is important to learn how this movement has evolved. Ecological restoration has its roots in work done by nineteenth- and early twentieth-century landscape architects and horticulturists who initially used native plants in various landscaping efforts but gradually broadened their focus to incorporate emerging ideas in plant community ecology. Among significant examples are Frederick Law Olmsted's 1879 development of the Back Bay Fens in Boston and various projects by Ossian Cole Simonds and Jens Jensen, particularly Jensen's attempts to "recreate" habitats experienced by Abraham Lincoln at Lincoln Memorial Gardens in Springfield, Illinois. Working with extension programs at the University of Illinois, Wilhelm Miller exhorted landowners in both urban and rural areas to "re-create as much of the local scenery as possible" and described restoration as guided by professionals to integrate invest-igations into systematic botany, state and local history, ecology, and ornithology (Miller 1915). Other academics in the 1920s also promoted a form of restoration in their teaching and experiments with their stu-dents. Notable was the work of Frank Waugh at Massachusetts Agri-cultural College (now the University of Massachusetts, Amherst) whose analysis of the landscape of western Massachusetts linked the study of place with creating new landscapes. Edith Roberts led efforts to create an experimental laboratory for restoration at Vassar College in Pough-keepsie, New York (Egan 1990; Grese 1990, 1992; Roberts 1933). The Depression era brought another round of restoration projects through the work of the Soil Conservation Service, Civilian Conservation Corps, and Tennessee Valley Authority. Some of these, however, did not neces-sarily use native plant material and were primarily focused on rural areas (Bratton 2000:54). These projects in particular did not have the same focus on connecting people to the native landscape as did the earlier work of Jensen, Waugh, and others.

A more modern phase of thinking about ecological restoration began with efforts to restore native prairie at the University of Wisconsin Arboretum in Madison in the 1930s (Egan 1990; Jordan 1989). More recent projects, such as the prairie restoration efforts at the Morton Arboretum in Lisle, Illinois, can be considered to be a direct outgrowth of the environmental movement of the late 1960s and 1970s. From these relatively small-scale projects, ecological restoration has increased in scale to include large-scale restoration of the Florida Everglades and Kissimmee River (Jordan 2003:113). Within more urban areas, the Volunteer Stewardship Network, founded by the Illinois Chapter of the Nature Conservancy in 1983, had grown by the mid-1990s to include over 5,600 volunteers working to restore and maintain over 67,000 acres of prairie, savanna, and wetlands, especially around the Chicago metropolitan area (Ross 1997). Now part of the larger Chicago Wilderness, volunteers work within the coalition of more than 170 public and private organizations that manages a regional reserve of over 200,000 acres.[1]

Restoration efforts of this magnitude would be impossible without the help of volunteers (Miles, Sullivan, and Kuo 1998:27). Understanding the current environmental state of an urban natural area requires that volunteers inventory endangered species and habitat, monitor water quality, and take soil samples. Ongoing monitoring conducted by volunteers allows environmental agencies and organizations to understand how these ecosystems are changing over time.

Volunteers' Relationship to the Natural World

Considering the busy time constraints of many urban dwellers, why do people volunteer their time with ecological restoration projects? One reason may be that all people have a strong attraction to nature. Studies have shown that urban residents have a strong, emotional affinity for urban trees, especially large specimen trees (Dwyer, Schroeder, and Gobster 1991:17–18). The public's preference for green spaces over buildings and other urban settings has been well documented (Kaplan and Kaplan 1996; Kaplan, Kaplan, and Ryan 1998), and volunteer stewardship programs build on this connection to nature. People get involved in urban tree planting projects because they want to help the environment (Westphal 1993:20). Our studies of Michigan volunteers who worked in ecological restoration projects in urban forests, watersheds, and other natural areas revealed that helping the environment and feeling useful were the most important motivations for both the initial decision to volunteer as well as continued participation. (Grese et al. 2000; Ryan, Kaplan, and Grese 2001:637). Ecological restoration allows people to take tangible steps to improve their local surroundings. A study of Chicago's Volunteer Stewardship Network found that volunteers enjoyed taking "meaningful action" to help the environment (Miles et al. 1998:31). Seeing the tangible effects of their work was also expressed in the newsletters of Chicago-area volunteer groups (Schroeder 2000). (The importance of meaningful action in motivating more environmentally beneficial lifestyles is discussed in chapter 12.)

Nature provides the opportunity for effortless fascination: the change of seasons, the kaleidoscope of wildlife and plants, and the sound of flowing water or stirring breezes. Participants in ecological restoration are motivated by this intimate contact with nature (Miles et al. 1998:32). Urban natural areas also provide the venue for learning more about the fascinating natural world. As we found in our two Michigan studies, volunteers are motivated by the opportunities that ecological restoration provides for observing nature and learning more about specific plants and animals (Grese et al. 2000; Ryan, Kaplan, and Grese 2001:637–638). Volunteering provides a new way to explore nature in a more hands-on manner than the traditional naturalist-led nature walk.

Does ecological restoration work indeed reconnect people to the land, as has been suggested by Bill Jordan (1989) and others (Ross 1994)? Volunteer stewardship programs give participants a chance to reflect (Grese et al. 2000; Roggenbuck et al. 2000), and reflecting about nature and its relationships to one's life may be the beginning point in developing an environmental ethic, as espoused by Aldo Leopold (1949). In particular, we found it interesting to explore how volunteering in ecological restoration projects has changed volunteers' environmental outlooks and actions.

Effects of Volunteering on Changing Attitudes toward the Environment

One of our studies of volunteers in Michigan explored the relationship between long-term volunteering and changes in environmental attitudes and behaviors, as well as other issues (Ryan, Kaplan, and Grese 2001). Our study was based on a mailed survey completed by 148 volunteers from three environmental stewardship groups: an urban watershed council, the natural areas division of the City of Ann Arbor Parks Department, and the state chapter of the Nature Conservancy. These volunteers monitored stream quality, inventoried terrestrial and aquatic plants and animals, cleaned out trash and other debris, and restored prairies, wetlands, and forest ecosystems. The ecological restoration work was generally part of a group workday with volunteers cutting and burning nonnative plants such as common buckthorn. Other days, volunteers collected the seeds of native grasses and flowers for planting new prairie areas in the spring. Workdays often include time to tour the natural area and learn about the native plants and animals. All of the volunteers surveyed had participated with these programs for at least a year, with some having up to 20 years of experience. The volunteers ranged in age from early twenties to sixties and seventies, with the median age in their forties. The sample was evenly divided between men and women.

Participants were asked to report how much their outlook and actions toward the environment had changed over the past few years and were given a list of items to rate. The results of the study strongly suggest that volunteering helps to build advocates for the environment. Seventy-five percent of the volunteers indicated that they had a much stronger interest in protecting local natural areas than they had held previously. This is particularly significant because many urban natural areas are not as charismatic as the tropical rain forest or African savanna.

These groups of volunteers also expressed a general increase in their appreciation for natural areas (79 percent) and reported visiting them more frequently (46 percent) and feeling more at home (44 percent) in these natural settings. Feeling more at ease in natural areas that may include forests, wetlands, and prairies is especially important for urban residents, who may have little familiarity with these more "wild" settings that differ markedly from traditional urban parks with their open lawns and manicured ornamental plantings. In fact, many urban residents, particularly from the inner city, find urban natural areas to be unkempt, overgrown, and dangerous (Bixler and Floyd 1997). Increased familiarity through volunteering in urban forest restoration projects increases appreciation for nature within the city. An urban watershed volunteer in our study noted that she had "gained a new appreciation of the environment and have found a new sense of worth while working on environmental projects."

Does volunteering build an emotional connection between urban residents and natural areas? Our study found that many volunteers (68 percent) developed a strong attachment to their volunteer sites. These urban forests, prairies, and wetlands were among their favorite places, and they would miss them if they moved away. The more committed the volunteers felt toward these ecological restoration programs, the stronger the attachment they had to their volunteer sites. A student working on rebuilding trails wrote, "I feel as if a part of me gets walked on every time a person travels on one of our trails." The volunteers' feelings of attachment were not simply limited to those places where they worked. Over a few years of involvement, 62 percent of the volunteers indicated that their attachment to other local natural areas also increased. Ecological restoration programs are unique in that volunteers often work in the same natural areas year after year. Just like farmers who develop an attachment to their land after a lifetime of farming, volunteers who nurture urban forests and prairies develop a strong attachment to those places that they have pruned, planted, and weeded. The simple acts of tending nature and watching it grow creates a powerful emotional bond that can energize volunteers into other environmental action.

Volunteers in our study indicated an increase in their level of environmental activism that may be associated with their volunteering (70 percent). In the past few years, they reported writing more letters about environmental issues (20 percent), telling their friends about environmental issues (56 percent), and becoming interested in protecting natural areas nationally (44 percent). In a separate question, volunteers indicated that they were especially protective of the natural areas in which they worked and would strongly protest any changes to these areas that they considered to be negative (83 percent). The more years that people had volunteered the more likely they would be to engage in environmental advocacy should their volunteer sites be threatened. For example, only 65 percent of the short-term volunteers (those with one year experience) were likely to protest negative changes to their volunteer sites, while 90 percent of long-term volunteers (those with two or more years experience) would protest such changes. Ecological restoration thus appears to be one route to building a strong group of advocates for the environment, both locally and nationally.

Ecological restoration work is also linked to transforming attitudes toward native landscapes in their home environment. Seventy percent of the volunteers in our study were more likely to landscape their own property with native plants and create backyard wildlife habitats. A majority of volunteers (55 percent) reported they were also more likely to discourage friends and neighbors from using invasive exotic species than they would have previously. Volunteering in ecological restoration had increased their ability to recognize specific plants and animals and to recognize landscapes that were environmentally unhealthy. The natural areas knowledge gained through these ecological restoration projects had opened volunteers' eyes to the often unhealthy state of urban forests and natural areas. Many became active in local native landscaping organizations.

Our study indicates that those who were drawn to ecological restoration work because it allowed them a chance to reflect about the natural world saw the greatest increase in their appreciation for natural areas in general and were more likely to create native landscapes at their homes. In other words, there was something transformative about volunteering in ecological restoration projects. Comments from study participants support these observations. In the words of an urban watershed volunteer, volunteering "has opened up a whole new world for me and for my family. It has also greatly increased my love and respect for this area and for many of the wonderful people with strong ethical values about the environment."

Ecological restoration allows people to contemplate the wonders of nature while engaged in meaningful activities. A volunteer working in an urban parks setting acknowledges, "I am more aware of the elements and am more at peace out-of-doors." In the words of another volunteer, "My usual approach to the out-of-doors is to do as much strenuous activity as possible. Engaging in volunteer activity necessarily slows me down and requires me to observe more closely the environment immediately around me rather than to concentrate on vistas [and to] observe the wildflowers."

In a related project, students at the University of Michigan in 2000–2001 involved in a freshman seminar and another course in environmental sustainability spent time during the semester volunteering on various ecological restoration projects in the university's Nichols Arboretum. Throughout the semester, the students kept journals recording their reactions and reflections about their work. Like the other volunteers we surveyed, many students reported feeling a strong sense of satisfaction about their work, both physically and emotionally. One student wrote: "I felt that the workday was a really productive way to spend my Saturday morning. Getting up and getting outside early in the morning actually made me feel better the rest of the day. It was also really good exercise and a great stress reliever. I felt like I was getting rid of all the built up tension from my classes." Another who worked rebuilding trails throughout a semester wrote: " I must say that I've become quite skilled with a shovel, pick ax, rake and handsaw. I really enjoyed spending time outside and putting my body to work. Most of the time, I enjoyed working in the Arb so much that it didn't really seem like work at all." Still, another student wrote, "My time in the Arb was enjoyable and relaxing. It was a great escape from the city, the human-built environment. I felt that it was a time for me to concentrate on the very physical and spiritual connection I feel between nature and myself. Having this time led to a greater feeling of physical, emotional, and spiritual time for me."

In sum, ecological restoration of degraded urban landscapes creates benefits for both people and the land. As one urban watershed volunteer stated eloquently, "Volunteering has filled in a part of that place we all have that isn't selfish, and needs to do the right thing. It has made me more aware, and both happier and sadder for my new knowledge of the environment and its condition." Urban restoration projects across the country have cleaned streams, restored native forests, planted prairies, and created new backyard habitats. Volunteering in ecological restoration projects builds environmental ethics as well as appears to transform volunteers' attitudes toward the environment. Volunteers have greater appreciation for urban natural areas, stronger attachment to nearby urban parks and natural areas, and an increase in their level of environmental activism. One of the students working in the Nichols Arboretum wrote, "I have . . . recognized the need for people such as myself who enjoy spending time in nature to be hands-on in conservation, restoration and maintenance of such areas as the Arb."

Facing the Challenge of Reconnecting People to Urban Natural Areas

While ecological restoration is one route for building a cadre of supporters for the environment, such programs are not without controversy that present several challenges to reconnecting people to urban natural areas.

Volunteers' preferences for native ecosystems in the form of prairies, savannas, wetlands, and forests do not necessarily reflect the preferences of the public as a whole. Local residents sometimes prefer urban parks and natural areas that appear more managed than do ecological restoration volunteers. In a study conducted by one of us in Ann Arbor, Michigan (Ryan 1997, 2005), urban forest areas that had been managed to have an open understory or smooth ground plain were more preferred by local residents than were unmown prairie areas or forests with an overgrown understory of twiggy shrubs and downed tree limbs. Volunteers who were involved in the ecological restoration of these prairies and forests had a stronger preference for these messier-appearing natural areas than did local residents. Ecological restoration programs, such as the restoration of Chicago's forest preserves, have at times become extremely controversial because members of the public objected to cutting down trees and large shrubs to restore prairies and savannas and did not perceive the planning process to be inclusive (Gobster 1997; Shore 1997). Simply copying nature as suggested by Bill Jordan (2003:24) is not an approach that will be often supported by the general public, especially when the resulting landscape is perceived to be messy, dangerous, or aesthetically unappealing. Particularly in urban areas, historic ecosystems are quite different from people's typical frame of reference—often the highly manicured and simplified landscapes of lawns and public parks they knew growing up.

Ecological restoration and the environmental movement in general have come under criticism for not reflecting the ethnic and racial diversity of many urban areas (Lodwick 1994:108–109). Ecological restoration of urban parks, especially replacing traditional plantings of lawn and trees with native prairies and forests, may be perceived as creating dangerous, overgrown, unmanaged places. In contrast, urban tree planting projects that visibly improve blighted neighborhoods may receive more support from inner-city residents (Still and Gerhold 1997:125), because the results of tree planting projects and vacant lot cleanups are more tangibly visible to local residents and enhance the sense of neatness and care to the neighborhood.

Volunteer programs, however, cannot replace civic investment in urban parks and natural areas, especially in the face of declining park programs and budgets. This is especially true in neighborhoods that may not have the social capital to mobilize volunteer groups to focus on urban forest issues when there are other pressing social issues to address. Linking the restoration of urban natural areas to larger recreational and social needs of urban residents is imperative for ecological restoration to benefit the larger society.

In order for ecological restoration projects to be accepted by local residents, project planners need to take into consideration the aesthetic and recreational desires of local natural area users and involve the larger public in the planning process (Ryan 2000). For example, workshops or surveys can be used to determine the characteristics of a place that are already appreciated by local residents. This information should be combined with a careful study of the aesthetic patterns found in natural ecosystems (Morrison 1987) as well as an adaptation of those patterns to how a site is to be used or experienced. Careful attention to edges, views from trails, and interpretation can greatly enhance the public's acceptability of the restored landscape. As suggested by landscape architect Joan Nassauer, providing "orderly frames to messy ecosystems" is one approach to building public support for ecological restoration (1995:161). In settings as diverse as suburban front yards and midwestern farm fields, Nassauer has found that framing ecologically beneficial improvements such as native prairie plantings with traditional mown lawns or including flowering plants and other "cues to care" has resulted in support by local residents for installing these improvements (1995:167).

The process of implementing a restoration project can also provide creative ways for engaging volunteers as well as the general public. Increasingly, artists are working with restorationists as an attempt to engage the public in new and different ways (Lambert and Kosla 2000). This can involve creating artistic willow wattles as part of a stream bank restoration or the careful documentation of the restoration process as a photographic exhibit. Barbara Westfall's "Daylighting the Woods" was such a project. Westfall carefully girdled aspen trees encroaching on Curtis Prairie in the University of Wisconsin-Madison Arboretum and recorded the changes as a photographic essay (Meekison and Higgs 1998).

Many groups working with volunteers have begun to develop rituals and enjoyable memorable events that can be easily incorporated with restoration activities (Holland 1994). For instance, as part of the efforts to replant prairie areas at the Neal Smith National Wildlife Refuge in

Jasper County, Iowa, staff organized a regular event they call "Sow Your Wild Oats Day" during which volunteers scattered seed and stomped the seed into the ground while dancing to the tune of an old-time band (Drobney 1994). Similarly, in a small prairie planting at Thurston Nature Center in Ann Arbor, Michigan, Bob Grese made the planting into a game activity where children matched their bags of seeds with zones painted on the landscape with lime. After each group carefully raked their seeds into the ground, everyone raced back and forth across the site to tramp down the seeds.

Exploring ways to make restoration activities more meaningful for the volunteer and helping them learn new things can recruit new volunteers as well as build a deeper engagement with the environment that results in longer-term volunteer service and increased activism. Holding interpretive walks as part of the workday, involving volunteers in the assessment of how their labors have made a difference, inviting the development of new techniques, and sharing photographs of special events—like a prairie fire—that volunteers can use as a screen-saver helps build a sense of commitment. Many volunteers want to feel that they are part of a social group, and ensuring that time during a workday is allotted to informal sharing and conversation may be important. In addition, separate events such as potlucks or seasonal celebrations (end of the fire season, for instance) can provide important ways of bringing volunteers together. Finding meaningful recognition is also critical. This can be as simple as acknowledging long-time volunteers at workdays, including features on them in newsletters, or providing small tokens of appreciation.

Volunteer programs require an ongoing commitment from both environmental organizations and government agencies. There is a need for a dedicated volunteer coordinator to ensure that programs run efficiently and that volunteers' time is used effectively. One way to do this is to form a regional network of volunteer stewardship groups. Such larger associations can provide a broader framework for offering training and workshops and encouraging a region-wide dialogue about how to care for local natural areas. Groups often benefit from learning from each other's successes as well as from their mistakes. Following on the success of the Volunteer Stewardship Network in Chicago, other networks are expanding across the country. In southeast Michigan, for instance, what began as a more localized network of groups working on natural areas around Ann Arbor in 1998 has expanded to include over 15 volunteer, nonprofit, governmental, and private organizations throughout southeastern Michigan. As a network, the organization sponsors localized "steward's circles" where representatives from individual groups can solve problems together. It also provides region-wide training in developing site restoration and management plans, invasive species control, and fire management and helps link groups to sources of funding and information. "I am grateful to be associated with the Stewardship Network. It has been another source of education for me in my life's work as a teacher, as a volunteer, as one who hopes to help empower others to make a difference in our world," says a volunteer steward who has been a part of the Southeast Michigan Stewardship Network.

Conclusion

Contact with nature can be a transformative experience, whether in the form of native ecosystems or simply the tree outside one's window. Understanding more about natural processes, native plants, and animals can lead to an appreciation for the natural world around us. One of the students working on ecological restoration at the University of Michigan's Nichols Arboretum wrote, "I definitely feel more connected and dedicated to nature.... Having experienced this new level and found myself more at home with nature than ever before, I would like to eventually see myself as a stronger, more active moving force for the course of sustainability and natural areas restoration." As our studies showed, ecological restoration, with its hands-on approach to healing nature, appeals to urban residents who feel overwhelmed by large-scale environmental issues, such as global warming (Ryan, Kaplan, and Grese 2001; Grese et al. 2000). Seeing one's efforts result in cleaner streams and rivers, prairies filled with native plants and animals, and urban forests blooming with spring wildflowers is more appealing than writing yet another check to a worthwhile environmental organization. Volunteer stewardship programs provide people with the opportunity to see tangible results from their efforts to heal the environment and at the same time reconnect them to the natural environment. Expanding these programs in a manner that appeals to a broader range of the population will go a long way to restoring nature in the city.

Acknowledgments

Thanks to the USDA Forest Service, North Central Forest Experiment Station, which funded our Michigan volunteer stewardship studies under Urban Forestry Unit Cooperative Agreement, # 23-94-53. We also thank Rachel Kaplan, who was co–principal investigator on this project and had a major role in developing each of these studies. Finally, we thank the program leaders and volunteers of the conservation agencies and organizations who participated in these studies.

Note

1. For the Web site, see http://www.chicagowilderness.org.

References

Benepe, Adrian. 2002. Presentation at the Humane Metropolis Conference: People and Nature in the 21st Century City, New York University, New York, June 6–7.

Bixler, Robert D., and Marion F. Floyd. 1997. Nature Is Scary, Disgusting and Uncomfortable. *Environment and Behavior* 29(4):443–467.

Botkin, Daniel, and Edward Keller. 1995. *Environmental Science: Earth as a Living Planet*. New York: Wiley.

Bratton, Susan P. 2000. Alternative Models of Ecosystem Restoration. In *Environmental Restoration: Ethics, Theory, and Practice*. W. Throop, ed. Pp. 53–65. New York: Humanity Books.

Chicago Regional Biodiversity Council. 1996. *Chicago Wilderness: An Atlas of Biodiversity*. Chicago: Chicago Regional Biodiversity Council.

Drobney, P. 1994. Iowa Prairie Rebirth. *Restoration and Management Notes* 12(1):16–22.

Dwyer, J. F., Herbert W. Schroeder, and Paul H. Gobster. 1991. The Significance of Urban Trees and Forests: Toward a Deeper Understanding of Values. *Journal of Arboriculture* 17(1):276–284.

Egan, D. 1990. Historic Initiatives in Ecological Restoration. *Restoration and Management Notes* 8(2):83–90.

Gobster, Paul H. 1997. The Chicago Wilderness and Its Critics. Part III, The Other Side: A Survey of Arguments. *Restoration and Management Notes* 15(1):32–37.

Grese, Robert E. 1990. Historical Perspectives on Designing with Nature. In *The Proceedings of the 1st Annual Conference of the Society for Ecological Restoration*. H. G. Hughes and T. M. Bonnicksen, eds. Pp. 39–48. Madison, Wis.: Society for Ecological Restoration.

Grese, Robert E. 1992. *Jens Jensen: Maker of Natural Parks and Gardens*. Baltimore, Md.: Johns Hopkins University Press.

Grese, Robert E., Rachel Kaplan, Robert L. Ryan, and Jane Buxton. 2000. Psychological Benefits of Volunteering in Stewardship Programs. In *Restoring Nature: Perspectives from the Social Sciences and Humanities*. Paul H. Gobster and R. Bruce Hull, eds. Pp. 265–280. Washington, D.C.: Island Press.

Holland, K. M. 1994. Restoration Rituals. *Restoration and Management Notes* 12(2):121–125.

Hough, Michael. 1995. *Cities and Natural Process*. New York: Routledge.

Jordan, William R., III. 1989. Restoring the Restorationist. *Restoration and Management Notes* 7(2):55.

Jordan, William R., III. 2003. *The Sunflower Forest: Ecological Restoration and the New Communion with Nature*. Berkeley: University of California Press.

Kaplan, Rachel, and Stephen Kaplan, S. 1996 [1989]. *The Experience of Nature: A Psychological Perspective*. Ann Arbor, Mich.: Ulrich's.

Kaplan, Rachel, Stephen Kaplan, and Robert L. Ryan. 1998. *With People in Mind: Design and Management of Everyday Nature*. Washington, D.C.: Island Press.

Lambert, A. M., and M. R. Khosla. 2000. Environmental Art and Restoration. *Ecological Restoration* 18(2):109–114.

Leopold, Aldo. 1949. *A Sand County Almanac*. New York: Oxford University Press.

Lodwick, Dorothy G. 1994. Changing Worldviews and Landscape Restoration. In *Beyond Preservation: Restoring and Inventing Landscapes*. A. D. Baldwin, Jr., J. De Luce, and C. Pletsch, eds. Pp. 97–110. Minneapolis: University of Minnesota Press.

Meekison, L., and E. Higgs. 1998. The Rites of Spring (and Other Seasons). *Restoration and Management Notes* 16(1):73–81.

Miles, Irene, William C. Sullivan, and Frances E. Kuo. 1998. Prairie Restoration Volunteers: The Benefits of Participation. *Urban Ecosystems* 2(1):27–41.

Miller, Wilhelm. 1915. *The Prairie Spirit in Landscape Gardening*. Circular no. 184. Urbana: Agricultural Experiment Station, Department of Horticulture, University of Illinois.

Morrison, Darrel. 1987. On Aesthetics and Restoration and Management. *Restoration and Management Notes* 5(1):3–4.

Nassauer, Joan I. 1995. Messy Ecosystems, Orderly Frames. *Landscape Journal* 14(2):161–170.

Roberts, Edith. 1933. The Development of an Out-of-Door Ecological Laboratory for Experimental Ecology. *Ecology* 14(2):163–223.

Roggenbuck, Joseph W., S. C. Haas, T. E. Hall, and R. Bruce Hull. 2000. *Motivation, Retention, and Program Recommendations of Save Our Stream Volunteers.* Blacksburg, Va.: Department of Forestry, Virginia Tech.

Ross, Laurel M. 1994. Illinois' Volunteer Corps: A Model Program with Deep Roots in the Prairie. *Restoration and Management Notes* 12(1):57–59.

Ross, L. M. 1997. Illinois Chapter of the Nature Conservancy, Volunteer Stewardship Coordinator. Personal conversation with author (Robert L. Ryan).

Ryan, Robert L. 1997. Attachment to Urban Natural Areas: Effects of Environmental Experience. Ph.D. dissertation, University of Michigan.

Ryan, Robert L. 2000. Attachment to Urban Natural Areas: A People-Centered Approach to Designing and Managing Restoration Projects. In *Restoring Nature: Perspectives from the Social Sciences and Humanities.* Paul H. Gobster and R. Bruce Hull, eds. Pp. 209–228. Washington, D.C.: Island Press.

Ryan, Robert L. 2005. Exploring the Effects of Environmental Experience on Attachment to Urban Natural Areas. *Environment and Behavior* 37:3–42.

Ryan, R. L., Rachel Kaplan, and Robert E. Grese. 2001. Predicting Volunteer Commitment in Environmental Stewardship Programmes. *Journal of Environmental Planning and Management* 44(5):629–648.

Schroeder, Herbert W. 2000. The Motivations and Values of Ecosystem Restoration Volunteers: An Analysis of Stewardship Group Newsletters. In *Restoring Nature: Perspectives from the Social Sciences and Humanities.* Paul H. Gobster and R. Bruce Hull, eds. Pp. 247–264. Washington, D.C.: Island Press.

Shore, D. 1997. The Chicago Wilderness and Its Critics. Part II, Controversy Erupts over Restoration in Chicago Area. *Restoration and Management Notes* 15(1):25–31.

Still, Douglas T., and Henry D. Gerhold. 1997. Motivations and Task Preferences of Urban Forestry Volunteers. *Journal of Arboriculture* 23(3):116–130.

Westphal, Lynn M. 1993. Why Trees? Urban Forestry Volunteers Values and Motivations. In *Managing Urban and High Use Recreation Settings.* General Technical Report NC–163. Paul H. Gobster, ed. Pp. 19–23. St. Paul, Minn.: USDA Forest Service.

Reclaiming Meanings

8

Nature, Memory, and Nation: New York's Latino Gardens and *Casitas*

Barbara Deutsch Lynch and Rima Brusi

In 1992 Daniel Perez planted corn on a Broadway median strip at 153rd Street; he thought he might get into trouble, and, in fact, a parks employee did object, but the general sentiment was favorable. Although a few ears disappeared, the crop was treated with respect by neighbors and passers by. Corn was not the Dominican immigrant's only crop. He cultivated garlic and tomatoes with the corn; the year before, he grew black beans and shared the harvest with neighbors. His was a one-man beautification project: "All I saw was bottles, old newspapers, garbage and weeds. I took a large garbage bag and cleared the land. I planted with the idea that this is my own little contribution, my own little Cibao" (quoted in Myers 1991b:B5).

Perez's act is one of numerous steps taken by Latinos to produce Caribbean landscapes and preserve Caribbean values in a cold, often hostile environment.[1] Some of these have been acknowledged and supported by city officials. An example is the Crotona Community Coalition in the South Bronx, led by Dominican labor activist and refugee Astin Jacobo, which reclaimed redlined housing and turned empty lots into community gardens and athletic fields.[2] Some, like the Tranquilidad Garden in the Loisaida neighborhood of Lower Manhattan, were created by informal groups of neighbors, and still others, like Perez's tiny plot, were individual reenactments of the practice of shifting cultivation common to precarious Caribbean landscapes and dating to the clandestine gardens of slaves and maroons (Price 1973; Sokolov 1992). In short, New York's Latino gardens have been shaped by specific historical conditions on the islands and in the city and by Caribbean patterns of interaction with nonhuman species.[3]

Perhaps the most interesting translation of the Caribbean garden to the New York environment is the *casita* complex, consisting of a small building, a swept yard (or *batey*), and garden. The casita complex is the product of a movement that paralleled and often converged with the community garden movement in New York City (see chapter 4). These seemingly simple rustic dwellings and adjacent gardens are meant to be places for leisure—safe places in which neighbors can celebrate, relax, share a meal, watch their children play, escape the heat of their apartments, drink a few beers, and connect to a carefully chosen set of companion plant and animal species.[4] Cross-species interaction within the spatial context of the casita complex is part of a larger strategy to preserve, create, and project national identities in an alien urban setting.

Whether individual or group statements, Latino gardens in New York City add up to a broader social movement. Common threads tying these efforts together are references to island life and landscapes and to the therapeutic effects of cultivation. However, if Latino gardens and garden complexes are expressions of nostalgia for a simpler island life, they are also critiques of the assumptions about open space and property that have informed municipal programs and policies. In this chapter, we describe the garden landscapes that Puerto Ricans—and to some extent, Dominicans—have produced in New York City and trace their island roots. We then discuss the notions of property that have undergirded the Latino garden movement in New York and ask about the potential for long-term survival of these gardens as New York City authorities and open-space advocates make choices about which gardens to preserve and which to sacrifice to alternative land uses.

Garden, *Batey*, and *Casita* in New York City

Interaction with other plant and animal species can take place in the structured vernacular landscape of the garden-batey-casita complex or in the context of seasonal appropriation of land for cultivation. In this section, we focus on the more elaborate end of the spectrum: the casita complexes that have grown up on empty lots in the South Bronx, Loisaida, El Barrio (Spanish Harlem), and other Hispanic neighborhoods in New York City. In these landscapes, oppositions between the built and the unbuilt, the natural and the artificial, humans and other species become complementarities that allow for sociable relations and the ongoing construction of ethnic and national identity.

Garden and Batey

Cultivation is a fundamentally important activity in the casita complex. When Winterbottom (1997:11) interviewed casita users in New York City, he found that fully 70 percent saw gardening as their primary reason for using the complex. Casita gardens contain an impressive array of cultivars. In the mid-1990s, Winterbottom found tomatoes, sweet peppers, chiles, corn, beans, eggplant, cucumber, zucchini, grapes, and strawberries in addition to apple, apricot, peach, and mulberry trees. In her 2001 survey of 20 Latino community gardens in New York City, Saldivar Tanaka identified 44 different food crops under cultivation during her summer-long investigation in addition to fruit trees, grape vines, blueberry bushes, and raspberry canes. Our own sitings of domestic fowl around casitas are confirmed by Sciorra (1996:76), who encountered ducks, chickens, geese, rabbits, and a goat in New York casita complexes. The planted component of Latino gardens, about half in most cases, is not just crops but grass, flowers, and trees (Saldivar Tanaka, 2002). In addition, ornamentals, including annuals, perennials, shrubs, and the occasional shade tree; herbs and medicinals (some used in the religious practice of Santeria); and opportunistic self-seeding species help to define the complex (Winterbottom 1977). Latino gardeners share with the broader garden movement a preference for fresher, healthier vegetables. Cultivator José García noted in 1991 that "chemicals can kill the flavor. I work in the market at Hunt's Point. You see these tomatoes, so nice, but not natural. They use gas to make them red. You grow it yourself, you get something fresh" (Raver 1991:C4). But even when gardeners eschew pesticides, they may encounter soils contaminated by lead and other toxins.[5]

That said, the primary purpose of Latino gardens is not to supplement income, enhance food self-sufficiency, or protect the environment. Cultivation is part of a broader set of cultural practices; its logic is mainly nostalgic and therapeutic rather than economic. Brook (2003) makes the general argument that "people connect to place through plants, and these emotional connections are often forged . . . through long association" with specific plants. Food too produces memories, and Caribbean memories are stimulated by *comida tipica*, dishes intimately associated with island provisioning grounds, or *conucos*. Saldivar Tanaka (2002) found the garlic, cilantro, tomatoes, and onions used in *sofritos* along with Cuban black beans and Dominican red beans or *habichuelas*. She even spotted pigeon peas (*gandules*), a crop that takes about eighteen months to mature on Dominican soil. Still, replication of neotropical farming systems in New York City is at best a quixotic effort. Soils are poor, and many gardens are shaded by tall buildings. In the venerable La Tranquilidad garden, we noted that only a tiny patch of land got enough sunlight for vegetables. Even devoted experimentalists have not succeeded in growing Caribbean dietary staples like *yuca*, *ñame*, *yautia*, and plantains or tropical fruits like mangos, *guayaba*, or papaya.

As in the case of Daniel Perez, nostalgia and therapy are closely linked. One cultivator working in an East Harlem casita complex, explained: "When I'm working in here among my corn and beans there is no danger . . . I feel like I am back in Puerto Rico, and that's important because I don't want to lose the affection I feel for my homeland" (Gonzalez 1990). Several years later, another Puerto Rican, looking out from the porch of his casita in El Barrio in Upper Manhattan, told a reporter, "We're in the mountains, looking out over Juahataca on the northern side of the island, an hour and a half from San Juan" (Griswold 1997). José Soto, one of the creators of the celebrated South Bronx casita, Rincón Criollo, speaking of his own motivation to create a new landscape out of a rubble-strewn lot, noted, "There were so many Puerto Ricans in this area, but you had nothing that looked like the place where you were born, except for your fellow countrymen on either side of you" (Sciorra 1996).

Thus, one key function of plants and animals in New York's Latino gardens is to evoke Caribbean landscapes. To do so, casita gardeners have introduced familiar-looking plant and animal species. Widely adaptable Caribbean cultivars like beans, corn, tomatoes, roses, and cilantro are planted along with stand-in species like Russian olive, which resembles a pigeon pea plant (Winterbottom 1997). Caribbean landscape architecture features are also used to evoke the islands. The batey, or swept yard, is one such feature.[6] Located close by the casita's front porch, this area is kept free of plants except for a few ornamental shrubs or flowers in containers. The batey separates spaces for food plant cultivation from the casita, and it is a major site for social interaction and child's play. Small animals or fowl, caged or loose, may also populate the batey.

Casita, Fence, and Flag: Built Elements in Garden Complex

The self-built casita stands at the heart of the complex. It is a one-story cabin, often built of found materials, with a front porch, or *balcon*, whose rail separates it from the adjacent batey. To casual observers, these colorful little buildings may appear as charming visual contradictions that lend interest to the urban fabric. To garden and open space advocates, they are a complication: their illegal status and vernacular architecture are obstacles to legitimation of the gardens that surround them.[7] The casita, a New York construction with antecedents, real and imagined, in the self-built dwellings of rural Puerto Rico, is often associated

Figure 8.1
Casita surrounded by flowers and fruit trees, flying the Puerto Rican flag, Loisaida, New York City (photo by Barbara Lynch).

with the *bohío*, a term used alternately to refer to round, thatched dwellings of the pre-Conquest Taino inhabitants of the island and to the rustic houses of Puerto Rican peasants, or *jibaros*. For Nuyoricans, the bohío and its surrounding landscape symbolize the lost homeland and the antithesis of a chilly New York (Sanchez Korrol 1983:78).

Casita complexes, even those relatively open to the public, are usually separated from the street by a chain-link fence. Whether erected by the owner of the vacant lot or the gardeners, the fence defines for gardeners an intermediate space that is neither public, like a park, nor entirely private, like a back yard. It is intended to include neighborhood families, but to exclude those perceived as delinquents or drug users. Gardeners and casita aficionados contrast the safety of the garden with the hostility of the street. But the fence does more than discourage unwanted intruders. By separating the constructed rural landscape from its urban surroundings, it creates a little territory. The territorial nature of the casita complex is usually emphasized by the presence of a Puerto Rican flag.

The Built and the Unbuilt

In the garden-batey-casita landscape, urban agriculture and open space preservation are intimately tied to memory and nation (Aponte-Pares 1997; Sciorra 1996; Vazquez 1992; Winterbottom 1997) and to an idea of well-being that is closely associated with national identity, land, and the possibility of relations with other species, especially those that recall the islands. As a whole, the built and unbuilt components of the mini-landscape foster preservation and re-creation of identity through leisure activity. While Latinos also interact with nonhuman species in the open spaces of Central Park or Bear Mountain, the safe, quasi-private landscape of the casita complex is valued more highly than the formal park.[8] Its seclusion makes it a favored site for child's play, birthday parties and other celebrations, music making, card playing, and dominos as well as for gardening—in short, for the performance of Puertoricanness. But what is the Puertoricanness or, more broadly, the Caribbeanness that is being performed? To answer this question, we need to inquire about the origins of various elements in the Latino garden landscape and their cultural meaning.

Island Origins

The New York garden-casita-batey complex closely resembles the traditional, vernacular casita-batey-dooryard garden complexes found in rural Puerto Rico (Kimber 1973), landscapes already well established by the late eighteenth century.[9]

Garden, Batey, and Casita in Puerto Rico

Caribbean gardens trace their cultural roots to the polycultural mounds of the Taino encountered by the Spaniards (Sauer 1966), to the clandestine plots of plantation slaves and escaped slaves called *cimarrones* or maroons, and to those of peasant cultivators known as *jíbaros* in Puerto Rico, and simply *campesinos* in the Dominican Republic. Mintz (1974) distinguishes two types of gardens in Caribbean rural landscapes. Provisioning grounds, typically located at some remove from the house, were places where slaves could escape for a while the brutal discipline of the sugar plantations. These *conucos* came to symbolize resistance to landscape changes and the political and economic forces that produced them.[10] Often associated with shifting cultivation, they enabled poor rural families to survive from one sugar harvest to the next (Jopling 1988:181).[11] Conucos were closely associated with the *viandas*, or starchy staples, that define Caribbean Latino cuisine. A subsistence necessity for the Puerto Rican landless population in the 1930s, conucos were integral to the design of the Puerto Rican land colonization programs and to the very concept of rural housing.

Cultivation also took place in dooryard gardens that constituted one component of a private but fluid space that includes three main elements: the house with its front porch or balcon, a swept yard or batey interspersed by shade trees and ornamentals, and the garden itself, usually dedicated to root crop–based polyculture. The batey, derived from the Taino ceremonial plaza (Jopling 1988), evolved into a swept yard dotted with potted plants and fruit trees that came to function as a locus of social and political activity. Flowering plants in well-defined beds surround the batey. Beyond the batey lie pens for small animals and a small vegetable plot. The complex is often surrounded by a living fence that creates a sense of seclusion. These vernacular gardens also resemble

Dominican patio gardens in the Zambrana-Chacuey region (Rocheleau et al. 1993). Kimber sees garden flora as defining the social and utilitarian spaces used for different outdoor activities. The social activities of the gardens that Kimber studied are those of the New York casitas— "gossiping, children's play, and partying" (1973:15). Men hang out on porches, while children play in the dirt clearings of the batey. Food preparation also takes place in the yard close to the house. As Jopling (1988:211) observes, "By bringing the natural environment into the private domain of the house for the personal enjoyment of residents, away from public view, the house is extended to incorporate property remaining unbuilt."

Like the conuco, the dooryard garden can be traced to plantations as well as to upland peasant settlements (Mintz 1974). In the latter, dooryard gardens became sites for domestic activity and social life. In rural Puerto Rico, the house and yard complex as a sociospatial whole assumed new importance during the first decades of the twentieth century when 70 percent of Puerto Rico's population was rural and largely landless.

The casita itself belongs to a tradition of vernacular architecture, self-building, and bricolage often associated with two types of jíbaro housing: bohíos and casitas that dotted rural landscape during the early twentieth century (Jopling 1988).[12] According to one New York gardener, "Back in Puerto Rico, casitas were built in the distant fields as shelters for the workers from the hot sun and downpours. Sometimes field workers would spend the night there during the harvest season" (Saldivar Tanaka 2002:44). Houses in this tradition, in both town and countryside, were self-built on connected lots large enough for vegetable plots and small animal pens. Folklorist Joseph Sciorra traces the casita's antecedents to the Taino bohío or circular dwelling, to jíbaro housing, and to the *arrabales*, or informal shantytowns, of urban Puerto Rico built by migrants who could not make a go of it in the countryside. In contrast, we argue that New York City casitas bear an even closer affinity to self-built houses on the agrarian reform parcels associated with the Puerto Rican and Dominican colonization programs of the 1930s and 1940s (see, for example, Jopling 1998:180–181). It is this association that gives them their political meaning. The straw hats and other jíbaro symbols that decorate New York's casitas recall not just a rural land-scape, but the populist rhetoric of the Muñoz Marín era in Puerto Rico, which established the right of rural Puerto Ricans to own land and legit-imated possession of unused state-owned lands for homes and gardens.

Gardens and *Parcelas*

Like the casita, the conuco is a potent symbol of the politics of land in Puerto Rico and of the idea of property associated with it. The follow-ing narrative by one of Brusi's informants from the Puerto Rican coastal community of La Parguera shows the association of the conuco with access to land in the early twentieth century:

"All this land belonged to one or two *hacendados*, they allowed some people to live in the land, and farm it. There were conucos in people's houses, and each one planted them to eat. They enclosed the conucos with aloe plants and a couple of wires. They planted pigeon peas, corn, squash, *viandas*."

Structural underemployment of agrarian workers and the Great Depression created an environment favorable to populism and land col-onization in Puerto Rico and the Dominican Republic (Morales-Carrión 1983:244; Turits 2003). Founder of the Popular Demonatic Party (PPD) Governor Muñoz Marín made the precarious economic status of *agre-gados* or landless rural workers, a focus of the 1940 Puerto Rican elec-tions. The party used the jíbaro emblem and the slogan *"Pan, Tierra y Libertad"* ("Bread, Land, and Liberty") as tools for political mobiliza-tion. He told the landless, "You have the land in the power of your votes" (cited in Edel, 1963:33). After winning the election, the PPD government implemented several land reform measures, including the 1941 Land Law. The law's Title V provided for relocation and assignment of land to *agregado* families (Edel 1963). The *parcela* program called for in the legislation allocated small parcels for house building and for subsistence and market gardening (Edel 1963:40). The Land Law also authorized a new Land Authority to aid families in home construction. Conucos, once a regular feature of *parcela* homesteads, are now disappearing. As one of Brusi's informants remarked, *"Los viejos son los que siembran"* ("The elderly are the ones who garden"). Nonetheless, the connection between casita, conuco, and access to land was firmly established in Puerto Rican culture by the time of the major postwar migrations from the island to New York City, and it is this connection that informs the Latino garden movement.

Thus, while the landscapes of memory that Puerto Ricans have created in New York include Taino, maroon, and jíbaro elements, they are in the first instance reflections of the progressive populist vision of the Muñoz Marín government and the parcela program. The physical landscape of the casita-batey-garden complex invokes the spatial and interspecies arrangements associated with the vernacular architecture of rural, small-town and peri-urban settings in Puerto Rico and the Dominican Republic—landscapes of the agregados and the parceleros—at the same time as the symbol of the jíbaro and the flag recall the right to land promised by the Muñoz Marín government.

Garden Wars and Garden Tenure

The right to cultivable land established in the 1940s in Puerto Rico informed Latino gardeners' struggles during the New York City "garden wars" of the 1990s.[13] The casita-batey-garden complex, like community gardens more generally, is an artifact of the urban crisis of the 1970s that saw redlining, abandonment, and demolition of buildings in Latino neighborhoods (Schmelzkopf 1995; Sciorra 1996). Rubble-strewn abandoned lots often reverted to the city. This patrimony became the land base for urban gardens. As the boom years of the 1990s created new development pressures, the administration of Mayor Rudolph Giuliani sought many of these lots for development. The resulting land use conflict was articulated, if not always accurately, as a zero-sum choice between affordable housing and community gardens.

Underlying this rhetoric, however, were fundamentally different concepts of property. The city saw its ownership rights in its vacant lands as absolute; it could, at its discretion, sell, lease, or alter the landscape of any lot in its inventory. Latino gardeners, however, subscribed to a idea of property that was more subtle and flexible. Casita and garden projects typically began with appropriation and improvement. From a Caribbean perspective, property was created by making of the garden, just as it was created when Dominican cultivators carved conucos from forested land in the public domain, when Puerto Rican urbanites created *casetas* on La Parguera's shores and low-lying lands near San Juan, or when rural landless appropriated public lands for parcelas.[14] Legitimation of claims to public lands was based not on titling and legal transfer but on investment in improvement.

Vazquez (1992:10) sees New York's casita projects as acts of "reclamation of traditional patterns of land use" through appropriation of unused land. Creation of a harmonious relationship between the built and the unbuilt, the house, the yard, and the garden, can, in the proper context, confer a right, albeit tenuous, to a parcel of land. In her interviews with Puerto Rican home owners living in urban subdivisions on the island, Jopling (1988) learned that in addition to whatever other symbolic content gardens and trees outside a house may have had, they symbolized ownership. "Those plain houses over there," said one of her informants, "they're just rented; the government owns them. Those houses with gardens, trees, walls, and so forth, belong to the people who live in them." Belonging is a function of improvement through building and gardening.[15]

Because these property rights are unenforceable, the survival of casita complexes depends on acknowledgment by city officials that rights to these lots are created through the labor invested in their improvement. In a North American context, however, creation of property through improvement is viewed as squatting. However pleasing or socially beneficial their products, squatters live in a state of chronic tenure insecurity. This insecurity was heightened when Mayor Giuliani ordered the razing of a number of gardens, including the Chico Mendez Mural Garden on the Lower East Side and the Garden of Love in Upper Manhattan (Ramirez 1997; Raver 1999).

One result of insecurity was differentiation among gardens on the basis of their perceived legitimacy. In their visually beautiful study of the gardens of the poor in New York City, Balmori and Morton (1993) offer a typology that helps us to understand the problems faced by Caribbean gardeners struggling for permanence. Their garden types represent different degrees of tenure security and formality. Formality may refer to garden design, but it also connotes recognition by a government agency

Figure 8.2
A GreenThumb assisted community garden, Loisaida (photo by Barbara Lynch).

or an organizational structure with clearly articulated rules for selecting managers, allocating space, assigning labor requirements, and policing. *Community gardens*, which lie at the formal end of the continuum, enjoy professional support and a quasi-legal status that offers a degree of stability. Their oak-leaf signs, high fences (often locked), dense plantings, raised beds, and geometric landscapes make them look like small parks. *Appropriated gardens* are the group efforts of neighbors who make gardens on patches of city land but do not engage in relationships with formal garden advocates. Interest in these gardens tends to be long term because their founders reside permanently in the neighborhood, but without the imprimatur of open space organizations, they are more vulnerable to expropriation. Casita complexes generally fall into this category, although a number have sought assistance from city agencies and open space nongovernmental organizations. To the extent that they entail illegal activities like building without a permit, harboring domestic animals, or allowing drinking on the premises, all essential to creating these landscapes of memory, they are less likely to get the imprimatur of GreenThumb, affiliated with the city's Department of General Services and, later, the Department of Parks and Recreation.

Squatters' gardens, congeries of individual plots cultivated by illegal occupants of abandoned buildings, are more transitory. To Balmori and Morton's typology, we would add *ephemeral gardens*: seasonal, individual appropriations of small patches of marginal land for cultivation on lands dedicated to other public uses, like Daniel Perez's plot on the Broadway median and gardens planted in the Metro-North railway right-of-way. By their very nature, these gardens lack permanence because they lack a constituency.

During the 1980s and 1990s, casita builders hoping to make their tenure more secure sought approval and support from the more formal governmental and nongovernmental institutions of the open space movement, including Operation GreenThumb, Bronx Green-Up, a program of the New York Botanical Garden, Cornell Cooperative Extension in New York City, the Trust for Public Land, and the New York City Council on the Environment. These organizations' more institutional connections and middle-class leadership enabled them to confer legitimacy on individual gardening efforts.[16] In particular, GreenThumb could

Figure 8.3
Tranquilidad Garden, Loisaida, which began as an appropriated garden (photo by Barbara Lynch).

lease city land, albeit on a short-term basis, to gardening groups, and the Trust for Public Land, together with singer and garden booster Bette Midler's New York Restoration Project, succeeded in buying outright a number garden parcels on city-owned land.

By registering with GreenThumb, some casita-batey-garden complexes became community gardens, eligible for free supplies, technical and design assistance, and a certain degree of permanence (Schmelzkopf 1995). In return, they were bound by city ordinances governing shelter construction, domestic animals, and consumption of alcoholic beverages. GreenThumb could not award recognition to gardens with enclosed or wired buildings constructed without building permits or inspections, and it could not work with a garden organization that allowed farm animals to roam on its site. Registry was by no means automatic. To succeed, garden advocates had to demonstrate that their garden served a broad constituency and provided social and ecological benefits that would not otherwise be provided. Appropriated gardens lacking a formal organizational structure were unlikely to gain even this small measure of security. Thus, in the hostile environment of the Giuliani administration, casita builders faced a dilemma: formalization of garden status offered greater, albeit still tenuous, security, but it committed gardeners to conform to building codes and park regulations that would alter the physical and social complexion of the casita complex.

Resolution and Prospects for Survival

If the garden wars of the 1990s were about whether rights to urban land might be acquired through cultivation and improvement, current debates may explicitly or implicitly revolve around the cultural acceptability of particular garden practices. As we have argued, Caribbean Latino communities brought to the garden movement a nostalgia infused with nationalism, an ambivalence about integration into North American urban society, coupled with an interest in maintaining island forms of social interaction, and a politically progressive stance supported by the populist ideology of the 1940s. The first two characteristics shaped the landscape of the garden-casita-batey complex, in its artifacts, and in its species composition. The third accounts for the central role that Latino organizations have played defining and implementing New York City's environmental justice agenda, which includes garden preservation.[17] The question at present is whether gardens whose physical form reflects Latino values will be deemed appropriate candidates for future preservation.

In response to the campaign for garden preservation spearheaded by the New York Restoration Project and the Trust for Public Land, the city's position on the gardens grew more nuanced under Mayor Michael Bloomberg. In what seemed like a win-win solution to the conflict between affordable housing and gardens, Mayor Bloomberg and New York State Attorney General Eliot Spitzer agreed in 2002 to preserve about 200 community gardens owned and run by city agencies and nongovernmental organizations and to offer another 200 gardens to the Parks Department without charge or to nonprofits for a nominal fee (Steinhauer 2002). In return, more than 150 gardens would be turned over to private developers for low-income housing. Response from the garden movement was generally positive, but the agreement did raise some concerns about the criteria for demolition. According to Steinhauer, "Residents near a garden slated for development on East Sixth Street between Avenues C and D were displeased to hear of its fate, and offered their own theories as to why it would soon be replaced with 75 units of housing. Manuel Valentine stared forlornly at a chicken strutting around the Sixth Street garden, where other neighbors were busy cooking dinner. 'We're going to find you a new home now' he told the chicken" (2002:B8). Valentine's illegal chicken is unlikely to find a home in a city-owned GreenThumb garden, and any garden that harbors his chicken may be less likely to survive.

As gardens come under the umbrella of the Department of Parks and Recreation or private entities legally recognized by the department, authority to designate uses within them is likely to lie with the city rather than gardeners. If this authority extends to aesthetic decision making, park architecture and artifacts will tend to reflect the taste and interests of administrators rather than users. In contrast, authority to make aesthetic decisions and designate appropriate uses in a casita complex or appropriated garden rests with those who have created property rights in the garden through their labor.[18]

It is likely that gardens that seek an affiliation with a city agency or a mainstream open space group will conform to city ordinances and open space movement aesthetics. They will come to look more like parks. On a visit to Loisaida gardens and casita complexes in the weeks following the 2002 accord, we found a sharpening distinction between gardens with parklike features—brick walks, arbors, unpainted wooden benches, iron fences, and even little stages—and those that had a Caribbean feel. Some of the latter had casitas; behind their fences, all featured bare-ground bateys, little rock-bordered beds of flowers and shrubbery, toys lying around, and patches of bare ground for picnics and partying. The former sought protection behind the Parks Department maple leaf; the latter displayed, as if in defiance, the Puerto Rican flag. A casita complex that conforms to city codes, one that looks like and is managed like a North American park, may be a less appropriate setting for the leisure activities and relations with other species associated with what Vazquez calls the "reclamation of memory." On the other hand, as city agencies and nongovernmental organizations adopt gardens for preservation, they may turn their back on casita complexes that cannot meet codes because they are built with a very Caribbean conception of the proper interaction between the natural and the social, the built and the unbuilt. The casita phenomenon shows the extent to which gardens, like other open spaces in the city, are cultural productions. They differ significantly because of the particular histories, sets of values, and aesthetics of their producers. We can only hope that the city and open space organizations, rather than impose a uniform set of garden landscapes through regulation, will embrace difference and protect Caribbean as well as parklike urban places.

Acknowledgments

In addition to the gardeners and open space advocates who have shared their gardens and their histories as well as their views, hopes, and dreams, we thank Laura Saldivar Tanaka, whose thesis research has helped to expand the range of our knowledge of Latino gardens, and Ann Margaret Esnard, whose help in the struggle to place the garden movement in theoretical perspective has been invaluable.

Notes

1. For accounts of Perez's achievement, see Meyers (1991a, 1991b). The story also appeared on National Public Radio's News Program, *All Things Considered*, Aug. 14, 1991.

2. Personal communication Astin Jacobo, May 2, 1992. See also Pace (2002).

3. It is not always possible to define New York City gardens as either Puerto Rican or Dominican. Saldivar Tanaka (2000:42) found that 90 percent of cultivators in the 20 gardens that she studied were Puerto Rican, 3 percent Dominican, and another 5 percent came from other Latin American nations. Puerto Rican influence is evident in flags planted in gardens of the Lower East Side, and the casita is a Puerto Rican cultural artifact. In the Caribbean, the distinction between Puerto Ricans and Dominicans is accentuated by the entry of the latter into Puerto Rico as illegal migrants, their stigmatization once on the island, and their relegation to jobs in construction and home care that many Puerto Ricans regard with disdain. In New York City, distinctions between the two populations are maintained through the census, parades, electoral campaigns, and baseball, but they become blurred at times, particularly as we enter the realm of

connections to nonhuman species. The rural cultures of both countries were similarly shaped by the sugar economy, *latifundia-minifundia* dualism, Taino influences that survived the biological and cultural onslaughts of colonialism, and migrations from Iberia, West Africa, and the Canary Islands. *Comida típica*, the plates that define the cuisine of both countries, is essentially similar in both places, as is the ubiquitous crow of the rooster raised for sport as much as for stew. So when we speak of the casita as an element in the garden, we are speaking of a very Puerto Rican artifact, but when we turn to cultivation, it is harder to assign traits to one population or the other.

4. I use Haraway's (2003) definition of companion species—those with which we share a set of partial connections that constitute "nature cultures" as well as "contingent historical foundations." In other words, the species encouraged or invited into the garden are simultaneously nature and culture. They shape and belong to us as we belong to and shape them.

5. Bronx Green Up, a program associated with the New York Botanical Garden, has provided community gardens with clean soil for raised beds, but this is an expensive undertaking and not easily replicable.

6. In New York City as in Puerto Rico, the term *batey* usually refers to the swept yard around the casita that is used for hanging out. See, for example, Sciorra (1996). Saldivar Tanaka (2002) uses this term to refer the garden area in its entirety. For Dominicans, the term *batey* connotes the area devoted to worker housing on the sugar plantations; it may also refer to the whole plantation, the worker settlement as a whole, or the land around the barracks.

7. This complication was made clear to Lynch as a result of meetings with GreenThumb and Cornell University extension staff working with the garden movement in the late 1990s.

8. Admittedly, her sample was limited to gardeners, but all of Saldivar Tanaka's informants claimed to prefer the *casita* to the park as a place for relaxation.

9. In his "Noticias de la historia geografica civil y politica de la Isla de San Juan de Puerto Rico" (1782), Fray Inigo Abbad y Lasierra noted that even the humblest peasant dwelling included a garden with plantain trees: "*El platanal lo tienen junto a las casas*" ("They have the plantain patch right next to their houses").

10. For a discussion of Caribbean gardens as resistance see Price (1973), Sokolov (1992), and Lynch (1993).

11. About 80 percent of the Puerto Rican population during this period was landless (Morales-Carrión, 1983). Many rural residents lived as *agregados* in landowners' property (Edel, 1963).

12. The main difference between the two lay in the quality and strength of the building materials, casitas having a zinc roof and wooden walls. The casita style is also common in the Dominican countryside.

13. Unlike the parcela program, the land colonization programs undertaken in the Dominican Republic under dictator Rafael Leonidas Trujillo did not provide

a basis for a claim to land. However, in the period immediately following Trujillo's assassination in 1961, large numbers of landless cultivators claimed lands that had reverted to the public domain, using the concept of improvement as a basis for their claims.

14. Macpherson (1978) distinguishes between property as a right and property as an enforceable claim, arguing that the societal right is prior to the enforceable claim. We argue that the property created by appropriators of the garden space takes the form of a societal right, but that it is not at the outset an enforceable claim.

15. This principle of legitimation of occupancy through improvement came north with migrants and was successfully transplanted in New York City. A notable example is Harding Park in the Bronx, an isolated cluster of small, once-ramshackle dwellings at the confluence of the East and Bronx rivers, whose history is summarized in Alvarez (1996). Beginning in the 1960s, Puerto Rican, Dominican, and Cuban settlers began buying the neighborhood's decrepit shacks on land owned by a real estate company and ultimately by the city. Through a process of self-building, Harding Park residents created a neighborhood of balconied houses on lots with vegetable gardens and chickens and entered into negotiations with the city for service delivery. In 1982, the city transferred its deed to the homeowners' association for $700,000, assumed responsibility for garbage collection, and exempted houses from building codes.

16. For information on these organizations see Fox, Koeppel, and Kellarn (1985), Saldivar Tanaka (2002), and Van Hassell (chapter 4, this volume).

17. For an interesting if controversial discussion of the role of the Young Lords and later El Puente in New York's environmental justice movement, see Gandy (2002).

18. In their study of Hmong Gardens in Sacramento California, Corlett, Dean, and Grivetti (2003) note a similar tension between Vietnamese refugee gardeners and municipal authorities.

References

Alvarez, Lizette. 1996. A Neighborhood of Homesteaders: Hispanic Settlers Transform Hardin Park in the Bronx." *New York Times*, December 31:B1.

Aponte-Parés, Luis. 1997. Casitas, Place and Culture. *Places* 11:53–61.

Balmori, Diana, and Margaret Morton. 1993. *Transitory Gardens, Uprooted Lives*. New Haven, Conn.: Yale University Press.

Brook, Isis. 2003. Making Here Like There: Place Attachment, Displacement and the Urge to Garden. *Ethics, Place and Environment* 6(3):227–234.

Corlett, Jan L., Ellen A. Dean, and Louis E. Grivetti. 2003. Hmong Gardens: Botanical Diversity in an Urban Setting. *Economic Botany* 57(3): 365–379.

Edel, Matthew. 1963. Land Reform in Puerto Rico. *Caribbean Studies* 2(3):28–60.

Fox, Tom, Ian Koeppel, and Susan Kellam. 1985. *Struggle for Space: The Greening of New York City, 1970–1984*. New York: Neighborhood Open Space Coalition.

Gandy, Matthew. 2002. *Concrete and Clay: Reworking Nature in New York City*. Cambridge, Mass.: MIT Press.

Gonzalez, David. 1990. "Las *casitas*": Oases or Illegal Shacks? *New York Times*, September 20:B1.

Griswold, Mac. 1997. Garden Notebook: World's Fair of Gardens Grow at the City's Doorstep. *New York Times*, September 25:F11.

Haraway, Donna. 2003. *The Companion Species Manifesto: Dogs, People, and Significant Otherness*. Chicago: Prickly Paradigm Press.

Jopling, Carol F. 1988. *Puerto Rican Houses in Sociohistorical Perspective*. Knoxville: University of Tennessee Press.

Kimber, Clariss. 1973. Spatial Patterning in the Dooryard Gardens of Puerto Rico. *Geographical Review* 63(1):6–26.

Lynch, Barbara D. 1993. The Garden and the Sea: U.S. Latino Environmental Discourses and Mainstream Environmentalism. *Social Problems* 40:108–112.

Macpherson, C. B. 1978. *Property: Mainstream and Critical Positions*. Toronto: University of Toronto Press.

Myers, Steven Lee. 1991a. Broadway's New Feature: Cornstalks. *New York Times*, August 13:B1–2.

Myers, Steven Lee. 1991b. Farmer Unearthed: He Planted the Corn. *New York Times*, August 15:B5.

Mintz, Sidney. 1974. *Caribbean Transformations*. Baltimore, Md.: Johns Hopkins University Press.

Morales-Carrión, Arturo. 1983. *Puerto Rico: A Political and Cultural History*. New York: Norton.

New York Times. 1999. Protesting the City's Plan to Sell Community Gardens. January 14:B8.

Pace, Eric. 2002. Astin Jacobo, 73, Unofficial Mayor of a Bronx Neighborhood. *New York Times*, March 20:A13.

Price, Richard, ed. 1973. *Maroon Societies*. Garden City, N.Y.: Doubleday.

Ramirez, A. 1997. Replowing a Garden for Housing. *New York Times*, August 31.

Raver, Ann. 1991. In a Mix of Cultures, an Olio of Plantings. *New York Times*. August 15:C1, C4.

Raver, Ann. 1999. Auction plan for gardens stirs tensions. *New York Times*. January 11:B1, B7.

Rocheleau, Dianne, Laurie Ross, Julio Morrobel, and Ricardo Hernandez. 1993. *Forests, Gardens and Tree Farms: Gender, Class and Community at Work in the Landscapes of Zambrana-Chacuey.* Worcester, Mass.: Clark University.

Saldivar Tanaka, Laura. 2002. Culturing Neighborhood Open Space, Civic Agriculture, and Community Development: The case of Latino Community Gardens in New York City. Master's thesis, Cornell University.

Sánchez Korrol, Virginia E. 1983. *From Colonia to Community: The History of the Puerto Ricans in New York City, 1917–1948.* Westport, Conn.: Greenwood Press.

Sauer, Carl Ortwin. 1966. *The Early Spanish Main.* Berkeley: University of California Press.

Schmelzkopf, Karen. 1995. Urban Community Gardens as Contested Space. *Geographical Review* 85(3):364–381.

Sciorra, Joseph. 1996. Return to the Future: Puerto Rican Vernacular Architecture in New York City. In *Re-Presenting the City: Ethnicity, Capital and Culture in the 21st Century Metropolis.* Anthony D. King, ed. Pp. 60–92. New York: New York University Press.

Sokolov, Raymond. 1992. Montserrat's Secret Gardens. *Natural History* (April):72–75.

Steinhauer, Jennifer. 2002. Ending a Long Battle, New York Lets Housing and Gardens Grow. *New York Times*, September 19:A1, B8.

Turits, Richard. 2003. *Foundations of Despotism: Peasants, the Trujillo Regime, and Modernity in Dominican History.* Stanford, Calif.: Stanford University Press.

Vazquez, Oscar. 1992. New York "Casitas": The Discourse of Nostalgia. Paper presented at Conference on Environment and Latino Imaginations, Cornell University, Ithaca N.Y.

Winterbottom, Daniel. 1997. "Casitas" Gardens of Reclamation. Paper presented at CELA (Council of Educators in Landscape Architecture) Conference, September. http://www.caup.washington.edu/larch/people/dan/casitas.php. Accessed Nov. 11, 2003.

9

On the Sublime in Nature in Cities

Robert Rotenberg

Meaning arises from difference. Considering the manner in which the majority of city folk evaluate nature, especially in the United States, one might be led to conclude that there is not much difference at all between nature and city. I first became aware of this disappearing contrast after writing my study of the meaning of landscape in Vienna, Austria. Returning to my teaching routine, I offered a course on the Chicago landscape in a context where the class could spend hours walking through the city's extensive park system. What I learned from that experience and subsequent conversations with hundreds of other city dwellers on this subject is that there appears to be a lack of a meaningful language to talk about connection to landscape among American city dwellers. Since urbanites constitute a significant portion of the public discourse on environmental values, the disconnection has social, economic, and political implications, as well as aesthetic ones. It also has implications for how social scientists, who are generally cosmopolitan, urbanized Americans, ask their questions about nature and analyze the responses.

The main contrast between my research partners in Vienna, 45 life-long home gardeners, and my neighbors in Chicago is that my neighbors lack a vocabulary for describing how their garden fits into the larger urban landscape. Urban gardening in Chicago exists on a continuum between the amateur and the agriculturalist. Amateurs include home gardeners who plant small beds for aesthetic enjoyment. Their labor input is highly variable, with retirees and young families generating the greatest time investment in their gardens. Their design rules and landscape tastes derive from popular media such as Martha Stewart's magazines and Home and Garden TV, on the one hand, and the more serious magazines, such as *Organic Living, Organic Gardening,* and *Horticulture Monthly.* The majority of domestic gardens within Chicago proper are suburban-style grass lawns with shrub borders and ornamental beds of annuals. A very small number of house gardens grow vegetables or engage in extensive development of perennials, flowering bushes, and bulbs. The urban agriculture end of the continuum is characterized by for-profit and nonprofit community gardening. Unlike the small home plots, these gardens are usually a city block in size or larger and tend to plant their crops in straight rows. The nonprofit version aims to build community and has the strongest investment in the movement side of urban agriculture (see chapters 5 and 6). This movement is characterized by such ideologies as sustainability through intensive soil building practices, integrated pest management with the avoidance of synthetic chemical additives, and crop rotation. The for-profit organizations supply locally grown, high-quality produce for restaurants and food pantries. For-profits are less likely to be wholly committed to any ideology.

In Vienna, my partners connected their home gardens to public gardens, and through public gardens to several different discourses, including the relationship between activity and health (Rotenberg 1993) and the relationship between the individual and the community (Rotenberg 1995). They had a vocabulary of urban landscape forms that were highly elaborated and that they used to describe and explain their public and private spaces. In Chicago, among my in-town neighbors, this particular conversation about public gardens does not exist, curtailing the development of public references and analogies in garden design. Gardening in America's cities also engages in multiple frames of discourse. For those who read *Horticulture Monthly,* it is about finding and successfully growing rare varieties. For those who watch Home and Garden TV and read *Martha Stewart Living,* it is about fashion in garden design and the patronage of boutique garden stores. For those who read *Urban Agriculture,* it is about the relative virtues of double-digging versus no-till drilling and other soil conservation issues. For those involved in community-based gardens, spiritual practices, like biodynamics, the planting and harvesting of plants according to celestial rhythms, or gardening throughout the four seasons using the techniques of Eliot Coleman, Kathy Bray, and Barbara Damrosch (2000) dominate the conversation.

What American gardeners in my research rarely talk about is the larger urban landscape and how their personal activities are part of both a natural system and a civic whole. The city is not referenced in the garden because the city is not referenced in the American experience through natural objects. Nature is generally of little consequence in the dominant discourse about the city. Systems of signs built from natural objects point to many kinds of social experiences but not to the urban per se. It is this contrast between the Viennese and Chicagoan understandings of nature in the city that provides me with an opening to unpack the idea of nature in the city.

My argument is that the discourse on nature in American urban communities that has developed since the eighteenth century has pushed the conceptual boundary between nature and culture so far in the direction of the wilderness that the discourse on nature in the city is marked by concerns of sanitation, civil order, and governmentality. Missing from this discourse for many urbanites is a consideration of nature as engendering a sensibility of the sublime, a disquieting awareness of forces beyond oneself that verges on the overwhelming. Perhaps in the privacy of their homes, gardeners talk of the power of natural cycles in their lives or the spiritual connection they feel toward the earth, as some have commented to me, but this is rare. The day-to-day experience of the sublime, unlike the quotidian experience of the beautiful, is extremely rare in ordinary conversation in American cities. Nature, even in the urban garden, has been sanitized even as it has been spiritualized. In those cases where nature intrudes on the urban cultural fortress, the sublimity that does ensue seems to take the form of terror.

This chapter begins with some background on the history of the idea of the sublime and its association with nature. Then I use two contrasting urban experiences to explore the dimensions of the sublime sensibility: confrontations with wild animals and extreme forms of weather. In describing these events, I want to show that the sublime in nature exists among urbanites, but not in ways that lend themselves to a conversation on nature in the city. In the final section, I explore some of the implications of this cultural predicament for our efforts at making sense of environmental issues.

On the Sublime

The American discourse on nature began no differently from the European discourse. If we were to somehow transport ourselves to the late 1700s, we would find ideas about nature that mirror those of Kant and Burke—that nature cannot be understood in human terms (Burke 1958; Kant 1911). Instead, nature provides people with the opportunity to transcend the ordinary limits of everyday life and enter a different realm. This realm cannot be apprehended with human knowledge alone. It lies beyond culture. When we enter it, we are often surprised by what we find, overwhelmed by a scale that is beyond human engineering and threatened by the sheer power of the unknown. Retreating back to the relative emotional safety of culture, we experience what the eighteenth-century philosophers thought the late Roman critic and rhetorician Longinus meant when he described the sublime sensibility and contrasted it to the sensibility of the beautiful. This was the basis of Longinus's approach to poetics, the branch of aesthetics that is concerned with our emotional response to literary works. The beautiful is the feeling we get when the importance of the human experience as a means for making sense is confirmed in the objects or scapes we see. The sublime is the feeling we get when we have escaped from the perception that our direct experience is sufficient for making meaning. It is this near-miss experience and the combination of relief and freight that we feel when reflecting on what might have been that constitutes the classical sublime. Longinus was primarily interested in showing how writers create a feeling of the sublime in their readers through various devices (Roberts 1907). In his day, the sublime was not associated with nature. In our day, we experience this sensibility through action-adventure or horror films when the camera pulls us into the danger the hero faces and then releases us to sublime reflection when the hero escapes.

The eighteenth-century philosophers wanted to develop a modern understanding of human emotions. For them, there was no hierarchy of emotion in which beauty trumped the erotic, or the sublime was more important than ordinary fear. Instead, they tried to distinguish between sense and sensibility, where the former was about experience of a feeling and the latter was about the making of meaning from that feeling. Kant, for example, wanted to create a system of aesthetics that would apply to all sensibilities and not merely the experience of literature that Longinus emphasized (1960). Burke explored how the emotions are invoked to political ends. In particular, he wanted to show that the use of power worked as political tactic because of its ability to engender terror, a significant component of the sublime (1958). Gilpin wanted to differentiate among three different sensibilities in our response to landscape painting. Building on the ideas of Kant and Burke, he divided the sensibilities among different responses to unexpected happenings and surprising recognitions. Thus, the beautiful arises when we suddenly become aware of some human quality in an object or experience where we least expect to find it. The picturesque is what we feel when we see artistry or the human hand in an object or landscape where we did not anticipate finding it. The sublime is what we feel when we are overpowered by the sheer magnitude of a perception (1794). In Gilpin's analysis, we have the first philosophical association of the sublime with nature. As the nineteenth-century preoccupation with the emotions as a source of meaning making progressed through Darwin, Wundt, and Freud, philosophers returned repeatedly to the distinctions between the beautiful and the sublime. Scholarly work on the sublime in twentieth century was even more extensive (Monk 1935; Nicolson 1959; Novak 1980; Weiskel 1976; Willey 1949).

Weiskel offers the most up-to-date formulation of the sublime sensibility. He argues that when we cross from culture into nature, there are two possibilities in the breakdown of meaning. His main points on this distinction provide the analytical framework for the discussion of wild animals and weather. The first possibility is most immediately understood as the feeling of being lost. One cannot grasp the signs or make sense of the relationships. There is "a massive under-determination that melts all oppositions or distinctions into a perceptual stream, or there is perceptual overload (1976:26)." The example he gives is that style of rock music where the back beat never varies, but the music gets louder and louder until something breaks. He cites Burke: "Excessive loudness alone is sufficient to overpower the soul, to suspend its action, and to fill it with terror" (1958:82). Because the sensibility is invoked through ratcheting up the scale of an otherwise ordinary stimulation, he calls this the mathematical phase of sublime. The imagery associated with the mathematic sublime is one of vastness. The horizontal and the vertical lose their ability to create relationships because their end points and intervals cannot be grasped. This is the image of the wilderness or, in eighteenth-century parlance, the wasteland. It is the first phase in a two-phase experience that results in the feeling of the sublime. The second phase begins when we return to the security of culture and an accustomed scale of stimulation. In this second phase, we make sense of the experience by associating it with something that is familiar. This is the metaphorical phase of the sublime. This is the sublime Kant described.

In Weiskel's second possibility, there is the feeling of everything being too familiar. Meaning is overwhelmed by the erosion of difference. An example of this experience of this sublime is the feeling of déjà vu. Meaning is suddenly arrested by the unrelenting sameness of experience that momentarily fixates the consciousness. While the first (mathematical-metaphorical) mode abrogates spatiality, this second mode erases temporality. Rather than being able to go with the flow, we become hung up on an image or word. We are blocked from moving beyond it. It possesses us. When the feeling passes, we try to make meaning of it, to try to find where the sources of difference may lie. In doing so, we seek to characterize the whole through the creative deployment of distinctive features. This effort disjoins meaning. Try to describe a déjà-vu moment to someone else. The whole is neither fully apprehended, nor could it be. Speech cannot keep up. This is the metonymical sublime, the sublime of such poets as Blake, Wordsworth, and Beckett.

These two possibilities for experiencing the sublime are not the end of the story. Philosophers and literary critics have developed nuanced discussions of how best to characterize the actual feeling of the sublime, and especially the best way to characterize how and why various writers describe this feeling differently. My concern here is to understand the meaning we give to nature in the city, and for that purpose, this discussion of Weiskel will suffice.

American Ways of Understanding Nature

The American urbanite's understanding of nature diverged from those of Europeans because the North American continent was open to settlement and the subsequent creation of a myth of the frontier, while Europe was not. Nineteenth-century American thinkers picked up on the sublime sensibility and developed it as theory of wilderness. If the wilderness lay at one extreme of the frontier, the city lay at the other.

This polarity was not available in Europe. For the Viennese in the eighteenth century, the nearby Vienna Woods or the Eastern Alps some 50 miles south of the city provided an immediate, familiar counter to urban life. When Romantic ideas about nature began to develop, they were projected locally. Nature was understood as both beautiful and useful, as possessions that are both sensuously desirable and economically profitable. The highest pleasure is the view of the inventory of possessions from the vantage point of a hillside vineyard (Küchelbecker 1730).

This perspective on nature changes by 1766. In a chapter entitled "On the Beauty of the Site of the City of Vienna and the Surrounding District," Fuhrmann uses Küchelbecker's account as a model to develop his own portrait of the Vienna surroundings. In his account, there is a change in viewpoint. Fuhrmann sees nature as not only beautiful, but also generous: it is the creator of lush visual sensations. A panoramic view from on top the mountain replaces the all-seeing bird's-eye view (1766:231). Both passages anchor the landscape from a specific viewing point. On top of the mountain, one no longer needs the rigorous grid plan of the emerging baroque city below in order to see what is valued. The eyes are permitted to wander through the boundlessness of the countryside. After hiking and climbing to the mountain top, one achieves that special outlook on the world. Nature, which up to that point has appeared as disordered, transforms itself into a coherent ensemble with the city embedded within it (Hajós 1989:24–25).

The increasing popularity of walking through the Vienna surroundings produced a profusion of guidebooks for hiking after 1790. The guides prompted the urbanite to take the family on long walks in the countryside on weekends, to find the culmination points from which the view was sublime in the metonymical mode. The familiar city as seen through the frame of nature left them speechless. Rather than polarizing the city and the wilderness as occupying separate ends of a space divided by a frontier, Viennese Romantics used nature to see the city better. They truly inhabited a city in a garden.

Two pieces of fiction on the urban experience from the mid-nineteenth century illustrate the contrast with nature in the American city. In Hawthorne's short story "Sights from a Steeple," the narrator takes up a position at the top of a church steeple and observes the circulation of people around his town for an entire day. Although the viewpoint is precisely what his Viennese counterpart would have considered sublime, Hawthorne's narrator has no time for nature's gifts to his town. He focuses on the billowy summer clouds initially and then refuses to look on them anymore. Instead, he uses his perch to hover "invisible round man and woman, witnessing their deeds, searching into their hearts" (Hawthorne 1974:192). In "The Man in the Crowd," Edgar Allan Poe treats us to a cinematographic tracking shot in words as his detective follows a derelict through the crowded streets of London for an entire day. The only references to nature in this popular story are nightfall and rain, both of which make the detective's business even more difficult. There is grass, but it is "rankly growing." The atmosphere "teemed with desolation" (Poe 1978:514). Both of these authors were adept at invoking the sublime in their stories. On the edge of the wilderness in Hawthorne's *House of the Seven Gables* or within the twisted minds of Poe's horrific protagonists, we find the proper location for the sublime sensibility in the mid-nineteenth century, but not in the city.

Although there were interesting physical features near their cities, the American Romantics journeyed to extreme landscapes in pursuit of their vantage points. Wordsworth went from London to the Simplon Pass between Switzerland and Italy in 1790. He characterizes this event as shaping the aesthetics of his poetry, which subsequently inspired several generations of Americans. Thoreau went from Concord, Massachusetts, to Mount Katahdin in Maine in 1846. John Muir went from Madison, Wisconsin, to Yosemite in 1868. What they found there was not a natural frame through which to view the city. Instead, they found "characters of the great apocalypse" (Wordsworth 1936:536) from a "divine manuscript" (Muir 1992:238), "such as man never inhabits" (Thoreau 1985: 640–641).

The Return of the Sublime

This American perspective on the location of the sublime may be the logical outcome of the cultural construction of national space. The frontier and its polarities are entirely of our making. Nature was never complicit in this construction. It "refuses" to stay put outside the urban zone. Sublime sensibilities are generated by nature in our cities in ways that obscure their "natural" context. The two confrontations I have in mind are weather events and wild animals. The former engenders the metaphorical sublime, while animals that we think belong more appropriately to the wilderness inspire the metonymic sublime.

Although wild animal sightings affect fewer people than the weather, their very rarity builds toward a different sensibility and understanding. I am not speaking of the ubiquitous squirrels in the park, or even of rats, though a particularly large rat can for some engender the sublime. Skunks nibbling carrot tops in the garden or wild rabbits hopping across a neighbor's lawn may grab our attention because of their rarity, but they do not leave us silenced with the awe and the terror I am trying to describe. A deer trapped by the fence in a backyard, an opossum illuminated by headlights scurrying across a driveway, a heron standing in a roadside creek, or a hawk gliding above a highway remind us that we share our cities with the "real" wilderness creatures. The parks of most northern cities are refuges for coyotes (McNeil 2003). From time to time, one can read an account of truly dangerous animals being found in apartments where irresponsible owners attempting to keep them as pets give up and let the authorities deal with the problem. Such were the recent cases of a fully grown tiger, poisonous snakes, families of foxes, and chimpanzees living in urban apartments (Barry 2003; Holtz 2003; Kelley 2003; Sheehan 1996). While we can wonder at the feelings of the police and animal control officers who had to deal with the tiger, we do not have to confront the cat ourselves. I have a memory of every encounter I have ever had with an animal I suspected was out of place. There was the raccoon the size of large German shepherd, sitting on a neighbor's porch and staring at me as I walked home late one evening. There was the deer that wandered into the courtyard of our building, became disoriented, and had to be subdued by tranquilizers. There was the rabbit that had a litter in a hole hidden under the sod of our backyard. The list stops.

I suspect that there are few urbanites whose encounter with wild animals exceeds my own. Among the more experienced are the animal control officers employed by cities and counties to maintain order in nature. Feature articles and public notices in local metropolitan newspapers make for interesting copy because interviews with these specialists reveal how they enjoy the special liminality of practicing a rural trade, trapping, in a city. These features inform us about the discourse among specialists on the sublime in nature, a discourse in which we rarely participate.

In one feature, Brian Miller, a commercial trapper and proprietor of a traveling petting zoo, recommends that people take steps to prevent nuisance animals from getting into their homes while on vacation, before they can damage property. These steps include not feeding them, either overtly or inadvertently. Home maintenance is crucial since raccoons will tear away loose siding or rotten wood to gain entry. Chimneys without screens bolted to the brickwork are common openings for birds. One should never try to dislodge the animal alone. Raccoons, skunks, groundhogs, and squirrels can be aggressive. It is illegal, as well as dangerous, to keep baby animals (Breckenridge 1999).

In an interview with Angel Litoborski, a suburban animal control officer and state licensed animal "rehabber," we learn that the wild animals she controls are either destroyed or relocated to the wild. She and her family have many pets, including three dogs, two cats, two ferrets, two opossums, and two hamsters (Thomas 1998).

Officer Alicia Wynick from Palos Hills, Illinois, reports that her main duties are removing nuisance animals and curbing the population of feral animals. The removal can keep her quite busy. In 1991, 91 percent of the 433 calls she received were to remove a raccoon from a home. By 1995, however, the number had dropped to 30 percent of 501 calls. She expects the problem to worsen in the next few years because "it goes in cycles according to the condition of the housing stock." Scaring the animals with flashlights or loud noises no longer works to scare them away because these animals have become acclimated to residential living. Her usual procedure for raccoons is to set a trap with food in the room and seal it. Usually, within a few days, the raccoon enters the trap to eat and can be removed. In one case, the animal held out for two weeks. "We used everything for bait: marshmallows, tuna, steak, even some homemade Italian meatballs the homeowner had made for her family dinner. Nothing worked." Groundhogs represent an average of 20 percent of her calls. They love fruit: "If you have an apple tree, you are going to have a groundhog." Animal control officers are also cognizant of the systemic dynamics between their efforts and the animal populations they seek to control. Efforts by officers in one county to control deer by introducing a few coyotes into the forest preserve system have led to a decline in the skunk problem. "But now the coyotes are the problem. . . . We have a couple of small dogs attacked and killed in back yards. . . . Small dogs are like an appetizer" (Sheehan 1996).

In an interview with Gerry LeLena, the senior warden for Dupage County in Illinois, we learn that stray cats are the department's biggest problem—1,900 of them in 1996! With the reporter in tow, the warden visits a suburban subdivision where wild turkeys have been chasing children. "The turkeys were fine here until recently. I think some of the kids were tormenting them. . . . Legally, turkeys are not considered wild life." This officer also does a lot of the traditional dog catching. Strays are kept for seven days. The decision to keep a dog for adoption or euthanize it after that period depends on the dog's temperament and health. Health is a big concern with feral animals. "While pet rabies is rare here now, it's still a real threat to our wildlife" (Mann 1997).

Finally, Carmen Wojcinski, a warden from Lombard, Illinois, informs us that she can relocate squirrels, chipmunks, coyotes, beavers, groundhogs, and muskrats but must euthanize raccoons and skunks for health reasons. The bait for the traps uses the animal's favorite food: "Squirrels love walnuts, while chipmunks prefer sunflower seeds. Raccoons love fish, except during mating season, when they prefer sweets. Muskrats go for apples. Carnivorous coyotes want meat. Opossums eat anything and everything, but especially like sardines. Skunks want lawn grubs during their grubbing season from August to October, but crave cheese year round. Groundhogs are vegetarians so they go for apples, cabbages, and broccoli." When asked to define an emergency, Wojcinski said, "An emergency is an animal in your house. A non-emergency is an animal wandering around your yard. Chances are, he'll wander away" (Mann 2002).

This language is not particular to Chicago. The *Washington Post* publishes an animal watch column in its suburban editions. In addition to the misdemeanors (and sometimes felonies) of dogs, cats, and owners, we can find notices of snakes in bedrooms and raccoons in the living room: "Animal control was called to a residence after a raccoon fell through a skylight into a living room" (Animal Wetch 2003). Through personal acquaintance, I know of an incident of two brown bears that wandered into some Washington, D.C., suburbs in the recent past. In Los Angeles, animal control is published in the police log. These entries include stories of wild cats: "A resident reported that a medium-size bobcat was heading toward some condos next door at 4:57 P.M. in the 21600 block. Animal Control suggested that the caller make it uncomfortable for the animal to stick around, adding that they could not do anything unless the animal was injured" (Swanson 2003). Mountain lions are also enough of a problem that the California Department of Fish and Game maintains a Web site of precautions people need to take when living in northern areas of Los Angeles (Dawson 2003). In Atlanta, the problem animals include deer (Haddocks 2003), wild dogs (Hill 1999; Ippolito 2003), raccoons, opossums, chipmunks, voles, and increasing amounts of road kill (McCarthy 2003). Seattle has its crows, coyotes, (Lewis 2002), and even buffalo (Give Them a Home 2002)!

The wild animals described in these newspaper accounts are a police problem. The officials charged with managing the problem are called officers and wardens. There are laws that they enforce and regulations that govern how they carry out their duties. There are licensing procedures that they must undergo. Their task is to rid civil society of nuisances—animals out of place. They attempt to control population growth through poisoning, culling, and sterilization. However, the primary activity of these officers is apprehending offending animals, especially those that invade property. To do so, they employ profiling techniques. They anticipate the behavior patterns, food preferences, and aversions of the animals and use this knowledge to entrap them. For those animals that are caught and impounded, one specialist was licensed to rehabilitate them. Others are released into special preserves. The most difficult animals and those that are most likely to be recidivists are euthanized. The discourse on wild animals in the city lies adjacent to the discourse on human criminality. It borrows many of the same concepts but stops short of criminalizing the behavior of wild animals by careful use of language. The journalists and the animal wardens seem very sensitive to anthropomorphism, even as they use human metaphors. The animals they describe do not know the difference between right and wrong, but they offend us nevertheless by invading our places. In fact, they induce terror precisely because they are outside morality. They are nature invading civilization.

The proximity of wild animals to urban life is terrorizing because it silences our efforts to make meaning. It erases the boundary construct between a nature governed by fundamental laws of survival and a culture governed by symbolic constructions of property, civility, and morality. The animal knows no such distinctions and in their obliviousness, they undermine our most closely held assumptions of order. When they invade our places, they erase difference, reduce us to their level (just another animal in the forest), and thereby arrest meaning with that unrelenting sameness of experience that abrogates the eons of time that separate the human from the animal. We must remove the animal, or we cannot go on. All other considerations remain frozen as long as the animal is present. At times, we are possessed by it. Only those of us who work with animals constantly—the wardens and rural specialists we employ precisely because they can evaluate the situation coolly and rationally—are free from this feeling of the metonymic sublime that animals produce in ordinary urbanites. This, then, is the final insult. By forcing us to feel emotion when we want most of all to reason a solution to the problem, animals subvert a cultural privilege claimed by many in urban life.

Invasions by wild animals happen to every urban resident. While we choose to ignore most of the insect invaders, the occasional spider or centipede will disturb us. Even then, the urbanite must have a predisposition to arachnophobia. Regionally, urbanites learn to grapple with scorpions, black widow spiders, hornets, and stinging ants. No one calls animal control for such pests. If we cannot handle the insects ourselves, we call the exterminators. There is no moral ambiguity here. Mammals, birds, and, in some parts of the country, lizards and alligators present a different problem, one that, like crime, is random and personal.

The other extreme of natural events for urbanities is weather. Atmospheric extremes affect entire populations simultaneously. Depending on where in the continent you happen to live, the city is as prone to extreme weather as its surrounding region. Anyone can recall how their life was shaped by weather; the same cannot be said for wild animals. For that reason, I will not describe the civil discourse on weather, as I did with animals. Oppressive heat or bone-chilling cold that lasts for weeks, wind storms, hurricanes, tornadoes, microbursts, flooding rains, lightning, and fire storms kill individuals, destroy communities, and devastate economies. Weather terrorizes us with its randomness, its unpredictability, and most of all its scale. Staring up at a thunderhead as it barrels its way into the city's atmosphere on a summer afternoon, we see a limitless black cloud, alive with flashes of internal lightning. Large, dangerous tornadoes bear down on us as we watch in helpless fascination. Fire storms move with a speed that is astonishing and lethal. The eye of a category 5 hurricane bends light and sound into otherworldly frequencies. At 20 degrees below zero, the ice cover on Lake Michigan does not merely crack; it roars. Sometimes specific features of the city's geography can become a weather-related threat. Chicago lies directly on Lake Michigan. In the late 1990s, the water level of the lake was at a historic high. During a particularly windy rainstorm one autumn day, I was surprised to see waves from the lake streaming over Lake Shore Drive, next to the lake, as I drove home. The water on the road was not particularly deep. I could drive through it without danger. It was deep enough, however, for the wind to drive waves across the roadway and into the park on the other side of the highway.

The discourse on weather is sustained by the periodic reports on radio and television. Newspapers carry weather reports, but mostly as a matter of record. Weather reports are a significant audience draw for media outlets. When the potential for extreme weather arises, the stations hype the extremity, milking their audience's attention as long as possible, while exposing them to the advertisements that pay the station's bills. The actual weather seldom lives up to its description. Weather events follow a normal distribution from the mildest summer shower to the life-threatening deluge, with most events occurring in a wide, middle range of the tolerable. The typical city dweller pays attention, makes whatever minimum preparation might be possible within the household schedule, but otherwise refuses to be terrorized by the hype. The weather reporters have cried wolf too often to be taken seriously. Over time, nonchalance toward weather events sets in, a form of tolerance of these events that leaves the status quo of urban life momentarily disrupted but unthreatened.

Extreme weather ought to terrorize urbanites. Contrary to the urban legend, tornadoes are not deflected by the concentration of high-rise buildings anymore than they are attracted to trailer parks. Severe snow-storms can be debilitating to urban life for days. The transportation network that supplies the food and fuel necessary for urban life can be ruptured. When Chicago received a particularly generous snowfall in 1978, the resulting paralysis was blamed on the mayor, not the snow! When hurricanes wipe out electricity or flood streets and homes, it is not awe at the storm's power that lingers, but impatience over the pace of the cleanup. When extraordinary summer rains caused floods in the Mississippi-Missouri watershed, it is the story of the engineering behind levees that either hold or do not hold that is highlighted. When New Orleans is threatened by flooding, it is the urban spirit of that city that ends the report. When fire storms sweep through subdivisions in California's fire belt, we marvel at the line of flames on our small screens, but cannot experience the scale of the devastation in frame of the camera. It is hard to see the difference between the randomness of fire damage in the chaparral and the city homes that burn down in electrical fires or gas explosions. Most city dwellers will criticize the judgment of planners who permitted homes to be built in the fire's path or blame the capriciousness of a random universe rather than gazing in awe at the fearsome power of nature.

The sublime in nature exists. Wild animals intrigue us with their unpredictability and their potential for random acts of violence and destruction. There is an experience of the sublime for everyone in a thunderstorm. Extreme weather presents the most powerful displays of nonhuman force on the planet. The city is powerless to prevent weather from disrupting its life. Yet neither of these features of nature lends itself to a conversation on nature in the city. Instead, it leads to a conversation about governmentality and civil engineering.

Revealing the Sublime in the City

As the examples of the wild animals and the extreme weather events show, the sublime in nature exists, even among urbanites, but not in ways that lend themselves to an understanding of nature in the city. Wild animals terrorize, but are extraordinary experiences. Most urbanites live their entire lives without an encounter with a menacing animal. Extremes of weather terrorize more people at once, but do so infrequently enough as to be mostly ignored. Most urbanites can count the number of extreme weather conditions that have directly impinged on their lives on their fingers. The sublime does not happen every day. This very quality of extraordinariness helps to convince us of how far from nature we live. The sublime sensibility is obscured through the institutions of city life. We do not expect to feel fear and awe where we live. When we want to experience the sublime, we go to the wilderness. What, then, are we studying when we do research on nature in the city?

The Romans and Romantic philosophers were concerned to describe the sublime sensibility accurately, because without it, a significant dimension of the human sensorium is disabled. Imagine living a life without the experience of beauty. The nineteenth century considered the experience of the sublime to be every bit as important as the experience of beauty. How might that influence the way people design space, decorate their homes, or learn about the lives of others? It seems absurd even to pose the question. How might the absence of grief or joy in the lives of the educated change the way questions about the human experience are asked and answered? It is precisely in this way that the muted experience of the sublime shapes the way questions about nature in the city are asked and answered.

The sensorium is a vital part of the anthropological concern with urban life. What does it do to us when our ability to make sense of the fearsome is dulled? In the theoretical essay that launched the study of urbanism at the turn of the twentieth century, Simmel writes that in accommodating to the structures of the metropolis, the city dweller's personality adjusts to the intensification of sensory mental imagery engendered by the stimulation of the speeding rhythm of life. The result is a blasé attitude as "reactions are shifted to that organ which is least sensitive and quite remote from the depth of the personality. . . . An incapacity thus emerges to react to new sensations with the appropriate energy" (1978: 411–412). Simmel could have been speaking of the sublime sensibility.

With no feeling for the potential terror of the forces that will forever lie beyond the grasp of human technical control, scholars focus far too often on either the margins of that control or the safe area far from the margins. What is a garden but a small plot of nature that we play at controlling, perhaps only to be disarmed by weeds and drought? For the city dweller, the garden is often materially inconsequential, even if it is emotionally satisfying. It is recreational farming whose real meaning in our lives is to relax us, suspend the control others have over us for a short portion of time, and help us acquire skills and recognition unrelated to our work activities (Habermas 1958). To this set of motives, we might add the pursuit of a sustainable relationship to nature and support for biodiversity among those who participate in the various environmental movements. In this book, we focus on gardens, urban forest preserves, and other forms of nearby nature because the spatial boundaries of the city define these pieces of nature as lying within the urban zone. While nature historically may have had little to do with nature in the city, these chapters document the emergence of this new, movement-based relationship.

By choosing to ask questions about a phenomenon for which we ourselves are debilitated from experiencing in its fullness, we reproduce the features of the discourse that deflect attention from the nature that really exists in the city. In his essay "The Trouble with Wilderness," Cronon indicts the environmental movement's use of wilderness as counterproductive. Invoking our lives as city dwellers, he states,

[To] the extent that we live in an urban-industrial civilization but at the same time pretend that our *real* home is in the wilderness, to just that extent we give ourselves permission to evade responsibility for the lives we actually lead. We inhabit civilization while holding some part of ourselves—what we imagine to be the most precious part—aloof from its entanglements. We work our nine-to-five jobs in its institutions, we eat its food, drive its cars (not least to reach the wilderness), we benefit from the intricate and all too invisible networks with which it shelters us, all the while pretending that these things are not an essential part of who we are. By imagining that our true home is in the wilderness, we forgive ourselves the homes we actually inhabit. In its flight from history, in its siren song of escape, in its reproduction of the dangerous dualism that sets human beings outside of nature—In all these ways, wilderness poses a serious threat to responsible environmentalism at the end of the twentieth century. (1996:81)

Can the same be said about the apprehension of nature in the city? This is not a flight from truth of history, but a flight from the truth of nature. To invigorate urban life with a more direct experience of nature means to embrace the sensibility of the sublime. The embrace of the sublime has already begun to occur in the reclaiming of spiritual and nonrational experience that is often associated with postmodern social movements. It may be merely a matter of time before our sense of the desirability of nature in the city has more to do with trembling fear than quiet beauty.

Acknowledgments

Amber Dewey, a master gardener who spearheads Chicago's Garfield Conservatory urban gardening outreach program, was kind enough to share her extensive experience of Chicago's gardeners and urban gardening movements with me. I am indebted to my colleague Randall Honold for valuable direction in discovering the nuances of the sublime. I also thank Peggy Barlett, Rachel Kaplan, and Steven Kaplan for their comments on an earlier draft of this chapter.

References

Animal Watch: Raccoon Drops In, Walks Out. 2003. *Washington Post*, November 2:C2.

Barry, Dan. 2003. About New York; Taking Down Savage Beast, Via Elevator. *New York Times*, Oct. 28:B1.

Breckenridge, Mary Beth. 1999. Whose House Is It Anyway? Keeping Critters from Making Your Home Their Home. *Chicago Tribune*, May 28:1.

Burke, Edmund. 1958. *A Philosophical Enquiry into the Origin of Our Ideas of the Sublime and the Beautiful.* J. T. Boulton, ed. London: Routledge and Kegan Paul.

Coleman, Eliot, Kathy Bray, and Barbara Damrosch. 2000. *Four-Season Harvest: Organic Vegetables from Your Home Garden All Year Long.* South Burlington, Vt.: Chelsea Green Publishing Company.

Cronon, William, ed. 1996. *Uncommon Ground: Rethinking the Human Place in Nature.* New York: Norton.

Dawson, Michelle. 2003. Sounding Off: Living in Mountain Lion Territory. *Los Angeles Times*, Oct. 31:2

Fuhrmann, F. 1766. *Historische Beschreibung und kurz gefasste Nachrichten von der Römisch, Kaiserl. und Königlichen Residemz-Stadt Wien und ihren Vorstädten.* Vienna: n.p.

Gilpin, William. 1794. *On Picturesque Beauty; on Picturesque Travel; and on Sketching Landscapes.* London: R. Blamire.

Give Them a Home Where the Buffalo Don't Roam. *Seattle Post-Intelligencer*, Apr. 29:1.

Habermas, Jürgen. 1958. Soziologische Notizen zum Verhältnis von Arbeit und Freizeit. In *Konkrete Vernunft: Festschrift für Rothhacker.* G. Funke, ed. Pp. 91–101. Bonn: H. Bonvier.

Haddocks, Robert. 2003. Subdivision Has Deer Problem. *Atlanta Journal Constitution*, Feb. 9:JJ1.

Hajós, Géza. 1989. *Romantische Gärten der Aufklärung: Englische Landschaft-skultur des 18. Jahrhunderts in und um Wien.* Vienna: Böhlau.

Hawthorne, Nathaniel. 1974 [1837]. Sights from a Steeple. In *Twice Told Tales.* Pp. 191–198. Columbus: Ohio State University Press.

Hill, Karen. 1999. Wild Dogs Become Bone of Contention: Decatur Residents: Police Fight Against Marauders. *Atlanta Journal Constitution*, Dec. 24:B4.

Holtz, Jeff. 2003. Worth Noting: A Runaway Chimpanzee Has the Law on Its Side. *New York Times*, Oct. 26(14CN):2.

Ippolito, Milo. 2003. Leaders of Pack Blamed on Cat Attacks Still Sought. *Atlanta Journal Constitution.* July 24(JN):1.

Kant, Emanuel. 1911. Analytic of the Sublime. In *Kant's Critique of Aesthetic Judgment.* New York: Oxford University Press.

Kant, Emanuel. 1960 [1764]. *Feeling of the Beautiful and Sublime*, J. T. Goldth-wait, trans. Berkeley: University of California Press.

Kelley, Tina. 2003. Metro Briefing, New York: Manhattan: Poisonous Snakes in Apartment. *New York Times*, Oct. 24:8.

Küchelbecker, J. B. 1730. *Allerneueste Nachrichten vom römisch-kayserlichen Hofe nebst einer ausführlichen historischen Beschreibung der kayserlichen Res-idenzstadt Wien, und der umliegenden Örter, theils aus Geschichten, theils aus eigener Erfahrung zusammengetragen, und mit sauberen Kupffern ans Licht gegeben.* Vienna.

Lewis, Mike. 2002. From Crows to Coyotes, Pests Proliferating Around Cities. *Seattle Post-Intelligencer,* July 6:1.

Mann, Leslie. 1997. Going to the Dogs . . . and Cats and Wild Turkeys Is All in a Day's Work for This Modern-Day Dogcatcher. *Chicago Tribune,* Apr. 13:1.

Mann, Leslie. 2002. The Trapper Takes a Walk on the Wild Side. *Chicago Tribune,* Dec. 13:7.

McCarthy, Rebecca. 2003. Roadkill Numbers Rising with Growth. *Atlanta Journal-Constitution,* May 20:JJ1.

McNeil, Brett. 2003. Unlike His Cartoon Pal, Coyote Gets Last Laugh. *Chicago Tribune,* Feb. 7:1.

Monk, Samuel. 1935. *The Sublime: A Study of Critical Theories in XVIII-Century England.* New York: Modern Language Association.

Muir, John. 1992. My First Summer in the Sierra (1911). In *The Eight Wilderness Discovery Books.* Seattle: Mountaineers.

Nicolson, Marjorie Hope. 1959. *Mountain Gloom and Mountain Glory: The Development of the Aesthetics of the Infinite.* Ithaca, N.Y.: Cornell University Press.

Novak, Barbara. 1980. *Nature and Culture: American Landscape Painting.* New York: Oxford University Press.

Poe, E. A. 1978 [1840]. The Man in the Crowd. In *Selected Works of Edgar Allan Poe, Tales and Sketches, 1831–1842.* T. O. Mabbott, ed. Pp. 506–518. Cambridge, Mass.: Belknap Press of Harvard University Press.

Roberts, W. Rhys. 1907. *Longinus on the Sublime.* Cambridge: Cambridge University Press.

Rotenberg, Robert. 1993. On the Salubrity of Sites. In *The Cultural Meaning of Urban Space.* Robert Rotenberg and Gary McDonogh, eds. Pp. 17–30. Westport, Conn.: Bergin & Garvey.

Rotenberg, Robert. 1995. *Landscape and Power in Vienna.* Baltimore, Md.: Johns Hopkins University Press.

Sheehan, R. A. 1996. Animal Control Officer's Duties Can Get a Little Wild at Times: Dangers of Palos Hills Job Come in Unlikely Places. *Chicago Tribune,* May 15:29.

Simmel, Georg. 1978 [1903]. The Metropolis and Mental Life. In *The Sociology of Georg Simmel.* K. Wolff, ed. Pp. 409–424. Glencoe, Ill.: Free Press.

Swanson, Mike. 2003. Police Log: Sunday: Ocean Vista Drive. *Los Angeles Times,* Oct. 31:1.

Thomas, Marilyn. 1998. Animal Control Officer. *Chicago Tribune,* May 1:1.

Thoreau, Henry David. 1985. The Main Woods (1864). In *Henry David Thoreau*. New York: Library of America.

Weiskel, Thomas. 1976. *The Romantic Sublime: Studies in the Structure and Psychology of Transcendence*. Baltimore Md.: Johns Hopkins Press.

Willey, Basil. 1949. *The Eighteenth Century Background: Studies on the Idea of Nature in the Thought of the Period*. London: Chattus and Windus.

Wordsworth, William. 1936. The Prelude (1808). In *The Poetical Works of Wordsworth*. T. Hutchinson, ed., Book 6. Oxford: Oxford University Press.

II

Consequences of Reconnection for Human Health and Functioning

10

Forest, Savanna, City: Evolutionary Landscapes and Human Functioning

William C. Sullivan

The careful study of perceptual experience unexpectedly began to make evident the hidden centrality of the earth in all human experience.
—David Abram, *The Spell of the Sensuous* (1996)

From David Abram's *The Spell of the Sensuous*, this quotation reminds us that evolution has shaped humans in ways that may not be immediately evident. Indeed, growing evidence shows that through evolution, the earth shaped not only our perceptions but also our very nature (Pinker 2002). To a striking degree, human nature includes being strongly attracted to places that include trees and other natural features. What are the consequences of living in places that have no resemblance to the landscapes that supported our evolution? Do humans today experience certain costs by living mostly disconnected from all traces of the natural world?

I explore these questions building on my work and that of my colleagues in the Human-Environment Research Laboratory at the University of Illinois. I begin by examining the habitats that supported human evolution and the notion that all animals seek particular habitats that enhance their functioning and reproduction. This examination generates three specific questions about the impact of living in barren urban settings that are answered by a series of recent studies. This chapter concludes by considering the implications for design and management of our current habitats and for human attachments to urban places.

Human Habitats

What were the characteristics of the habitats that supported human evolution? The answer depends on what period of human evolution is under consideration. During the past 10 million years, the earth has undergone extreme, repetitive shifts in climate, plant, and animal life (Potts 1996). The dramatic, repetitive alteration of the surface of the earth grew from an interaction between earth's orbit and geology. Dramatic climate change resulted not only from oscillations in earth's orbit of the sun (ranging in scale from 20,000 to 100,000 years), but also from volcanic outpourings, convulsions in the terrain, and a repetitive freezing and thawing of the polar ice caps. It was in this highly unpredictable environment that human intelligence, language, and creativity emerged.

Let us take a closer look at how the surface of Africa changed over time. Five million years ago, or roughly 250,000 generations ago, our ancestors lived in an enormous tropical forest.[1] It was in this forest that our evolutionary break from chimpanzees occurred and in which our fully upright, bipedal ancestors (*Australopithecus afarensis*) emerged some 185,000 generations ago. The famous "Lucy" was a member of this group.

Roughly 100,000 generations ago, a period of global cooling driven by polar glaciations fragmented the vast tropical forest of Africa into a patchy mosaic of forest interspersed with grassland (Burenhult 1993). The fragmentation of the forest and the introduction of large, grassy areas put pressure on many species to adapt to these new conditions (Megarry 1995). It was out of this landscape that the first members of the genus *Homo—Homo habilis*—evolved roughly 90,000 generations ago. *H. habilis*, or handy man, as they are commonly known, retained tree-climbing adaptations such as curved finger bones (Megarry 1995).

From *H. habilis* and a landscape that was more forest than grassland, we jump forward to approximately 45,000 generations ago when *H. erectus* flourished in east Africa. *H. erectus* faced considerable challenges from another peak of glacial activity brought on by global cooling that resulted in harsh conditions and seasonal variation in climate and thus availability of food (Walker and Shipman 1996). The cooling also broke up the tropical landscape into even patchier areas, which by now were dominated by savanna and interspersed with forest.

This process of punctuated change in the landscape of our evolution occurred again during another great ice age—beginning about 5,700 generations ago (115,000 years ago), just after the first anatomically modern humans (*Homo sapiens*) had emerged (Foley 1995; Groves 1993). The result of 100,000 years of global cooling was what we now think of as the typical East African savanna—grassland dotted with clumps of trees (Burenhult 1993). Behaviorally modern humans, who emerged from this landscape roughly 2,000 generations ago, lived as nomadic hunter-gatherers in small bands of a few dozen people.

In but the blink of an eye in geological time, the next significant landscape changes occurred. But this time the changes were not due to the repercussions of global climate change; they occurred due to human activity. Around 250 generations ago (5,000 years ago), half the world's population had access to agriculture and thus a more stable, predictable supply of food, fiber, and medicine. Since the dawn of agriculture, the pace of change in the human habitat has accelerated. Beginning a mere 11 generations ago, the Industrial Revolution brought the advent of large cities and, for much of the world's human population, the beginning of a profound shift away from the intimate, daily contact with other species that had characterized human existence for millennia. This trend has been reinforced recently with the advent of the computer revolution, a transition that began only a generation ago.

My point here is obvious: we humans have spent 99 percent of our time on earth living in tremendously close contact with forests, grasslands, and other intact ecosystems. Indeed, until recently, each of our ancestors participated in what can be called from today's perspective a life-long camping trip (Orians 1986). A life-long camping trip stands in stark contrast to the amount of nature that many modern humans experience. With our center cities often devoid of green space or even street trees and new suburban developments that dot the countryside on what was recently corn or bean fields, too many Americans live today without the hint of the savanna or forest. Are there costs to living so far removed from the landscape of our evolution?

Habitat Selection

To begin to address this question, it is helpful to consider the scholarship on habitat selection. Biologists have shown that all organisms capable of moving on their own will seek specific habitats. Although seagulls can fly, they do not fly everywhere. Rather, they search for particular environmental conditions that support their functioning. The same is true of dolphins, bees, and every other animal.

Biologists call this general phenomenon *habitat selection*—the process by which animals find settings that support a significant part of their life cycle, if not their entire life. Because habitat selection powerfully influences survival and reproductive success, the mechanisms involved in choosing a habitat have been under strong selection pressure for millennia (Orians 1986). According to the basic biological argument underlying habitat selection theory, natural selection has favored individuals who were motivated to explore and settle in environments likely to afford the necessities of life and to avoid environments with poorer resources or that pose higher risks (Orians 1980, 1986; Orians and Heerwagen 1992). The brain mechanisms involved in habitat selection were shaped by natural selection because individuals who sought out supportive environments produced, on the average, more progeny than did individuals who were indifferent to such concerns.

There is compelling evidence that it is not simply their reproductive success that suffers when animals occupy unfit habitats. When cats, for instance, are placed in unfit habitats, they become antisocial and a great deal more aggressive. They stop playing, and there is continuous hissing, growling, and fighting (Leyhausen 1965). For rats, the social impacts of being in an unfit habitat are even more pronounced. Wilson catalogues the consequences as including "hypertension, . . . cannibalism, and atypical and nonfunctional nest construction, with infant mortality rising to 96%" (1975:255). Thus, the evidence suggests that unfit habitats lead to unhealthy patterns of behavior and functioning in which social and psychological breakdowns occur.

This analysis leads us to our main question: If humans are adapted to the savanna, forest, and a close connection to the natural world, do we show social and psychological impacts or even breakdowns when we live with very little nature? Several studies conducted by the scientists at the Human-Environment Research Lab shed light on this question. Our research measured various dimensions of social and psychological functioning, while holding constant the broad cultural impact on daily life. Our studies do not intend to deny the importance of culture in shaping urban life; the learned patterns of social interaction and meaning with regard to nature are important. We seek to explore, however, whether patterns can be seen within one cultural context when contact with the surrounding natural world is varied.

The Neighborhoods

When we set out to study the effect of green neighborhood landscapes on individuals and communities, we faced a major challenge: selecting neighborhoods that would allow us to make comparisons between individuals with more or less contact with green landscapes (Sullivan and Kuo 2000). Ideally, we wanted neighborhoods that met four criteria. First, the neighborhoods must have variation in the amount of green cover—from places that were full of plants to places that were barren. Second, besides the amount of vegetation, other environmental and cultural features should be held constant within the neighborhood. Third, residents should be randomly assigned to the areas that had more or less green cover. And finally, the residents should have no influence over the maintenance of the vegetation near their home.

We found two public housing developments in Chicago that met these criteria: Robert Taylor Homes and Ida B. Wells. Each development has pockets of trees and grass and expanses of barren territory (figure 10.1). Each is strikingly consistent in its architecture and because of their neighborhood scale, residents reported no building-wide or neighborhood-wide patterns of cultural variation. At the time of our studies, Robert Taylor Homes consisted of 28 identical 16-story apartment buildings laid out in a single file line along a 3-mile corridor. Each building at Robert Taylor Homes is bordered on the west by an interstate highway and railroad tracks and on the east by a six-lane municipal thoroughfare and wide sidewalk. Ida B. Wells included 124 low-rise (two- to four-story) apartment buildings laid out on a typical grid pattern.[2] Because of its

Figure 10.1
Apartment buildings at Robert Taylor Homes *(top)* and Ida B. Wells *(bottom)*, without trees *(left)* and with trees *(right)*.

size (40,700 housing units in 1,479 buildings), Chicago Housing Authority policies result in de facto random assignment of residents to particular apartment buildings for both developments. While housing applicants can specify their choice of development, they have little choice of where they will be assigned within a development (for a fuller discussion and analysis of this issue, see, Kuo and Sullivan 2001a). We found, for example, no evidence that residents who had been assigned to apartments with views of trees or grass were systematically different from their neighbors who had been assigned to apartments in more barren settings in terms of tenure in their apartments, number of children, age, education, employment, or other characteristics that are known to be associated with social functioning.

The residents in both neighborhoods are overwhelmingly African American and are among the poorest of the poor in the United States (Ihejirika 1995). Other than some trees and grass, the neighborhood

Table 10.1
Characteristics of Robert Taylor Homes and Ida B. Wells

	Robert Taylor Homes	Ida B. Wells
Buildings	28	124
Building height in stories	16	2–4
Number of apartment units	4,419	2,788
Residents	12,300	5,700
Percent African American	91	97
Percent of residents under 14 years old	51	44
Rank of poorest neighborhoods in United States	3	12
Resident control over trees and grass	none	none
Landscape amenities (e.g., benches, water features)	2 benches	none

landscapes have a striking lack of other amenities such as benches, drinking fountains, and water features. Table 10.1 compares the two neighborhoods on a variety of features.

Strength of Community

When animals are placed in unfit habitats, their social behavior suffers. We sought to test whether neighborhood settings that lack nature have a similar impact on human social functioning. We first explored the extent to which neighborhood spaces with and without trees affect the strength of social ties among neighbors by conducting structured interviews with 145 residents of the high-rise Robert Taylor Homes. Participants had been randomly assigned to apartments with different levels of nearby vegetation. Interviews were conducted by three individuals who lived in a portion of the Robert Taylor Homes that was not part of the study. The interviewers were African American women between the ages of 24 and 50. Each had 96 hours of training in interview techniques. Each also had an easy rapport with residents. The interviewers did not interview individuals with whom they were familiar. (For a more complete discussion of the procedures and methods used in this study, see Kuo et al. 1998.)[3]

What we found was striking: the greener the neighborhood common spaces, the stronger were the neighborhood social ties near those spaces (Kuo et al. 1998). Compared to residents living adjacent to relatively barren spaces, individuals living adjacent to green common spaces reported that they had more social activities and more visitors, knew more of their neighbors, felt their neighbors were more concerned with helping and supporting one another, and had stronger feelings of belonging. These results were replicated in a study of older adults living at Robert Taylor Homes (Kweon, Sullivan, and Wiley 1998).

What might account for this pattern? There is evidence indicating that neighborhood green spaces enhance ties among neighbors because they draw residents from their homes and provide settings in which neighbors greet and get to know one another (Coley, Kuo, and Sullivan 1996; Sullivan, Kuo, and DePooter 2004). The contrary is also true: residents avoid barren outdoor spaces and in doing so miss opportunities to create a stronger neighborhood social fabric. In short, by increasing the opportunities for residents to meet and interact, greener neighborhood spaces facilitate the development and maintenance of neighborhood social ties. Compared to barren neighborhood settings, greener settings are considerably more supportive patches of human habitat.

Domestic Violence

When animals have been caged or placed in otherwise unfit habitats, they often become aggressive and even violent. Are individuals who have little access to nearby nature also more aggressive and violent than their counterparts who live in greener surroundings? To examine this possibility, we interviewed 145 women residents of Robert Taylor Homes about the strategies they had used to solve conflicts with their partner. We used the well-known Conflict Tactics Scale (Straus 1979) to measure the frequency and aggressiveness of the strategies employed. The Conflict Tactics Scale begins with socially acceptable ways of dealing with a conflict (e.g., talked it over, called in someone to help), moves to aggressive actions (e.g., threatened to hit or throw something), and ends with violent tactics (e.g., used a gun or a knife).

As can be seen in figure 10.2, we found that residents living in greener surroundings reported significantly less overall aggression against their

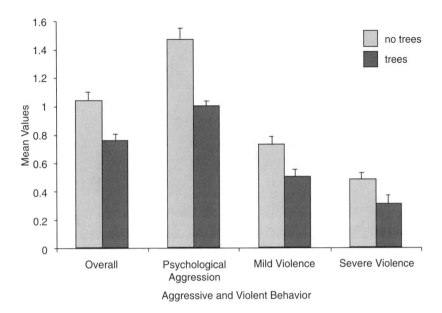

Figure 10.2
Mean rates of aggression against partner during past year in green versus barren conditions.

partners than did their counterparts living in more barren conditions (Kuo and Sullivan 2001a). This pattern held when we examined specific categories of aggressive and violent behaviors: women living in greener conditions reported significantly less psychological aggression, mild violence, and severe violence than their counterparts living in more barren settings.

In this study, we found that residents living in relatively barren buildings reported engaging in more aggression and violence than did their counterparts in greener buildings. These findings provide evidence that treeless, barren neighborhood settings have a considerable cost in terms of human behavior and functioning.

Crime

It seemed plausible that neighborhood residents would experience less crime in their neighborhood if they knew, trusted, and were able to count on their neighbors and if they were less prone to aggressive and violent

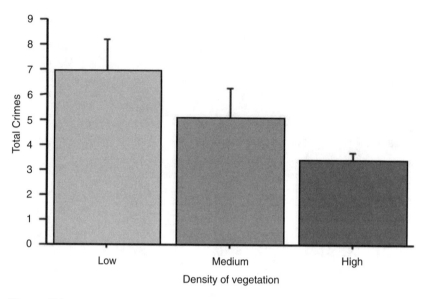

Figure 10.3
Total crimes over two years by level of vegetation for 98 apartment buildings.

behavior themselves (Sullivan and Kuo 2000). Thus, we wondered whether the greenness of neighborhood common spaces would be related to lower rates of crime. To examine this question, we collected two years of police data on crime for 98 low-rise apartment buildings in one inner-city neighborhood, Ida B. Wells. Would the greenness of the landscape outside each building predict the number of crimes reported for that building?

We found it did. As can be seen in figure 10.3, there was a consistent, systematically negative relationship between the greenness of the land-scape and the number of crimes per building reported to the police. That is, the greener a building's surroundings, the fewer total crimes were reported. Moreover, this relationship extended to both property crimes and violent crimes. The greenness of the neighborhood landscape explained 7 to 8 percent of the variance in the number of crimes reported per building (Kuo and Sullivan 2001b).

To summarize these studies, we found that higher levels of greenness in neighborhood landscapes yield not only stronger ties among neigh-bors, but also the additional benefits of less aggressive and violent behavior and lower rates of crime. To a middle-class observer, surrounded daily by reasonably pleasant settings, a small number of trees and some grass may seem only marginally better than an otherwise barren inner-city landscape. The findings from this body of work, however, suggest that to residents of inner cities, green neighborhood landscapes are profoundly important. The surprising connection between neighborhood green spaces and the strength of neighborhood social ties, lower levels of aggression and violence, and lower levels of reported crimes provides compelling evidence that nearby nature is a necessary component of a healthy human habitat.

The Broader View

One might wonder how the findings described compare to theories and evidence that other scholars have produced. Are the findings here consistent with the work of others who have examined the benefits of exposure to nearby nature, or do they stand alone? Let me explain very briefly the connections as I see them in two categories.

First, there are a number of connections to theory. More than a handful of scholars have argued that people have an innate attraction to natural landscapes that enhance health and functioning (e.g., Kaplan and Kaplan 1989; Frumkin 2001; Kellert and Wilson 1993; Wilson 1984; Ulrich 1993). Others have suggested that the converse is also true—that time spent solely in barren urban environments is detrimental to human health and well-being (Stilgoe 2001). Also consistent with the arguments presented here is the notion that there is a genetic basis to this affiliation with, and attraction for, nature (Kellert 1997; Newell 1997; Kellert and Wilson 1993). In fact, there are compelling arguments that regular contact with nearby nature is a requirement for mental health (Roszak 1995).

Second, there are a number of connections to the ideas presented above and the empirical findings from other scholars and other chapters in this book. People across nations and cultures are drawn to and prefer natural environments (particularly those that have savanna-like characteristics) more than urban settings (Herzog et al. 2000; Newell 1997; Parsons 1991). The great majority of places that individuals describe as favorite places are natural or contain a considerable numbers of other species (Herzog et al. 1997, 2000; Kaplan and Kaplan 1989; Korpela and Hartig

1996; Rohde and Kendle 1997). A large number of studies now show that settings that contain nearby nature, even urban environments that have trees and grass, foster recovery from mental fatigue and restore mental functioning (Cimprich and Ronis 2003; Hartig, Mang, and Evans 1991; R. Kaplan 1990, 2001; S. Kaplan 1995; Kuo and Sullivan 2001a; Taylor, Kuo, and Sullivan 2001, 2002). And finally, exposure to nearby nature enhances the ability to cope with and recover from physiological stress, cope with subsequent stress, and even recover from surgery (Parsons 1991; Ulrich 1984; Ulrich et al. 1991).

How does this growing body of evidence square with the fact that humans are the one species that can live anywhere—on the South Pole, inside caves in Afghanistan, under the sea, on the International Space Station? The answer is clear. Although individuals *can* live in such settings, humans function most effectively when they have regular exposure to natural features such as trees, grass, and water. What is striking from the body of evidence discussed here, and throughout this book, is the diversity and significance of the benefits that humans gain from having regular exposure to green settings.

Greening Our Habitats

The landscapes we inhabit have far-reaching and profound impacts on our behavior and functioning. For well over 99 percent of human evolution, our ancestors lived in extremely close association with the natural world. Their lives and capacity to transmit their genes to the next generation depended on selecting habitats that simultaneously contained the natural elements that supported their functioning and reduced the threats to their survival. Today, agriculture, industrialization, and technology have removed these constraints. Thus, it is possible to live and reproduce with little or no contact with nature. Although such a life is possible, we should not lose sight of the costs of living without nearby nature, for as the research summarized here demonstrates, the costs of living in an unfit habitat are significant and pervasive.

In the light of the research, it is altogether appropriate to enact policies to protect and enhance the green infrastructure of our cities. Such policies should encourage nature at every doorstep. Four concrete steps can be taken immediately:

• The U.S. Department of Housing and Urban Development (HUD) should amend its recently released *Principles for Inner City Neighborhood Design* to include goals and guidelines for the development and maintenance of green neighborhood spaces in all HUD-supported developments.

• Every city, county, and state should adopt an urban forestry program that provides for the comprehensive planning, implementation, and management of green neighborhood spaces.

• Every physical planning agency in the country, from school boards to the Bureau of Land Management, should include a green infrastructure layer in their planning process.

• Organizations committed to design, planning, and management of urban environments (e.g., the American Society of Landscape Architecture, American Planning Association, and International Society of Arboriculture) should make it a policy to teach municipal officials, housing authority directors, and police chiefs about the value of having nature at every doorstep.

By taking these actions, cities, professional organizations, and individuals will make considerable progress toward producing healthy human habitats.

Notes

1. Over the course of human evolution, the interval between generations has increased. Early in our evolution, the interval was likely 15 to 20-years. Today, a generation is defined as 30 to 35 years. In order to be consistent, generations here have been calculated at 20-year intervals.

2. In the studies described here, no comparisons are made between the low-rise and high-rise neighborhoods. All comparisons are made within a single housing development.

3. We selected 18 of the 28 buildings in the complex to be in the study (10 buildings were excluded for various reasons that might affect the validity of the comparison). In these 18 buildings, we sought to interview all the women heads of households who lived on floors two through four (there were no apartments

on the first floor). We invited 207 women to participate, and 145 did (a 70 percent response rate).

References

Abram, David. 1996. *The Spell of the Sensuous*. New York: Vintage Books.

Burenhult, Goran. 1993. Towards Homo Sapiens: Habilines, Erectines, and Neanderthals. In *The First Humans: Human Origins and History to 10,000 B.C.* Goran Burenhult, ed. Pp. 55–59. New York: HarperCollins.

Cimprich, Bernadine, and David L. Ronis. 2003. An Environmental Intervention to Restore Attention in Women with Newly Diagnosed Breast Cancer. *Cancer Nursing* 26(4):284–292.

Coley, Rebekah L., Frances E. Kuo, and William C. Sullivan. 1997. Where Does Community Grow? The Social Context Created by Nature in Urban Public Housing. *Environment and Behavior* 29(4):468–492.

Foley, Robert. 1995. *Humans Before Humanity*. Cambridge, Mass.: Blackwell.

Frumkin, Howard. 2001. Beyond Toxicity: Human Health and the Natural Environment. *American Journal of Preventative Medicine* 20:23–24.

Groves, Colin. 1993. Our Earliest Ancestors. In *The First Humans: Human Origins and History to 10,000 B.C.* Goran Burenhult, ed. Pp. 42–45. New York: HarperCollins.

Hartig Terry, M. Mang, and G. W. Evans. 1991. Restorative Effects of Natural Environment Experience. *Environment and Behavior* 23(1):3–26.

Herzog, Thomas R., Andrea M. Black, Kimberlee A. Fountaine, and Deborah J. Knotts. 1997. Reflection and Attentional Recovery as Distinctive Benefits of Restorative Environments. *Journal of Environmental Psychology* 17(2): 165–170.

Herzog, Thomas R., Eugene J. Herbert, Rachel Kaplan, and C. L. Crooks. 2000. Cultural and Developmental Comparisons of Landscape Perceptions and Preferences. *Environment and Behavior* 32(3):323–337.

Ihejirika, Maudlyne. 1995. CHA Has Nation's Poorest, Study Says. *Chicago Sun Times*, Jan. 26: 3–4.

Kaplan, Rachel. 2001. The Nature of the View from Home: Psychological Benefits. *Environment and Behavior* 33(4):507–542.

Kaplan, Rachel. 1990. Restorative Experience: The Healing Power of Nearby Nature. In *The Meaning of Gardens: Idea, Place and Action*. M. Frances and R. T. Hester, Jr., eds. Pp. 238–243. Cambridge, Mass.: MIT Press.

Kaplan, Rachel, and Stephen Kaplan. 1995 [1989]. *The Experience of Nature: A Psychological Perspective*. Cambridge: Cambridge University Press.

Kaplan, Stephen. 1995. The Restorative Benefits of Nature: Toward an Integrative Framework. *Journal of Environmental Psychology* 15:169–182.

Kellert, Stephen R. 1997. *Kinship to Mastery: Biophilia in Human Evolution and Development*. Washington, D.C.: Island Press.

Kellert, Stephen R., and Edward O. Wilson. 1993. *The Biophilia Hypothesis*. Washington, D.C.: Shearwater Books/Island Press.

Korpela, Kalevi, and Terry Hartig. 1996. Restorative Qualities of Favorite Places. *Journal of Environmental Psychology* 16:221–233.

Kuo, Frances E., and William C. Sullivan. 2001a. Aggression and Violence in the Inner City: Impacts of Environment and Mental Fatigue. *Environment and Behavior* 33(4):543–571.

Kuo, Frances E., and William C. Sullivan. 2001b. Environment and Crime in the Inner City: Does Vegetation Reduce Crime? *Environment & Behavior* 33(3): 343–367.

Kuo, Frances E. 2001b. Environment and Crime in the Inner City: Does Vegetation Reduce Crime? *Environment and Behavior* 33(3):343–367.

Kuo, Frances E., William C. Sullivan, Rebekah L. Coley, and Liesette Brunson. 1998. Fertile Ground for Community: Inner-City Neighborhood Common Spaces. *American Journal of Community Psychology* 26(1):823–851.

Kweon, Byoung-Suk, William C. Sullivan, and Angela R. Wiley. 1998. Green Common Spaces and the Social Integration of Inner-City Older Adults. *Environment and Behavior* 30(6):832–858.

Leyhausen, Paul. 1965. The Communal Organization of Solitary Mammals. *Symposia of the Zoological Society of London* 14:249–263.

Megarry, Tim. 1995. *Society in Prehistory: The Origins of Human Culture*. New York: New York University Press.

Newell, Patricia Brierl. 1997. A Cross Cultural Examination of Favorite Places. *Environment and Behavior* 29:495–515.

Orians, Gordon H. 1980. Habitat Selection: General Theory and Applications to Human Behavior. In *The Evolution of Human Social Behavior*. Joan S. Lockard, ed. Pp. 49–66. New York: Elsevier.

Orians, Gordon H. 1986. An Ecological and Evolutionary Approach to Landscape Aesthetics. In *Landscape Meaning and Values*. Edmund C. Penning-Rowsell and David Lowenthal, eds. Pp. 3–25. London: Allen and Unwin.

Orians, Gordon H., and Heerwagen, Judith H. 1992. Evolved Responses to Landscapes. In *The Adapted Mind: Evolutionary Psychology and the Generation of Culture*. Jerome H. Barkow, Leda Cosmides, and John Tooby, eds. Pp. 555–579. New York: Oxford University Press.

Parsons, R. 1991. The Potential Influences of Environmental Perception on Human Health. *Journal of Environmental Psychology* 11:1–23.

Pinker, Steven. 2002. *The Blank Slate: The Modern Denial of Human Nature*. New York: Viking.

Potts, Rick. 1996. *Humanity's Descent: The Consequences of Ecological Instability*. New York: Morrow.

Rohde, C. L. E., and A. D. Kendle. 1997. Nature for People. In *Urban Nature Conservation: Landscape Management in the Urban Countryside*. A. D. Kendle and Stephen Forbes, eds. Pp. 319–335. London: E and FN Spon.

Roszak, Theodore. 1995. Where Psyche Meets Gaia. In *Ecopsychology: Restoring the Earth, Healing the Mind*. Theodore Roszak, Mary E. Gomes, and Allen D. Kanner, eds. Pp. 1–17. San Francisco: Sierra Club Books.

Stilgoe, John R. 2001. Gone Barefoot Lately? *American Journal of Preventative Medicine* 20:243–244.

Straus, Murray A. 1979. Measuring Intrafamily Conflict and Violence: The Conflict Tactics (CT) Scales. *Journal of Marriage and the Family* 41(1):75–88.

Sullivan, William C., and Frances E. Kuo. 2000. Far Reaching Benefits of Green Neighborhoods: Evidence from the Inner City. In *Proceedings of the Conference Does the Neighborhood Landscape Matter?* University of California at Berkeley, Department of Landscape Architecture and Environmental Planning.

Sullivan, William C., Frances E. Kuo, and Stephen DePooter. 2004. The Fruit of Urban Nature: Vital Neighborhood Spaces. *Environment and Behavior* 36(5):678–700.

Taylor, Andrea Faber, Frances E. Kuo, and William C. Sullivan. 2001. Coping with ADD: The Surprising Connection to Green Play Settings. *Environment and Behavior* 33:54–77.

Taylor, Andrea Faber, Frances E. Kuo, and William C. Sullivan. 2002. Views of Nature and Self-Discipline: Evidence from Inner City Children. *Journal of Environmental Psychology* 22:49–63.

Ulrich, Roger S. 1984. View through a Window May Influence Recovery from Surgery. *Science* 224:420–421.

Ulrich, Roger S. 1993. Biophilia, Biophobia, and Natural Landscapes. In *The Biophilia Hypothesis*. Stephen R. Kellert and E. O. Wilson, eds. Pp. 74–137. Washington, D.C.: Shearwater Books/Island.

Ulrich, Roger S., R. F. Simons, B. D. Losito, E. Fiorito, M. A. Miles, and M. Zelson. 1991. Stress Recovery During Exposure to Natural and Urban Environments. *Journal of Environmental Psychology* 11:231–248.

Walker, Alan, and Shipman, Pat. 1996. *The Wisdom of the Bones: In Search of Human Origins*. New York: Knopf.

Wilson, Edward O. 1975. *Sociobiology*. Cambridge, Mass.: Harvard University Press.

Wilson, Edward O. 1984. *Biophilia*. Cambridge, Mass.: Harvard University Press.

11

The Health of Places, the Wealth of Evidence

Howard Frumkin

Some places are romantic, and some places are depressing. There are places that are confusing, places that are peaceful, places that are frightening, and places that are safe. We like some places better than others.

"Sense of place" is a widely used term that remains difficult to define. John Brinckerhoff Jackson, the founder of *Landscape* magazine, wrote that the antecedent Latin term, *genius loci*, referred not to a place itself but to the guardian divinity of that place. In modern, more secular times, Jackson went on, the term connotes "the *atmosphere* to a place, the quality of its *environment*." This idea matters because "we recognize that certain localities have an attraction which gives us a certain indefinable sense of well-being and which we want to return to, time and again" (Jackson 1994:157–158).

The features of a place affect us in many ways (Eyles 1985). We gain our spatial orientation—our sense of where we are and how to get where we are going—from place cues (Kaplan and Kaplan 1982; Tuan 1977). Places can evoke memories, arouse emotions, and excite passions (Lippard 1997; Walter 1988). Some have spiritual resonance; every religion has sacred places—some natural, such as the Himalayas for Buddhists and Hindus (Bernbaum 1991), and some built, such as the great Catholic cathedrals. Legends are grounded in places (Abram 1996). Places affect our performance as we work and study. Some places—the social gathering spots that sociologist Ray Oldenburg (1989, 2000) has called "great good places"—help us to connect with other people. Some places, as every vacationer knows, seem to enhance well-being. Some places may even promote good health.

There is every reason for those who care about public health to care about place. If places have such varied and far-reaching effects on people, we would expect some places to surpass others in promoting health and well-being. There is an analogy to medications, for which we consider both efficacy and safety. The field of environmental health has focused much attention on safety, defining the dangers of such places as cliff edges, hazardous waste sites, and lead smelters. But what about efficacy? How do we know what makes a good place?

The Evidence of Good Places

There is no shortage of guidelines on how to recognize, design, and build a good place. Where do these guidelines originate? Sources range from personal opinion to compelling data.

First, some guidelines appear as ex cathedra pronouncements—an especially common finding in the architecture and planning literature, where declarations of the "right way" to build are the norm. Authors declare what is beautiful and what is not, what works well and what does not, and how places ought to be built. James Howard Kunstler, for instance, declares that

eighty percent of everything ever built in America has been built in the last fifty years, and most of it is depressing, brutal, ugly, unhealthy, and spiritually degrading—the jive-plastic commuter tract home wastelands, the Potemkin village shopping complexes, the "gourmet mansardic" junk-food joints, the Orwellian office "parks" featuring buildings sheathed in the same reflective glass as the sunglasses worn by chain-gang guards, the particle-board garden apartments rising up in every meadow and cornfield, the freeway loops around every big and little city with their clusters of discount merchandise marts, the whole destructive, wasteful, toxic, agoraphobia-inducing spectacle that politicians proudly call "growth." (Kunstler 1993:10)

Conclusions such as these are often intuitively appealing and lively to read, but the reader may wonder: Says who? By what authority? Does the writer's advice actually work? Does it make people happier or healthier? How would success be measured?

Second, some guidelines emerge out of deductive inference, from overarching premises about how things arise to specific recommendations for placemaking. An example is feng shui, the ancient Chinese belief that good and evil spirits reside in natural features of landscape, and the associated geomancy that determines proper placement of homes, offices, graves, and other places (Collins 1996; Hale 1999). For instance, one feng shui guide offers the following advice when a large tree is located in front of a house: "This tree is overpowering the house. A convex mirror on the front door or a polished door knob will disperse its energy. Gateposts symbolically reverse the flow and send it back to the tree" (Hale 1999:44). The only firm conclusion we can draw is that the specific recommendations flow from a general theory.

Third, some guidelines emerge from qualitative observational research. Towering exemplars of this approach are Jane Jacobs, author of the classic *Death and Life of Great American Cities* (1961), and William Holly Whyte, author of *The Social Life of Small Urban Spaces* (1980) and *City: Rediscovering the Center* (1988). "Cities are thoroughly physical places," Jacobs wrote. "In seeking understanding of their behavior, we get useful information by observing what occurs tangibly and physically, instead of sailing off on metaphysical fancies" (Jacobs 1961:124). Living in Greenwich Village during the 1940s and 1950s, walking its streets, visiting its shops, lingering in its cafés, and extending her scrutiny through visits to other cities, Jacobs proved herself a trenchant observer. Several decades later, Whyte's Street Life Project used direct observation and still and video photography to study the sidewalks, parks, playgrounds, and streets of New York, yielding rich and textured descriptions. Writers like Jacobs and Whyte went on to reach firm conclusions.

For example, Jacobs was an early and influential advocate of mixed-use neighborhoods, a belief that grew in part out of her observation of parks. She noted that parks in purely residential or commercial neighborhoods did not fare well, while parks in mixed-use neighborhoods thrived. Thus, she noted that Philadelphia's Rittenhouse Square was ringed by a mix of housing, schools, offices, a library, retail shops, restaurants, and galleries. She argued that "this mixture of uses of buildings directly produces for the park a mixture of users who enter and leave the park at different times . . . because their daily schedules differ" (Jacobs 1961:125). This created a lively, safe, and wholesome public place, a setting for physical activity, social interaction, relaxation, and reflection. Through such close observation, a mode of inquiry familiar to field anthropologists, Jacobs generated a broad range of recommendations for urban placemaking.

Fourth, empirical studies of stated preference, published for the most part in the environmental psychology literature, have yielded conclusions about what makes good places. Rachel and Stephen Kaplan of the University of Michigan, pioneers in this research, have reviewed much of their work and that of others in *The Experience of Nature* (1995) and *With People in Mind* (1998). In a typical study, respondents are shown photographs of places with varying built and natural features, and asked to rate them according to their preference. In one study, for example, Rachel Kaplan (1985) surveyed 268 residents of multiple-family housing complexes to identify preferred configurations of nature. The survey revealed that parkland and other large, natural areas were preferred to large expanses of mowed lawn and small, "faceless" green patches. In other studies, respondents favor clear borders, alluring paths that curve out of sight, and a balance of trees and pasture. Such research has identified general features of preferred places, such as spatial definition, coherence, legibility, and mystery (the promise of learning more through exploration, as described in more detail in the next chapter).

Finally, empirical research has demonstrated associations between certain aspects of place and behavioral and health outcomes (Catalano and Pickett 2000). This approach, which resonates with modern medical and public health science, offers the prospect of evidence-based guidelines for healthy places. For example, architect Ernest Moore (1981–82) took advantage of a natural experiment by studying the State Prison of Southern Michigan, a massive, Depression-era structure. Some prisoners resided in cells along the outside wall, with a window view of rolling farmland and trees, while others had a view of the prison courtyard. Assignment to one or the other kind of cell was random. The prisoners in the inside cells had a 24 percent higher frequency of sick call visits than those in exterior cells. Unable to identify any design feature to explain this difference, Moore concluded that the outside view "may provide some stress reduction."

Another study (Ulrich 1984) also took advantage of an inadvertent architectural experiment, this one in a health care setting. On the surgical floors of a 200-bed suburban Pennsylvania hospital, some of the rooms faced a stand of deciduous trees, while others faced a brown brick wall. Postoperative patients were assigned essentially randomly to one or the other kind of room. Ulrich reviewed the records of all patients who underwent gall bladder removal over a 10-year interval, restricting attention to the summer months when the trees were in foliage. Patients with tree views had statistically significantly shorter hospitalizations (7.96 days compared to 8.70 days), less need for pain medications, and fewer negative nurses' notes compared to patients with wall views.

A third example of a study was a true randomized clinical trial (Diette et al. 2003). Investigators at Johns Hopkins University studied patients receiving fiberoptic bronchoscopy, a diagnostic procedure that involves inserting a flexible tube down the throat and into the lungs. Patients remain awake for this procedure and can experience some discomfort. The investigators randomly assigned the patients to "distraction therapy" with nature scene murals and with recorded nature sounds before, during, and after the procedure, or to a control group that did not receive these interventions. The two groups received the same amount of anesthetic medication. The patients in the intervention group were 43 percent more likely to report "very good" or "excellent" pain control and 63 percent more likely to report a "very good" or "excellent" ability to breathe, compared to those in the control group.

Studies such as these suggest that views of the natural world have a salutary effect and, together with other evidence, support the notion that trees are part of a "good place." Studies such as these also conform to modern standards of evidence in medicine and public health.

Place as a Public Health Construct

The appreciation that place matters for health is not new. Twenty-five centuries ago, in *Airs, Waters, and Places*, Hippocrates helped his readers distinguish unhealthy places (such as swamps) from healthy places (such as sunny, breezy hillsides). Frederick Law Olmsted, the preeminent landscape architect and planner of the nineteenth century, explicitly placed human health at the heart of his work (Jackson 2001; Szczygiel and Hewitt 2000). A half-century ago, the American Public Health

Association (APHA) issued a set of standards, *Planning the Neighborhood*, that addressed "the physical setting in which homes should be located." "In recent years," the committee declared, "it has been clearly recognized that the effect of substandard environment extends beyond direct threats to physiological health, and that it involves quite as significant detriments to mental and emotional well-being" (APHA 1960). The APHA standards addressed site selection, sanitary infrastructure, planting and landscape design, street layout, lighting, residential density, and community amenities. More recently, urban planners have recognized the implications of their work for public health (Dube 2000; Duhl 2002; Northridge and Sclar 2003), and the field of medical geography has been reinvigorated (Kearns 1993).

But today's challenges are different from those of the past. The built environment is far more complex, with more materials used in construction, more elaborate building systems, and more intricate urban networks. In some ways, technical advances have reduced health risks (indoor air is now far cleaner than in the days of wood- and coal-burning stoves), but new risks need to be better defined. At the same time, in a highly mobile society, traditional links to place may be weakened. If a sense of place has benefits for health and well-being, then understanding how to design for it may have real public health value. In a further change from years past, many more aspects of design, construction, and transportation are regulated, if not by law then by voluntary standards. This requires that our knowledge of how places affect health and well-being, including the evidence base, be codified as well. And in an age of electronic communication, such information is widely and instantaneously accessible. If it is useful in advancing public health, it can be useful on a large scale.

Members of the public increasingly value their health, consider that the environment is an important source of such risks, and want to avoid these risks. Both professionals and members of the public increasingly expect solid data to support health recommendations. For all these reasons, then, members of the medical and public health professions should refocus on the health implications of place. We need a broad, vigorous research agenda, and we need to apply research findings to practice.

Research on Place and Health

If health research needs to focus more on place and if empirical research can profitably be applied to questions of place and health, what are the topics to be investigated? Four aspects of the built environment offer promising opportunities for health research: nature contact, buildings, public spaces, and urban form.

Nature Contact

Contact with nature seems to be good for health, at least for some people in some circumstances (Frumkin 2001; chapter 10). There is a theoretical basis for this effect in E. O. Wilson's "biophilia" hypothesis (Wilson 1984, 1993; Ulrich 1993; Kellert and Wilson 1993; Kellert 1997). Biophilia is the notion that humans have an "innately emotional affiliation . . . to other living organisms." There is also empirical support for the benefits of nature contact. As noted above, studies have suggested that views of natural settings decrease sick call visits among prisoners and speed recovery among postoperative patients. In other studies, contact with nature has been associated with improved attention among children with attention deficit disorder (Faber Taylor, Kuo, and Sullivan 2001), improved self-discipline among inner-city girls (Faber Taylor, Kuo, and Sullivan 2002), decreased mortality among senior citizens (Takano, Nakamura, and Watanabe 2002), and lower blood pressure and less anxiety among dental patients (Heerwagen 1990). There is evidence that nature contact enhances emotional, cognitive, and values-related development in children, especially during middle childhood and early adolescence (Kellert 2002). Nature contact has been credited with reducing stress and enhancing work performance (Kaplan and Kaplan 1995). In fact, given the accumulated body of empirical evidence, it is remarkable that health researchers have not been more assiduous in follow-up studies.

If nature contact indeed promotes health, there are important implications for the design of the built environment. Should gardens be incorporated into housing? Should windows in offices offer views of trees? Should neighborhood parks include certain kinds of plantings? Should hospitals offer healing gardens to patients and their families? But before such questions can be answered, research needs to be carried out. This research needs to include careful operational definitions of nature contact, including the kinds of nature (flowers? trees? animals?) and the kinds of contact (viewing? touching? entering?). It needs to include careful operational definitions of health end points. It needs careful specification of the populations that are studied, and of personal attributes of study subjects, to help clarify individual and group variations in responses to nature contact. It also needs careful control of potential confounders. For example, wilderness experiences may be salutary because of the benefits of bonding with companions, being physically active, taking a vacation, or meeting a challenge, and not because of nature contact per se. As evidence emerges, we will have a clear basis for guidelines on incorporating nature contact into the built environment.

Buildings

Building design is a second arena in which health research offers great promise. Recent interest in "sick buildings" has focused attention on indoor air quality as a determinant of health (Bardana 2001; Hodgson 2002). Indeed, choosing building materials, furnishings, and cleaning agents that minimize indoor emissions, designing and operating effective ventilation systems, and maintaining air circulation and humidity at optimal levels are all recognized as important design strategies to protect health. Evidence-based recommendations are available (Bearg 1993; U.S. Environmental Protection Agency 1994; Seppanen and Fisk 2002; Wargocki et al. 2002).

Broader public health considerations apply as well. First, the design principles known as "green building" (Earth Pledge Foundation 2001; Stitt 1999), geared primarily toward environmental sustainability, may offer substantial (if indirect) public health benefits.[1] For example, designing for energy conservation may reduce the demand for energy, in turn reducing the emission of air pollutants from power plants. Similarly, using sustainably harvested wood may help reduce deforestation, slowing global climate change and preserving biodiversity. Public health research that takes full account of the health benefits of such environmental building practices will yield important insights.

Second, some aspects of building design are not generally recognized as having direct health impacts, but they deserve renewed attention. For example, despite the established health benefits of physical activity (U.S. Surgeon General 1996), most modern buildings with more than two or three floors have conspicuous elevators in their lobbies and staircases that are concealed and unappealing. Could the return of prominent, graceful, well-lit staircases seduce people into walking instead of riding to higher floors? Similarly, although there is some evidence on the role of natural lighting in promoting comfort and performance (Boyce 1981), not enough is known about how lighting can be designed to promote health. With the advent of energy-efficient, compact, fluorescent bulbs, this question takes on added importance. Finally, although substandard housing is clearly bad for health (Krieger and Higgins 2002), a recent review found that evidence of the health benefits of specific housing interventions is scarce (Thomson, Petlicrew, and Douglas 2003). How to design and build good homes, schools, and workplaces remains a pressing, and largely unanswered, health question.

Public Places

Many of the best places are neither home nor work, but "third places" in the public realm: streets and sidewalks, parks and cafés, theaters and sports facilities (Oldenburg 2000). Such public places are important venues for a wide variety of activities, of which some, such as social interaction and physical activity, have clear health implications (Kuo et al. 1998; Ulrich and Addoms 1981).

What makes a good street? There is no shortage of design guidelines issued by government agencies and private groups. Those issued by state departments of transportation typically aim to maximize motor vehicle traffic flow and prevent crashes. Guidelines from other sources are oriented more toward pedestrians. Some, such as Dan Burden's *Street Design Guidelines for Healthy Neighborhoods* (1999), explicitly focus on health. Such sources typically recommend streets that are narrower and incorporate traffic-calming strategies; sidewalks with sufficient width, buffers, continuity, and connectivity; safe crosswalks; and bicycle lanes.

What about parks? Parks exist in a variety of settings, from urban pocket parks to waterfronts, to large expanses like Cullen Park in Houston, Fairmont Park in Philadelphia, and Griffith Park in Los

Angeles to reclaimed transportation corridors like the C&O Canal (Altman and Zube 1989; Garvin and Berens 1997). Research on how people use parks suggests that several design features play a role, including the amount and type of vegetation; the presence of interesting, meandering pathways; quiet areas for sitting and reading; recreational amenities; adequate information and signage; and the perceived level of safety (Marcus et al. 1998). People's conceptions of parks, the expectations they bring to them, and the ways they use them vary greatly by age, gender, ethnicity, and other factors (Francis 1987; Burgess, Harrison, and Lamb 1988; Loukaitou-Sideris 1995).

What features of street and park design predict social interactions and physical activity? A large literature provides some answers with regard to physical activity (Brownson et al. 2001; Craig et al. 2002; Handy et al. 2002; Humpel, Owen, and Leslie 2002; Sallis, Baumann, and Pratt 1998). Destinations that are reasonably close, accessible, and well designed and that feature attractive scenery, maintained paths, good lighting, toilets, and drinking water seem to predict physical activity. Less information is available regarding social interactions, but studies have suggested that "sense of community" increases when neighborhoods are walkable (Glynn 1981; Leyden 2003; Lund 2002), and when well-maintained public spaces are located near homes (Skjaeveland and Garling 1997).

Again, much remains to be learned. If a sidewalk is built, will people walk? If a park is built, will people come? Which park designs are most restorative? What are the best ways to site, design, and build public places in ways that attract people, lift their spirits, encourage them to socialize, and promote physical activity?

Urban Form

Urban form results from design, transportation, and land use decisions at a larger scale than buildings and public places. In recent decades, the growing dominance of the automobile, the migration from central cities to suburbs, and zoning codes that segregate different land uses have resulted in the pattern known as urban sprawl. Principal features of sprawling communities include low residential and employment density; separation of housing, employment, recreation, services, and other land uses; low connectivity among destinations; weak and dispersed activity centers and downtowns; and heavy reliance on automobiles with few available transportation alternatives (Ewing, Pendall, and Chen 2002; Gillham 2002; Frumkin, Frank, and Jackson 2004).

What kinds of places result? There is no simple answer, as suburban and exurban communities vary widely. Some are relatively dense while others are sparse, some have sidewalks while others do not, some have viable downtowns while others lack any commercial districts, and some have parks while others comprise only private property (Ewing et al. 2002; Gillham 2002). Accordingly, the social and political composition of suburban communities varies widely (Orfield 2001).

Meanwhile, in many metropolitan areas, the mirror image of suburban growth has been the decline of central cities. As jobs and economic activity migrated from the center to the periphery, the neighborhoods left behind became different kinds of places, with neglected and abandoned buildings, dilapidated and dangerous parks and streets, dysfunctional transportation systems, and failing infrastructure (Fitzpatrick and LaGory 2000; Wilson 1987). Poor people and members of minority groups are concentrated in such environments, raising profound social justice concerns.

Research has suggested that the land use and transportation patterns that characterize urban sprawl have health implications (Frumkin 2002; Frumkin et al. 2004). Heavy use of motor vehicles contributes to air pollution, which increases respiratory and cardiovascular disease as well as overall mortality. Declining physical activity, related to decreased walking, contributes to obesity, diabetes, and related ailments. Increased time in traffic raises the risk of traffic crashes, and roads built for cars but not pedestrians pose a risk of pedestrian injuries and fatalities. Factors as diverse as road rage and physical inactivity threaten mental health, and social capital—an important predictor of health both directly and mediated through income inequality—may decline. At the same time, the complex of physical and social risk factors in the central city—the concentration of poverty, the dearth of social and medical services, the prevalence of substandard housing, the threats of crime and drug use, the squalor of many places—is so well recognized that it has spawned a subfield, urban health, with its own research centers, journals, and specialists (Andrulis 1997; Andrulis et al. 1995; Andrulis and Goodman 1999; Ford 1997; McCarthy 2000).

Urban form has much to do with health. Attention to health problems of the center city has focused largely on social and organizational factors rather than features of the built environment. Similarly, health research on the consequences of suburban sprawl has been limited. Research is needed on a variety of issues. What urban arrangements, what zoning codes, what transportation plans, and what industrial policies lead to the most livable and healthy cities and suburbs? Of the many sweeping plans for urban design—and urban renewal—that have come and gone over the years, which do the most for human health and welfare?

Conclusion

Medicine and public health can and should contribute to a growing recognition of the importance of place. From nature contact to buildings, from public places to cities, there are research needs and unmet opportunities to design and build healthy places. As health professionals collaborate with urban planners and architects, transportation engineers and real estate developers, environmental psychologists and geographers, we will ask and answer these research questions with solid evidence, and we will envision, plan, and build healthier, more sustainable human environments.

Note

A version of this chapter was published as "Healthy Places: Exploring the Evidence" in *American Journal of Public Health*, 2003, vol. 93, pp. 14351–14355.
1. For information on green building, go to the Web site of the U.S. Green Building Council (www.usgbc.org) or the Energy and Environmental Building Association (www.eeba.org).

References

Abram, David. 1996. *The Spell of the Sensuous*. New York: Pantheon.

Altman, Irwin, and Ervin Zube, eds. 1989. *Public Places and Spaces*. New York: Plenum Press.

Andrulis, Dennis P. 1997. The Urban Health Penalty: New Dimensions and Directions in Inner-City Health Care. In *Inner City Health Care*. Philadelphia: American College of Physicians. http://www.acponline.org/hpp/pospaper/andrulis.htm. Accessed Sept. 16, 2004.

Andrulis, D. P., C. Ginsberg, Y. Shaw-Taylor, and V. Martin. 1995. Urban Social Health. Washington, D.C.: National Public Health and Hospital Institute.

Andrulis Dennis P., and Nanette J. Goodman. 1999. *The Social and Health Landscape of Urban and Suburban America*. Chicago: American Hospital Association.

American Public Health Association, Committee on the Hygiene of Housing, Subcommittee on Environmental Standards. 1960. *Planning the Neighborhood*. Chicago: APHA.

Bardana, Emil J., Jr. 2001. Indoor Pollution and Its Impact on Respiratory Health. *Annal of Allergy Asthma Immunology* 87(6 Suppl. 3):33–40.

Bearg, David W. 1993. *Indoor Air Quality and HVAC Systems*. Chelsea, Mich.: Lewis Publishers.

Bernbaum, Edwin. 1991. The Himalayas: Realm of the Sacred. In *The Power of Place: Sacred Ground in Natural and Human Environments*. James A. Swan, ed. Pp. 107–119. Wheaton, Ill.: Quest Books.

Boyce, Peter R. 1981. *Human Factors in Lighting*. London: Applied Science Publishers.

Brownson, R. C., E. A. Baker, R. A. Housemann, L. K. Brennan, and S. J. Bacak. 2001. Environmental and Policy Determinants of Physical Activity in the United States. *American Journal of Public Health* 91:1995–2003.

Burden, Dan. 1999. *Street Design Guidelines for Healthy Neighborhoods*. Sacramento, Calif.: Local Government Commission.

Burgess, J., C. M. Harrison, and M. Lamb. 1988. People, Parks, and the Urban Green: A Study of Popular Meanings and Values for Open Spaces in the City. *Urban Studies* 25:455–473.

Catalano, Ralph, and Kate E. Pickett. 2000. A Taxonomy of Research on Place and Health. In *Handbook of Social Studies in Health and Medicine*. G. Albrecht, R. Fitpatrick, and S. Scrimshaw, eds. Pp. 64–83. Thousand Oaks, Calif.: Sage.

Collins, Terah Kathryn. 1996. *The Western Guide to Feng Shui: Creating Balance, Harmony, and Prosperity in Your Environment*. Carlsbad, Calif.: Hay House.

Craig, C. L., R. C. Brownson, S. E. Cragg, and A. L. Dunn. 2002. Exploring the Effect of the Environment on Physical Activity: A Study Examining Walking to Work. *American Journal of Preventive Medicine* 23(2):36–43.

Diette, G. B., N. Lechtzin, E. Haponik, A. Devrotes, and H. R. Rubin. 2003. Distraction Therapy with Nature Sights and Sounds Reduces Pain during Flexible Bronchoscopy: A Complementary Approach to Routine Analgesia. *Chest* 123:941–948.

Dube, P. 2000. Urban Health: An Urban Planning Perspective. *Review of Environmental Health* 15:249–265.

Duhl, Leonard. 2002. Health and Greening the City: Relation of Urban Planning and Health. *Journal of Epidemiology and Community Health* 56:897.

Earth Pledge Foundation. 2001. *Sustainable Architecture White Papers*. New York: Earth Pledge Foundation.

Ewing, R., R. Pendall, and D. Chen. 2002. Measuring Sprawl and Its Impact. http://www.smartgrowthamerica.org/sprawlindex/MeasuringSprawl.PDF. Accessed Jan. 19, 2005.

Eyles, John. 1985. *Senses of Place*. Warrington, U.K.: Silverbrook Press.

Faber Taylor, Andrea, Frances E. Kuo, and William C. Sullivan. 2001. Coping with ADD: The Surprising Connection to Green Play Settings. *Environment and Behavior* 33:54–77.

Faber Taylor, Andrea, Frances E. Kuo, and William C. Sullivan. 2002. Views of Nature and Self-Discipline: Evidence from Inner City Children. *Journal of Environmental Psychology* 22:49–64.

Fitzpatrick, Kevin, and Mark LaGory. 2000. *Unhealthy Places: The Ecology of Risk in the Urban Landscape*. New York: Routledge.

Ford, Amasa B. 1997. *Urban Health in America*. New York: Oxford University Press.

Francis, M. 1987. Some Meanings Attached to a City Park and Community Gardens. *Landscape Journal* 6:101–112.

Frumkin, Howard. 2001. Beyond Toxicity: The Greening of Environmental Health. *American Journal of Preventive Medicine* 20:234–240.

Frumkin, Howard. 2002. Urban Sprawl and Public Health. *Public Health Reports* 117:201–217.

Frumkin, Howard, Lawrence Frank, and Richard Jackson. 2004. *Urban Sprawl and Public Health: Designing, Planning, and Building for Healthy Communities*. Washington, D.C.: Island Press.

Garvin, Alexander, and Gayle Berens. 1997. *Urban Parks and Open Space*. Washington, D.C.: Urban Land Institute and Trust for Public Land.

Gillham, Oliver. 2002. *The Limitless City: A Primer on the Urban Sprawl Debate*. Washington, D.C.: Island Press.

Glynn, Thomas. 1981. Psychological Sense of Community: Measurement and Application. *Human Relations* 34:789–818.

Hale, Gill. 1999. *The Practical Encyclopedia of Feng Shui*. London: Hermes House.

Handy, S. L., M. G. Boarnet, R. Ewing, and R. E. Killingsworth. 2002. How the Built Environment Affects Physical Activity: Views from Urban Planning. *American Journal of Preventive Medicine* 23(2):64–73.

Heerwagen, Judith H. 1990. The Psychological Aspects of Windows and Window Design. In *Proceedings of the 21st Annual Conference of the Environmental Design Research Association*. K. H. Anthony, J. Choi, and B. Orland, eds. Oklahoma City: EDRA.

Hodgson, Michael. 2002. Indoor Environmental Exposures and Symptoms. *Environmental Health Perspective* 110(4):663–667.

Humpel, N., N. Owen, and E. Leslie. 2002. Environmental Factors Associated with Adults' Participation in Physical Activity: A Review. *American Journal of Preventive Medicine* 22:188–199.

Jackson, John Brinckerhoff. 1994. *A Sense of Place, a Sense of Time*. New Haven, Conn.: Yale University Press.

Jackson, Richard Joseph. 2001. What Olmsted Knew. *Western City* 6(3):12–15.

Jacobs, Jane. 1961. *The Death and Life of Great American Cities*. New York: Random House.

Kaplan, Rachel. 1985. Nature at the Doorstep: Residential Satisfaction and the Nearby Environment. *Journal of Architectural Planning Research* 2:115–127.

Kaplan, Rachel, and Stephen Kaplan. 1995. *The Experience of Nature: A Psychological Perspective*. New York: Cambridge University Press.

Kaplan, Rachel, Stephen Kaplan, and Robert L. Ryan. 1998. *With People in Mind: Design and Management of Everyday Nature*. Washington, D.C.: Island Press.

Kaplan, Stephen, and Rachel Kaplan, eds. 1982. *Humanscape: Environments for People*. Ann Arbor, Mich.: Ulrich's Books.

Kearns, R. 1993. Place and Health: Towards a Reformed Medical Geography. *Professional Geographer* 45:139–147.

Kellert, Stephen R. 1997. *Kinship to Mastery: Biophilia in Human Evolution and Development*. Washington, D.C.: Island Press.

Kellert, Stephen R. 2002. Experiencing Nature: Affective, Cognitive, and Evaluative Development in Children. In *Children and Nature: Psychological, Sociocultural, and Evolutionary Investigations*. Peter H. Kahn, Jr., and Stephen R. Kellert, eds. Pp. 117–151. Cambridge, Mass.: MIT Press.

Kellert, Stephen R., and Edward O. Wilson, eds. 1993. *The Biophilia Hypothesis*. Washington, D.C.: Island Press.

Krieger, James, and Donna L. Higgins. 2002. Housing and Health: Time Again for Public Health Action. *American Journal of Public Health* 92:758–768.

Kunstler, James Howard. 1993. *The Geography of Nowhere: The Rise and Decline of America's Man-Made Landscape*. New York: Simon & Schuster.

Kunstler, James Howard. 1996. Home from Nowhere. *Atlantic Monthly* 278(3):43–66.

Kuo, Frances E., William C. Sullivan, Rebekah Levin Coley, and Liesette Brunson. 1998. Fertile Ground for Community: Inner-City Neighborhood Common Spaces. *American Journal of Community Psychology* 26:823–851.

Leyden, Kevin M. 2003. Social Capital and the built environment: The importance of walkable neighborhoods. *American Journal of Public Health* 93:1546–1551.

Lippard, Lucy R. 1997. *The Lure of the Local: Senses of Place in a Multicentered Society*. New York: New Press.

Loukaitou-Sideris, Anastasia. 1995. Urban Form and Social Context: Cultural Differentiation in the Uses of Urban Parks. *Journal of Planning and Educational Research* 14:89–102.

Lund, Hollie. 2002. Pedestrian Environments and Sense of Community. *Journal of Planning and Educational Research* 21:301–312.

Marcus, Clare Cooper, Clare Miller Watsky, Elliot Insley, and Carolyn Francis. 1998. Neighborhood Parks. In *People Places: Design Guidelines for Urban Open Space*. 2nd ed. C. C. Marcus and C. Francis, eds. Pp. 85–148. New York: Wiley.

McCarthy, Mark. 2000. Social Determinants and Inequalities in Urban Health. *Reviews on Environmental Health* 15:97–108.

Moore, E. O. 1981–1982. A Prison Environment's Effect on Health Care Service Demands. *Journal of Environmental Systems* 11:17–34.

Northridge, Mary E., and Elliott Sclar. 2003. A Joint Urban Planning and Public Health Framework: Contributions to Health Impact Assessment. *American Journal of Public Health* 93(1):118–121.

Oldenburg, Ray. 1989. *The Great Good Place: Cafés, Coffee Shops, Community Centers, Beauty Parlors, General Stores, Bars, Hangouts and How They Get You through the Day*. New York: Paragon House.

Oldenburg, Ray. 2000. *Celebrating the Third Place: Inspiring Stories about the "Great Good Places" at the Heart of Our Communities*. New York: Marlowe & Company.

Orfield, Myron. 2002. *American Metropolitics: The New Suburban Reality*. Washington, D.C.: Brookings Press.

Sallis, James F., Adrian Baumann, and Michael Pratt. 1998. Environmental and Policy Interventions to Promote Physical Activity. *American Journal of Preventive Medicine* 15:379–397.

Seppanen, Olli, and W. J. Fisk. 2002. Association of Ventilation System Type with SBS Symptoms in Office Workers. *Indoor Air* 12(2):98–112.

Skjaeveland, Oddvar, and Tommy Garling. 1997. Effects of Interactional Space on Neighboring. *Journal of Environmental Psychology* 17:181–198.

Stitt, Fred. 1999. *The Ecological Design Handbook*. New York: McGraw-Hill.

Szczygiel, Bonj, and Robert Hewitt. 2000. Nineteenth-Century Medical Landscapes: John H. Rauch, Frederick Law Olmsted, and the Search for Salubrity. *Bulletin of the History of Medicine* 74:708–734.

Takano, T., K. Nakamura, and M. Watanabe. 2002. Urban Residential Environments and Senior Citizens' Longevity in Megacity Areas: The Importance of

Walkable Green Spaces. *Journal of Epidemiology and Community Health* 56:913–918.

Thomson, H., M. Petticrew, and M. Douglas. 2003. Health Impact Assessment of Housing Improvements: Incorporating Research Evidence. *Journal of Epidemiology and Community Health* 57:11–16.

Tuan, Yi-Fu. 1977. *Space and Place: The Perspective of Experience*. Minneapolis: University of Minnesota Press.

Ulrich, Roger S. 1984. View through a Window May Influence Recovery from Surgery. *Science* 224:420–422.

Ulrich, Roger S. 1993. Biophilia, Biophobia, and Natural Landscapes. In *The Biophilia Hypothesis*. Stephen R. Kellert and Edward O. Wilson, eds. Pp. 73–137. Washington, D.C.: Island Press.

Ulrich, Roger S., and D. L. Addoms. 1981. Psychological and Recreational Benefits of a Residential Park. Journal of Leisure Research 13:43–65.

U.S. Environmental Protection Agency. 1994. *Indoor Air Pollution: An Introduction for Health Professionals*. Washington: EPA.

U.S. Surgeon General. 1996. *Physical Activity and Health: A Report of the Surgeon General*. Atlanta, Ga.: Department of Health and Human Services.

Walter, Eugene Victor. 1988. *Placeways: A Theory of the Human Environment*. Chapel Hill: University of North Carolina Press.

Wargocki, P., J. Sundell, W. Bischof, G. Brundrett, P. O. Fanger, and F. Gyntelberg. 2002. Ventilation and Health in Non-Industrial Indoor Environments: Report from a European Multidisciplinary Scientific Consensus Meeting (EUROVEN). *Indoor Air* 12(2):113–128.

Whyte, William H. 1980. *The Social Life of Small Urban Spaces*. New York: Conservation Foundation.

Whyte, William H. 1988. *City: Rediscovering the Center*. New York: Doubleday.

Wilson, Edward O. 1984. *Biophilia: The Human Bond with Other Species*. Cambridge, Mass.: Harvard University Press.

Wilson, Edward O. 1993. Biophilia and the Conservation Ethic. In *The Biophilia Hypothesis*. Stephen R. Kellert and Edward O. Wilson, eds. Pp. 31–41. Washington, D.C.: Island Press.

Wilson, William Julius. 1987. *The Truly Disadvantaged: The Inner City, the Underclass, and Public Policy*. Chicago: University of Chicago Press.

12

Preference, Restoration, and Meaningful Action in the Context of Nearby Nature

Rachel Kaplan and Stephen Kaplan

Images of cities are more likely to emphasize the vibrancy and excitement, the noise, crowds, and fast pace than tranquility. Yet cities also have tranquil places. Where might such places be? Perhaps beneath the canopy of a large tree, a vest pocket park, a colorful garden, or along a riverside trail.

More than likely, such respites are nature places. They are unlikely to be nature on a grand scale or what would qualify as "nature" for a wilderness purist. Far from being untouched by humans, urban nature is at the mercy of people. But at the same time, people are at the mercy of such nature. Nature plays a vital role in their lives. People are often passionate about the bits of nature they find nearby. They nurture it, defend it, and mourn its loss. Why such strong emotions?

These same passionate people are, after all, the source of enormous environmental degradation. They might own gas-guzzling vehicles that make their cities less healthy places. They might choose to live in suburbs that use up precious agricultural land and require endless hours for daily commuting. They might vote for candidates whose priorities are contrary to a healthy, sustainable world.

But nature, and especially nearby nature, seems to be a different matter. What is it about such nature places that can make this strong difference in human lives? We offer some answers to this puzzle in the form of a conceptual framework that examines the relation between environmental factors and people's behavior. We call the framework the reasonable person model (RPM) because we think it is useful in explaining the circumstances that help bring out the best in people (R. Kaplan, 2004; S. Kaplan 2000; S. Kaplan and Kaplan 2003). As it turns out, even small nature places can help do just that.

The RPM also speaks to health impacts in a broader context. Traditionally, discussion of health has focused on disease. The health issues one hears about all the time concern the big killers (heart disease, cancer, stroke) and numerous dreaded symptoms. Concomitants of urban life and dependence on the auto can be seen in the steady rise of diabetes, obesity, and asthma (Frank, Engelke, and Schmid 2003; Frumkin 2002). Good health, however, is not merely the lack of major illness. It seems inappropriate to consider people as healthy when they are exceptionally irritable, feel impaired in making plans, are unusually error prone, and feel less competent than usual. Though not qualifying as symptomatic of major illness, such behaviors and reactions can range from the mild to the dangerous, from needing a rest to violence. From the RPM perspective, good health is about feeling effective, being clear-headed, and resilient. Furthermore, health extends beyond personal well-being to community well-being. If people are less frustrated, they are more likely to be civil with each other, to be cooperative and helpful, and perhaps even to take care of their environment (S. Kaplan and Kaplan 2003).

In the next section, we provide a brief discussion of each of the RPM domains, with particular emphasis on the way this framework can help identify what lies behind the benefits offered by nature experiences. We then apply the model to other chapters in the book, as well as other research concerning the psychological benefits of nearby nature. In the context of the RPM, these examples facilitate an understanding and appreciation of the broad spectrum of benefits that nature provides, as well as the diverse settings and activities that make them possible. In the final section, we explore some implications of the model. In particular, we look at the theme of reconnecting from two perspectives: the context of nearby nature and the domains of the RPM framework. There is ample need for reconnection; fortunately, while the benefits it promises are substantial, the changes are manageable.

The Reasonable Person Model

The dominant economic paradigm would have us believe that people are rational actors—that they know all the possible choices and weigh all their costs and benefits in reaching decisions. This is not the place to expound on the many flaws of the rationality position (Shafir and LeBoeuf 2002). Rather, suffice it to say that the intention of the RPM is to point to a more appropriate framework for understanding humans, their actions, and convictions. We come to this framework from a cognitive, information-processing perspective, integrated with the study of human needs, and enriched by many other disciplines and viewpoints. We see humans as active organisms, devoid of the strength, speed, or size of others in the animal kingdom, making their way in an uncertain world (S. Kaplan and Kaplan 1989a). In contrast to the rationality position, we see people as having far less than perfect knowledge and insufficient capacity to weigh all possible alternatives, yet having deep concern about a wide range of issues extending far beyond the maximization of gain.

People can be reasonable; they often are. But as we all know, there is much that people do that is short of reasonable. They can be destructive, irrational, uncooperative, and quite unpleasant to be near. Interestingly, the same person might be reasonable one moment and difficult the next. And that may well be true of all of us. The RPM posits that the difference is often in the environment, and more specifically, that people are more reasonable when the environment supports their basic informational needs (S. Kaplan and Kaplan 1982, 1989a).

Before we turn to informational needs, we should make clear what we mean by information. Information, much more than money, is the stuff that runs our lives. Humans are information-based creatures (R. Kaplan 1995). We yearn for it, we horde it, we are overwhelmed by it, we trade it, we hide it. We ask questions such as "How do I get there?" "What's your point?" "Do you have something cheaper?" While a great deal of our information-rich lives depends on spoken and written material, information is by no means limited to such sources. The environment conveys information. We examine it to learn what is going on. The objects in the environment provide information (e.g., a park, a busy intersection, a gated community). The arrangement of the objects also provides information. For example, finding one's way in a subdivision of cul-de-sacs or in one based on a grid system can be a very different experience; a trail system with no landmarks can be discouraging, and obstructed views can increase fear and apprehension.

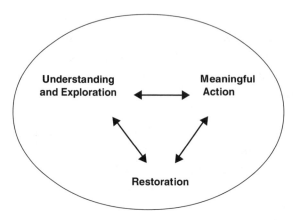

Figure 12.1
Reasonable person model: interrelated domains

The RPM focuses on three domains of informational needs. *Exploration and understanding* are about the dual human needs to make sense and to extend what one already understands. *Restoration* is necessary for maintaining the capacity to respond appropriately to the abundance of information surrounding us. *Meaningful action* concerns the need to participate, to be an active part of the information-rich world around us. We next discuss each of these as a separate domain; in practice, however, they are strongly interrelated. It is hard to act meaningfully without understanding, exploration can facilitate restoration, and being restored can make us more effective in our actions (figure 12.1).

Exploration and Understanding

We came to appreciate the profound role of these two concepts through our research on environmental preference, begun in the 1960s. At that time, as far as we knew, there was no empirical evidence to support what was certainly widely believed—that people prefer natural places. Since our first study that showed this (S. Kaplan, Kaplan, and Wendt 1972), this effect has been a consistent finding across many settings and demographic differences (R. Kaplan and Kaplan 1995). In the present context, it is particularly pertinent that this preference holds not only for glorious, distant, nature places that most of us experience only through glossy

	Understanding	Exploration
Immediate	Coherence	Complexity
Inferred	Legibility	Mystery

Figure 12.2
The preference matrix

books or posters; unspectacular, everyday nearby nature is also highly preferred. Even a tree outside the window, a place to grow a few flowers, or some plants in a courtyard between buildings can serve as "nearby nature." Watching squirrels chase each other, spotting the first robin in spring or a cardinal on a wintry day can all contribute to our well-being.

That is not to say, however, that all nature settings are equally beloved. The research that we and many others conducted led us to have a clearer notion of some of the factors that explain preference. In time, we also came to appreciate that these factors apply not only to scenes, but to many other domains of preference. We have summarized these factors in the preference matrix, shown in figure 12.2 (see R. Kaplan and Kaplan 1995 for fuller discussion).

Understanding and exploration form one axis of the matrix. Understanding is about making sense, about increasing one's sense of familiarity. Sometimes understanding is achieved through formal knowledge or education; more often, it is gained through direct or indirect experience. Consider arriving in a town or a building for the first time with no maps or directions. This can be a daunting and confusing experience. There may be cues, however, that make the experience seem more comfortable and familiar. For example, one may have a sense for where to find lodging, or food, or a particular room for a meeting. Exploration is about negotiating a space (or idea) to find out more about it. Such exploration can take place in the "real world," or virtually, or in one's mind. Brainstorming can be a group-based exploration; planning may involve exploration of a future time or place.

In addition to the identification of understanding and exploration as key issues, the matrix points to a second dimension that affects how we perceive the environment. This involves the degree of inference that is required in judging the situation. Some aspects of the environment are judged almost instantly. The sense that it is overwhelming or chaotic comes very fast (i.e., a lack of coherence), conveying difficulty in making sense of the situation. The judgment that "there is nothing going on," and therefore nothing to explore (i.e., a lack of complexity), also tends to be made very rapidly. While such seemingly immediate judgments may prove false if one has substantial exposure to the setting, the initial reaction can certainly make us more reluctant to find out. For example, finding oneself disoriented in a particular environment, whether an unfamiliar forest or a math class, may not only motivate the decision to leave if one can but also to avoid the setting in the future.

Other aspects of our judgment are based on inference of what might be. For example, one might be fearful in a particular environment if one anticipates difficulty in being able to find one's way to a destination and back again (i.e., legibility). Other situations suggest that our exploration will be rewarded by new opportunities or information, motivating us to explore further (i.e., mystery). A good storyteller can hold us spellbound by the expectation of what is yet to come, signaling that the trip will be safe while at the same time adventurous. Similarly, a meandering path in the woods can compel us to keep going to find out what lies beyond each bend. With sufficient distinctive places along the path, we can feel secure that we will be able to find our way back.

Even very familiar places, for which we have considerable understanding, can continue to invite exploration. Places for which we have a strong attachment are likely to be comfortable because we know them intimately, while at the same time they offer new insights and opportunities for further exploring. A personal or community garden is unlikely to become boring; though highly familiar, it can offer endless fascination and exploration.

Restoration

Time comes when one feels worn out. Managing all the information we humans crave, as well as the abundance of information bombarding us that we did not seek, can lead to feeling overwhelmed and exhausted. Strangely, when we think we could not handle even one more bit of information, there are some kinds of information that are not bothersome and perhaps even enjoyable. While some environments can be the cause of our distress, others can provide the solution.

One way to explain this puzzle is provided by attention restoration theory (S. Kaplan 1995, 2001), which views attention as playing a key role not only in why mental fatigue occurs, but also in how restorative environments can foster recovery. Critical to this analysis is differentiating between two kinds of attention. One of these, which is called on much of the time, is attention that requires effort (e.g., listening to a challenging lecture, intently pursuing a task, juggling concurrent demands). The necessities of acquiring, managing, delivering, and remembering information generally take effort. We need to focus our attention on what we are doing, despite information surrounding us that may be irrelevant or actually be interfering. There are times when we need to hear what others are saying, while remembering what we do or do not want to let them know. We may need to relay information without letting what is on our mind get in the way. Humans are capable of sustaining a great deal of such focus, of using their directed attention. Sooner or later, however, the ability to direct attention becomes fatigued. While such mental fatigue often goes by the popular term of feeling "stressed out," there are important distinctions between reduced attentional capacity and stress in general. The distinctions are particularly pertinent in considering ways to regain directed attention.

Recovering from fatigued directed attention calls on the other kind of attention. This second kind requires no effort; in fact, it is often difficult to turn off. Consider activities and places that are fascinating and compelling, times when one feels in tune with one's surroundings and the demands of the moment. Paying attention to a waterfall or indoor aquarium is distinctly different from paying attention to an uninspired speaker. (It is possible that the concept of the sublime emphasized by Rotenberg in chapter 9 is a particularly intense instance of the fascination concept.) Exploring things that are intriguing usually seems effortless. The attention restoration theory posits that time spent in such effortless pursuits and contexts is an important factor in the recovery of mental fatigue. In other words, restoration involves activities and settings that are compelling and allow directed attention to rest.

The natural environment has a particularly strong restorative effect for many people. Nature places are often sought for respites, for regaining one's capacity to face demands. Particularly telling is the role of nature places at times of loss or grief. It is noteworthy that as a consequence of the September 11, 2001, terrorist attacks, Congress requested that the U.S. Forest Service create the Living Memorials Project—places that "bring people together and create living memorials to foster healing" (U.S. Forest Service 2003). As the Web site attests, these projects capture both the physical and symbolic power of nature as a restorative force. Special nature places, places for which we have a strong attachment, are particularly likely to hold such restorative properties.

Meaningful Action

Information is a source of insight, intrigue, and innovation. It can be enriching and wondrous. There are many times, however, when it is none of these. The daily news provides an all-too-common example of an abundance of information that leaves us helpless, and possibly even hopeless. We learn about events of great significance and major consequences, yet the opportunities for our doing anything about them are minimal. Feelings of helplessness, not surprisingly, are harmful and demoralizing (Seligman 1975).

By contrast, opportunities for exercising one's effectiveness serve as important examples of meaningful action. Many of the chapters in part I of this book offer rich imagery of transformations through meaningful action. Such actions may involve livelihood or food security, struggles for justice, or efforts to build community. By achieving and using competence, one is less likely to feel helpless and worthless. One is also likely to gain the respect of others and feel that one is contributing to a larger goal.

Both the experience of competence and achieving respect are profoundly important sources of meaningful action. At the same time, meaningful actions may be of modest scale yet of great symbolic and even practical importance. Thus, while one can gain great satisfaction from participating in a stewardship activity, participating by voting can also be meaningful and have an important impact. Here too "nature" seems to be a particularly meaningful domain to urban people. This is exemplified not only by activities that bring us in contact with natural places, but even by a considerably more remote involvement with the natural environment. Across the nation for many years, ballot initiatives to protect open space and natural places have been remarkably successful. A 70 percent success rate is reported for conservation-related initiatives between 1998 and 2002. Despite a weak economy and an off-year election, the voting record in November 2003 was even more positive: 83 percent of 77 state and local ballots received positive votes (Trust for Public Land 2003). These outcomes speak clearly not only to the public's awareness of nature's role in their lives, but also to the potential meaningfulness of an apparently remote form of participation.

Special places, places for which we have a strong attachment, are likely to be ones where we are invested in meaningful action. They are places where we can feel needed, where our participation can contribute to their long-term viability.

Nearby Nature and the Reasonable Person Model

We began by pointing to the special role played by nature that is nearby, even if not grand or vast. We then suggested that the RPM might offer some insights about why these bits of nature can play such an important role. The RPM, in turn, builds on three interrelated themes that articulate ways in which the environment can be supportive of human informational needs. In this section we examine a series of studies and examples that support the importance of nearby nature in the context of the RPM.

Nature's role in human well-being seems sweeping in its reach. The connection to nature places and their health impacts cuts across numerous demographic categories, as seen by the many examples in previous chapters. These and scores of other examples provide a cumulative wealth of insight and evidence (Frumkin 2001). At the same time, however, support from systematic research is essential (see chapter 11), not only because of its attention to randomized procedures to preclude threats to internal validity, but equally because of the need for careful conceptualization and construct validity (R. Kaplan 1996). Many of the studies we discuss here are commendable for speaking to these issues. They are striking for supporting the strong power of engagement with nature while focusing on distinctly different populations. In discussing each of these, we highlight the relation of the results to the RPM framework.

Illusory Passivity

Connecting with nature evokes images of doing something in a natural setting. There is a vast range of activities that involve moving through a natural setting (e.g., walking, biking, canoeing), or modifying the setting (e.g., gardening, clearing brush), or somehow partaking of the setting (e.g., camping, nature photography). Some forms of connecting with nature, however, take place without being in it. Pictures of nature are everywhere—on walls, in books and magazines, in commercials, even in our mind's eye. In contrast to nature activities, such indirect contact with nature might be considered passive. But the consequences of the mental activity that accompanies such seeming inactivity can be enriching and far-reaching, suggesting that passivity is a poor way to conceptualize these nature opportunities.

In this section, we consider two areas of research that have documented surprising consequences of connecting with nature, although the contact with nature was largely indirect or passive. The two areas also have in common that the "nature" is hardly grand or awesome, unlikely to be seen as a picture on a wall, in a magazine, or as part of an advertisement. Finally, though the consequences are significant, they often go unnoticed.

View from the Window   One of the most pervasive interactions people have with nearby nature comes from looking out the window. It is hardly surprising that many of us find windowless environments to be problematic. There is substantial research to document the psychological benefits of having nature in the view from the window (R. Kaplan 2001). As highlighted in the previous chapter by Frumkin, this has been shown in a variety of settings, including not only workplaces and residential settings (including dormitories), but even hospitals and prisons (R. Kaplan, Kaplan, and Ryan 1998). For example, nature views have been found to be related to prisoners' reduced needs for medical attention, speedier recovery following surgery, greater patience and sense of health in the workplace, and a reduced sense of being distracted and disorganized.

The striking results of these studies are not that people like to have windows, but that what they can see out the window makes a difference. The view out the window can provide a respite from what one is doing. Such brief, micro-restorative experiences occur when there is something compelling or fascinating to look at—drawing on the effortless kind of attention and giving the fatigued directed attention a moment to recover. Nature elements serve this purpose well. Even a single tree outside the window can be a special place, a whole little world for that moment. Not only does this provide a chance for directed attention to recover, it also provides opportunities for exploring that little world and feeling connected to it. When viewed from the window, these connections to the natural world may occur in very short bursts of time, but they nonetheless lead to effects that are positive and substantial.

Public Housing and Some Trees   Sullivan (chapter 10) presents findings from a series of studies that compared public housing residents who differed with respect to the availability of nearby nature. These studies, noteworthy examples of sound experimental research (e.g., de facto random assignment) and careful conceptualization of outcome measures, have shown the following advantages for those whose residence has a few trees and lawn adjacent to the high-rise dwelling:

• More social interaction among youth and adults (Coley, Kuo, and Sullivan 1997)

• Greater sense of community among older adults (Kweon, Sullivan, and Wiley 1998)

• Greater sense of safety and feeling of belonging (Kuo et al. 1998)

• Better ability to cope with challenges (Kuo 2001)

• Lower levels of fears, fewer incivilities, and less aggressive and violent behavior (Kuo and Sullivan 2001a)

• Less chronic mental fatigue, which means less likely to be impulsive and irritable (Kuo and Sullivan 2001b)
• Greater self-discipline and ability to concentrate on the part of girls (Taylor, Kuo, and Sullivan 2002)

Who would have ever imagined such a wide range of positive outcomes related to the availability of some trees amid the desolate concrete and asphalt where some 12,000 people live along a three-mile stretch consisting of 28 identical buildings? As Kuo, Sullivan, and their associates have demonstrated, the living conditions of these extremely poor African Americans have a devastating impact on directed attention. With so little to alleviate their mental fatigue, the presence of even a little bit of nature offers opportunities for restoration.

At the same time, the trees and lawn are a magnet, an oasis in an urban desert. These areas draw others from the building, and gradually residents get to know their neighbors. With greater familiarity come, greater trust and a stronger sense of community. There is increased understanding of the social fabric and exploration of social patterns. The greater ability to concentrate further enables these residents (and the girls especially) to take stock of their lives, face peer pressures, and cope with the challenges that surround them.

Greater civility and less violence are strong evidence of increased reasonableness. As these findings suggest, these consequences of nature experiences go far beyond recovery from fatigue as the term is usually used. The benefits extend to what often are considered moral issues, suggesting the need for rethinking the conditions that support prosocial behavior (S. Kaplan 2004).

Active Restoration

The studies we highlight in this section involve active engagement with nature in three distinctly different contexts and by diverse groups. AIDS caregivers (Canin 1992), like so many other caregivers, are likely to neglect their own needs as their lives are immersed in the more intense needs of others. Cancer patients (Cimprich 1993) have more than their physical health to contend with; the illness takes a substantial toll on their psychological energy and outlook. The young children Grahn et al.

(1997) studied can hardly be expected to appreciate that time in nature is quite different from time spent playing elsewhere, yet they too showed the remarkable benefits of nature activities. These and other studies have shown that nature activities can be restorative and at the same time enhance competence.

Caregiving and Self-Care   Caregiving can be exhausting and emotionally draining. Canin's (1992) study, including 200 AIDS caregivers, looked at factors that might help explain why some of these volunteers are more resilient and others feel more burned out. From an RPM perspective, these categories are closely linked to the fatigue of directed attention and the need for its recovery. Canin did in fact find that the two groups show different patterns in their orientation toward leisure, and thus to facilitating the recovery process. The participants in her study who rated themselves as functioning more effectively (based on an 18-item scale Canin called "Robust Functioning") were significantly more likely to have positive Restorative Evaluation (10-item scale including feeling "tranquil," "gained some perspective on things"). Those who showed more Caregiver Fatigue (11 items including "overburdened," "work frustrating") were more likely to indicate guilt and anxiety about taking free time.

  Canin's work also explored the patterns of leisure activities that her study participants engaged in by asking them to indicate how frequently they pursued each of 36 activities. Factor analysis yielded eight types of activities. Of particular interest was a nature-based pattern, which consisted of two items: "walking, hiking, running, boating, biking in a nature area" and "watching t.v." Although its reliability coefficient is rather low, the juxtaposition of these two items as an empirically generated factor is interesting in its own right, offering some support for the antithetical aspects of these two types of pursuits. Furthermore, those scoring high on the "active nature" factor (i.e., spending more time in nature activities and less watching TV) scored significantly higher on the Robust Functioning measure.

Cancer and Mental Fatigue   Cimprich's (1993; Cimprich and Ronis 2003) studies are notable for their experimental rigor as well as the insights they provide about the restorative benefits of time spent in nature for postsurgery cancer patients. Using a battery of measures to assess the attentional capacity of the study participants, the earlier study showed that those in the experimental group (committed to carry out at least three 20-minute restorative activities each week) showed significantly greater recovery from directed attention fatigue than the control group. The experimental group participants in time showed superior performance on the cognitive tasks Cimprich included and also reported higher levels of "executive functioning" (e.g., ability to make plans and carry them out effectively). While Cimprich provided a long list of potential restorative activities, the study participants tended to engage in nature activities such as gardening or walking. In terms of the RPM, Cimprich's work provides strong support for the restorative effects of nature experiences for cancer patients, an illness recognized for its concomitant fatigue (Lesage and Portenoy 2002; Mock 2001).

The research results are pertinent to each of the domains of RPM. Cimprich's research was motivated in part by the puzzling consequences often found in association with cancer. Patients who are considered to be well on their way to recovery report difficulties in social relationships, performing everyday tasks, and returning to work (Meyerowitz, Sparks, and Spears 1979). Cimprich hypothesized that these difficulties were due to mental fatigue. Participants in the experimental group showed recovery from mental fatigue and, in addition, went back to work sooner and were more willing to initiate new projects (Cimprich 1990)—behaviors that are indicative of not feeling helpless and of pursuing personally meaningful actions, such as self-improvement and self-discovery.

The Very Young and Nature   Grahn et al. (1997) compared the attentional capacity of kindergartners attending schools that differed with respect to the opportunities the children had for outdoor play. One school had a traditional urban playground with play equipment, while the other school provided access to a forested natural environment. The attention measures showed the expected results, with access to nature accompanied by a greater ability to concentrate.

This study, as well as the work of Fjørtoft, shows that children attending kindergartens with greater emphasis on the natural setting perform significantly better on a variety of motor fitness measures, including balance and coordination. Fjørtoft attributes these differences to the diverse affordances provided by the natural landscape and the "versatile play in a stimulating playscape" (2001:116). From the perspective of the RPM, the natural settings provide extensive opportunities for exploration and foster greater competence. It may also be the case that these settings make it easier for children to find the balance they need between times with their peers and time by themselves.

Community-Based Nature Activities
Many of the examples described in earlier chapters in this book involve nature in the context of a community. To describe these as social activities, however, emphasizes only one dimension of the impacts of each of these projects. Other strong themes that pervade many such community-based nature activities include learning and achieving greater understanding and competence, empowerment that comes from participation, and making a difference. These activities are particularly significant because of their positive effects for many individuals, their community, and even beyond the bounds of the project itself.

Learning and Teaching   Barlett's discussion of the Piedmont Project in chapter 2 offers an example of the many themes of community-based nature activities and of the RPM as well. Although the project involved substantial concentration, and hence effort, for the participants, the daily walks provided a time for restoration. The walks also introduced the participants to places they could return to for restorative experiences in the future.

The project included many dimensions of meaningful action. Participants started to be more concerned about their personal lifestyles, and some became more active in environmental issues. The single most striking aspect of meaningful action comes in the successful realization of the project's underlying intention of enhancing the environmental curriculum. Such actions depend on the participants' increased sense of competence to organize new courses and change their existing ones.

These curricular changes could hardly have been achieved without the many forms of understanding and exploration that occurred during the workshop and were stimulated by it. Not only did the participants feel sufficiently confident to offer new courses, but they also ventured into new ways of teaching. Their new explorations thus ramified, generating greater understanding and exploration on the part of many others.

The Piedmont Project, as Barlett illustrates, had connections to community on many levels. Workshop participants discovered that the plant species they were so intent on identifying had implicit bonds to the university and the city. They also formed communities based on sharing meaningful experiences that could lead to future joint explorations. In addition, the participants found new ways to connect to both their existing local community and a larger community that shared their concern for the future of living systems.

Stewardship and Participation   The desire for exploration and for learning new things that was strong in the Piedmont Project is also evident in research on environmental stewardship (chapter 7). Not only are new volunteers eager to learn (Grese, Kaplan, and Ryan 2000), but long-term volunteers continue to derive these benefits as well (Ryan, Kaplan, and Grese 2001). In addition, stewardship volunteers indicate that their involvement gives them a "feeling of peace of mind" and a chance to reflect, qualities that suggest that the restoration applies to the volunteers as well as to the ecosystems they are protecting (Grese et al. 2000).

Stewardship activities are necessarily specific to a place. At the same time, for many devoted environmental stewards, volunteering reflects a deep conviction about restoring nature; their attachment may be as much for the cause as the specific place. For them, neither the learning that takes place (understanding and exploration) nor the increased competence and sense of contributing to a larger good depends on place specificity. As Ryan (2000) points out, the volunteers' attachment may be in sharp contrast to the attachment that local users may have for the same place. "Community" may be an important concern for both groups; in the one case, however, it is the community battling the invasives to restore biodiversity (Schroeder 2000), while in the other the relevant community is one's homeplace and its surroundings.

The RPM postulates that people are more reasonable when the environment supports their needs for understanding and exploration, meaningful action, and restoration. The nearby woods where residents take many walks and that are central to their views from home are likely to be supportive of these needs. Some of these residents may not be sensitive to the species growing there or even to the greater density of vegetation beyond their familiar paths. By contrast, the mission of stewards is clearing the invasive species and removing the nonnative trees. Their understanding of appropriate ecosystem management provides a supportive context for the ecological restoration activities. As the Chicago restoration controversy vividly demonstrated, reasonable behavior is undermined when one's world is dramatically changed without warning (Gobster and Hull 2000). Discovering that their nearby, familiar, favored natural spaces have been "destroyed" in the name of authentic reconstruction of forests and prairies with native species was deeply painful for some residents. Central to meaningful action is participation (S. Kaplan and Kaplan 1989b, 2003). This is true not only with respect to the restoration activities, but also for those who will be affected by the changes.

Neighborhood tree planting initiatives offer a somewhat different example of community nature. Austin (2002) used surveys and interviews to learn about the impacts of tree planting projects on vacant lots in 11 Detroit neighborhoods. Prior to the festivities of planting day, these vacant lots were not only blots on the landscape, but were unsafe as well. They were often garbage filled, and their very tall weeds served as good hiding places. The transformation that took place in each of these communities involved more than a physical change (Austin and Kaplan 2003). The presence of an attractive, highly visible location enhanced the community's sense of pride, a result noted by von Hassell in chapter 4 as well. It also provided a place to meet with neighbors and learn of community events. Participation in creating and sustaining a meaningful local resource can enhance personal identity and connectedness, as Lynch and Brusi show in chapter 8. The sense of competence gained from these experiences, moreover, may facilitate further involvement and participation in neighborhood improvement. As was the case for participants in Stuart's therapeutic gardens (chapter 3), daily contact with such treasured local nature places can foster greater self-esteem, trust, and hope.

Gardening and Community   Lewis (1996:54) uses the heading "Growing self-esteem" to tell of similar transformations in a context quite different from the Detroit tree plantings. While also involving inner-city residents, Lewis's story is about a flower competition, sponsored by the New York City Housing Authority, "the largest landlord in the world" (p. 55). As a judge for this competition in the early 1960s, Lewis observed many lovely flower gardens grown by public housing tenants. He found far more remarkable, however, what these efforts yielded in terms of individual and community outcomes. Attempts to protect the gardens from vandalism led to an assortment of creative solutions that brought neighbors together, even permitting a meaningful role for those who might otherwise have been the offenders. The gardeners explored color themes and patterns that extended beyond the garden plot to the building facade behind it. The gardens led to fixing up the surroundings, to creating attractive settings that symbolized better things to come.

The competition has continued for over four decades, now including not only flowers but vegetable gardens and children's theme gardens. Interestingly, more of the entries in the competition are flower than vegetable gardens (228 versus 199 in 2003) (Williams 2003). The tenants' names for their gardens reflect the wealth of intangible benefits that come from their tiny plots—Sweet Success Gardeners, The Neighborhood Garden, Nature's Wonder Garden, New Beginning Garden, Renew Your Spirit Garden, and Love, Care and Respect (chapters 4 and 7 provide similar examples).

Whether on a community plot or at home, gardening has long been a popular outdoor activity. Clearly food production is an important reason for gardening, but many gardens provide colorful testimony that the rewards exceed the produce. Our research on the psychological benefits of gardening documents the diverse satisfactions gardeners obtain from their efforts (R. Kaplan 1973; R. Kaplan and Kaplan 1995). For those who grow food, the tangible benefits are important, but no more important than the restorative qualities of gardening. Feelings of peacefulness and tranquility were the highest-ranking source of satisfaction in a study that included 4,297 gardeners responding to a mailing of the American Horticultural Society membership as well as 240 readers of what was then called *Organic Gardening and Farming* magazine (R. Kaplan and Kaplan 1995).

A very close second in ranking for both samples was a cluster of items that we labeled "Nature fascination." While such fascination clearly reflects the restorative domain of the RPM (i.e., a way to rest directed attention), it is also an example of the other two domains of the framework. Understanding is reflected by items such as "working in the soil" and "close to nature," while "checking to see how the plants are doing" has a strong dose of exploration. The Nature fascination cluster also included an item about liking "the planning involved" in gardening, an indication of meaningful action. (The means for the "peacefulness and quiet" and the "nature fascinations" themes for the two samples were all between 4.2 and 4.5 on a 5-point scale.)

These benefits are equally likely to accrue to the gardeners in the New York City gardening competition and, to varying degrees, to the thousands of individuals who participate in community gardening programs. Community gardening has been described as a movement (Hynes 2002). Glover (2003:192) aptly observes that "community gardens are often more about *community* than they are about gardening." Various writers have described the movement in terms of empowering people; the gardens have the potential to lead members, individually and collectively, to a multitude of activities whose reach is far beyond the plants. They are catalysts, seeds of hope, of success, of brighter futures.

The place focus of community gardens is central to their far-reaching benefits. It is not just any place, but a nature place, and a special nature place in its daily promise of growth and change. It is also an activity-based place, calling for action, responsibility, and nurturing. The activities depend on some knowledge and understanding, and these are often fostered by the stories others tell of their experiences.

While not involving direct participation with gardening, many of these qualities have also been fostered by new ways of relating people to how food is grown. For many urban residents local food has long meant a purchase at a local supermarket. By contrast, Andreatta (chapter 5) and Barham, Lind, and Jett (chapter 6) tell of new patterns and connections to food systems in North Carolina and Missouri, respectively. In Ohio, "Thanksgiving Boxes" containing fresh organic turkeys as well as locally grown seasonal vegetables and herbs have served to link farmers and consumers through food, increased awareness, and the spiritual bond of the holiday. Carol Goland (2002), director of O.U.R. Food, has also orchestrated farm tours, learning circles, courses for undergraduates at Denison University, and other networking opportunities to foster understanding and exploration of local food systems.[1] A national conference hosted at Denison University in 2001, "Farming: People, Land and Community" launched a magazine by the same name.[2] The magazine has become a rich source of information on meaningful actions that lead to more sustainable agriculture. As with community gardens, one could hardly find better examples of the many relationships among the RPM domains.

Reconnecting

The Power of Nature

Many of the studies and examples we have discussed, as well as others throughout this book, demonstrate the multifaceted power of nearby nature in the urban context. These findings are noteworthy for their effects across a great variety of activities and very different kinds of "nature." The activities can be solitary or with others, of long or short duration, planned or by chance. Some forms of involvement, like looking out the window, are physically passive yet can lead to intense mental activity and reflection. Other activities may be physically demanding, such as removing invasives. Some require extensive knowledge; others need no special training.

The findings of these nature-based studies are particularly encouraging given the magnitude of their impact relative to their modest financial requirements. The view of a single tree from the window can bring restorative moments to many people, many times each day. The chance to engage in stewardship activities can lead to learning new skills and meeting people. The opportunity to grow some flowers can help people's sense of personal competence and their trust in their neighbors. Taking walks can build psychological health. Nearby nature has the capacity to promote reasonable behavior, foster community, and bring joy to people's lives.

Yet despite all these benefits and values, the diversity of ways of providing nearby nature opportunities and the high return on investment, many people rarely, if ever, connect with nature. In some cases, this is because they do not seek nature opportunities despite acknowledging the benefits they would bring. For others, lack of knowledge of local resources may preclude their seeking opportunities. Unfortunately an all-too-common reason stems from the absence of nature places that are within ready access. Regardless of the reason, for many of these people, the failure to reconnect with nature may represent an unrealized opportunity to escape a life of "quiet desperation." Approaches to these different circumstances call for a variety of solutions. In the next section we examine some ways that the RPM might prove useful.

Reconnecting with Reasonableness
The theme of this book—reconnecting—may be appropriate not only with respect to our relationship with nature, but in terms of many other reasonableness-supporting aspects of life. From this perspective, the resurgence in interest in reconnecting with nature may be an expression of the yearning for a return to basic values and needs. The RPM may provide some assistance and structure in identifying where things have gone awry and how they could be corrected.

While information is central to reasonableness, it is also the source of much that prevents it. Many aspects of communication, notably the media, provide all-too-common examples of costly changes that have resulted in a less humane environment. In principle, the media provide a source of useful information wherein people can explore aspects of their world not otherwise apparent to them and achieve an increased understanding. Postman (1985) provides a perceptive analysis of how the role of media has shifted; in colonial times, it was a source of useful information, while in our contemporary situation, the emphasis is on entertainment. This has led to a focus on unusual, amazing, and disturbing events gathered from all corners of the earth. In contrast to the information in early American newspapers, which was local, relevant, and useful, the new emphasis is on things that most people can do nothing about. There is thus a growing sense of both helplessness and being in a world that is dangerous and out of control, since there is an oversampling of the disturbingly fascinating as different media compete with each other. The resulting sense of helplessness is the opposite of the meaningful action that people long to participate in.

The explosion of opportunities to experience mass entertainment has had other consequences as well. Families once routinely ate dinner together and shared the experiences of the day. Participation in creating one's own entertainment was once more common, as were times when people talked with each other rather than watching television together. Interestingly, in Canin's (1992) study of what was restorative and pre-ventive of burnout in AIDS caregivers, "Quiet activities" (listening to music, reading for pleasure, and spending quiet time with family or friends) was second only to active nature experiences as a positive factor. Watching television, by contrast, was the strongest negative factor. In other words, commercial entertainment has contributed to the under-mining of restoration and meaningful action, as well as understanding and exploration.

Even when such undermining effects of modernist culture (Ray and Anderson 2000) are clear, breaking away from these patterns can be enormously difficult. They tend to get in the way of time in nature and other restorative activities, leading to mental fatigue. The irony here is that breaking away requires the very mental resource that has been undermined. Despite this substantial hurdle, the actual changes required are generally small—spending time outdoors instead of time as a couch potato, reading instead of shopping. But making the changes requires an appreciation of their benefits, and since these may be subtle and delayed in effect, they are easily overlooked. A little bit of record keeping can be very useful as a way to track the positive effects. Once acknowledged, these benefits need to be taken seriously.

Results of a recent survey commissioned by Hallmark (Gaffen 2003) showed that a vast majority of those queried "feel refreshed, happy, and healthy" after they have spent time outdoors. And while survey partici-pants indicated that they preferred outdoor to indoor activities, they spent less than 40 minutes outdoors a day. The primary reason given for not acting on their preference was lack of time. Given the amount of time Americans are reported to spend watching television, this pattern is, to say the least, troublesome. Herzog's laboratory study showed remarkably strong parallels. Participants were asked about what to do when one is feeling fatigued and needs to be alert for a coming activity or event. When asked about what they would suggest to a friend "that would restore the ability to work effectively" (2002:298), their advice was that the person should spend time in outdoor activities. When asked what *they* would do under the same circumstances, they listed such activities as watching television and going to a movie. Their reflections about their own behavior certainly correspond to anecdotal observations: people know what is good for them but they do not do it and *know* that they are not doing it.

One means of achieving the benefits of time outdoors is to integrate it with activities that tap people's desire to be purposive and useful. The purpose can take many forms, such as walking to work or running an errand (as noted by Frumkin in chapter 11), or a sufficiently compelling health threat that leaves no doubt of the meaningfulness of the activity, or a social contract that provides a sense of obligation to another person or group. Involvement as a volunteer provides an excellent context for such purpose and meaning. "Helper's high," coined by Luks and Payne (1991), refers to the "rush of good feelings" that can be brought on by volunteering. Luks (2003) discusses several studies that show that volunteers not only report increased self-worth, but reduced stress and a sense of calm. Presumably, volunteering in the context of nature-based activities, though pursued for reasons that may differ from the personal contact Luks emphasizes, would be an effective way of obtaining such restorative benefits. For those who acknowledge the benefits of nature but cannot get themselves to engage in it, nature-based volunteering might provide a valuable option.

Volunteer activities may also provide an interesting way to connect with nature for those who are not aware of local nature options. Seeking a place for taking a walk entails a very different quest from learning of ways to help out in the community garden. Individuals who may not explore the availability of nature places may nonetheless be enthusiastic about opportunities to be helpful and may have time on their hands that they wish to use meaningfully.

From the perspective of the RPM, the vulnerable status of community gardens is particularly shortsighted. They frequently lack permanence, being viewed as a temporary use of vacant land (Breslav 1991; Hall 1996). Urban planners more readily recognize the need for open space or parks than for these microcosms of activity that can be catalysts for building community, self-sufficiency, and a host of other benefits for the economically disadvantaged.

The RPM domains also provide a useful framework at the organizational level. Some leaders are intuitively aware of factors that make the experiences of group members more satisfying. Successful leadership, however, is no more ensured in community efforts than in any organization. Groups struggling to sustain volunteer participation might find greater success if they understood their members' desire to learn, to be asked for their input, and to be reminded of the meaningfulness of their activities. Being able to identify the factors that enhance reasonableness with greater confidence may make their implementation more likely.

As it turns out, there are many relatively straightforward ways to bring out the best in people. People are uncomfortable when they fail to understand their world and frustrated when they have no opportunities to explore; at the same time, they are eager to be listened to and to be given a chance to be helpful. With attention to these conditions, and nearby places for respites from pressures and demands, the better side of all of us is more likely to emerge. As we have seen, a great variety of nature-related places and activities can be exceptionally effective in meeting these human needs. The multitude of evidence and examples provided in these pages will, we hope, be an inspiration for increasing support and extending the reach of nature opportunities, as well as for fostering other activities that bring exploration and understanding, meaningful action, and restoration back to their rightful role at the center of both civic and family life.

Acknowledgments

We are grateful for the Cooperative Agreements with the U.S. Forest Service, North Central Forest Research Station, Urban Forestry Project, that have funded different aspects of the work discussed here.

Notes

1. For the Web site of O.U.R. Food, go to http://www.our-food.org.
2. For the conference Web site, go to http://www.denison.edu/enviro/farming/.

References

Austin, Maureen E. 2002. Partnership Opportunities in Neighborhood Tree Planting Initiatives: Building from Local Knowledge. *Journal of Arboriculture* 28(4):178–186.

Austin, Maureen E., and Rachel Kaplan. 2003. Identity, Involvement and Expertise in the Inner City: Some Benefits of Tree Planting Projects. In *Identity and the Natural Environment: The Psychological Significance of Nature*. Susan Clayton and Susan Opotow, eds. Pp. 205–225. Cambridge, Mass.: MIT Press.

Breslav, Marc. 1991. The Common Ground of Green Words. *Community Greening Review* 1(1):4–9.

Canin, Lisa H. 1992. Psychological Restoration among AIDS Caregivers: Maintaining Self-Care. Ph.D. dissertation, University of Michigan.

Cimprich, Bernadine. 1990. Attentional Fatigue and Restoration in Individuals with Cancer. Ph.D. dissertation, University of Michigan.

Cimprich, Bernadine. 1993. Development of an Intervention to Restore Attention in Cancer Patients. *Cancer Nursing* 16(2):83–92.

Cimprich Bernadine, and David L. Ronis. 2003. An Environmental Intervention to Restore Attention in Women with Newly Diagnosed Breast Cancer. *Cancer Nursing* 26(4):284–292.

Coley, Rebekah Levine, Frances E. Kuo, and William C. Sullivan. 1997. Where Does Community Grow? The Social Context Created by Nature in Urban Public Housing. *Environment and Behavior* 29(4): 468–494.

Fjørtoft, Ingunn. 2001. The Natural Environment as a Playground for Children: The Impact of Outdoor Play Activities in Pre-Primary School Children. *Early Childhood Education Journal* 29(2):111–117.

Frank, Lawrence D., Peter O. Engelke, and Thomas L. Schmid. 2003. *Health and Community Design: The Impact of the Built Environment on Physical Activity*. Washington, D.C.: Island Press.

Frumkin, Howard. 2001. Beyond Toxicity: Human Health and the Natural Environment. *American Journal of Preventive Medicine* 20(3):234–242.

Frumkin, Howard. 2002. Urban Sprawl and Public Health. *Public Health Reports* 117(3):201–217.

Gaffen, Eileen. 2003. New Survey Reveals Americans' Love of Nature and Lack of Time. http://pressroom.hallmark.com/Bastin_spring_survey.html. Accessed Dec. 10, 2003.

Glover Troy D. 2003. The Story of the Queen Anne Memorial Garden: Resisting a Dominant Cultural Narrative. *Journal of Leisure Research* 35(2):190–212.

Gobster, Paul H., and R. Bruce Hull, eds. 2000. *Restoring Nature: Perspectives from the Social Sciences and Humanities*. Washington, D.C.: Island Press.

Goland, Carol. 2002. Community Supported Agriculture, Food Consumption Patterns, and Member Commitment. *Culture and Agriculture* 24(1):14–25.

Grahn, Patrik, Fredrika Mårtensson, Bodil Lindblad, Paula Nilsson, and Anna Ekman. 1997. *Ute på dagis. Stad & Land #45*. Alnarp, Sweden: Movium, Sveriges Lantbruksuniversitet.

Grese, Robert E., Rachel Kaplan, and Robert L. Ryan. 2000. Psychological Benefits of Volunteering in Stewardship Programs. In *Restoring Nature: Perspectives from the Social Sciences and Humanities*. Paul H. Gobster and R. Bruce Hull, eds. Pp. 265–280. Washington, D.C.: Island Press.

Hall, Diana. 1996. Community Gardens as an Urban Planning Issue. Master's thesis, University of British Columbia.

Herzog, Thomas R. 2002. Perception of the Restorative Potential of Natural and Other Settings. *Journal of Environmental Psychology* 22(3):295–306.

Hynes, H. Patricia. 2002. Urban Gardens and Farms: Community Benefits and Environmental Risks. In *Urban Agriculture: Emerging Opportunities in Science, Education, and Policy: Proceedings of the Symposium*. Tim D. Davis and Victor A. Gibeault, eds. Pp. 97–108. Dallas: Texas A & M University.

Kaplan, Rachel. 1973. Some Psychological Benefits of Gardening. *Environment and Behavior* 5(2):145–152.

Kaplan, Rachel. 1995. Informational Issues: A Perspective on Human Needs and Inclinations. In *Urban Forest Landscapes: Integrating Multidisciplinary Perspectives*. Gordon A. Bradley, ed. Pp. 60–71. Seattle: University of Washington Press.

Kaplan, Rachel. 1996. The Small Experiment: Achieving More with Less. In *Public and Private Places*. Jack L. Nasar and Barbara B. Brown, eds. Pp. 170–174. Edmond, Okla.: Environmental Design Research Association.

Kaplan, Rachel. 2001. The Nature of the View from Home: Psychological Benefits. *Environment and Behavior* 33(4):507–542.

Kaplan, Rachel. 2004. The Social Values of Forests and Trees in Urbanised Societies. In *Forestry Serving Urbanised Societies*. Cecil C. Konijnendijk, Jasper Schipperijn, and Karen H. Hoyer, eds. Pp. 167–178. Vienna, Austria: International Union of Forest Research Organizations.

Kaplan, Rachel, and Stephen Kaplan. 1995 [1989]. *The Experience of Nature: A Psychological Perspective*. Republished by Ann Arbor, Mich.: Ulrich's.

Kaplan, Rachel, Stephen Kaplan, and Robert L. Ryan. 1998. *With People in Mind: Design and Management of Everyday Nature*. Washington, D.C.: Island Press.

Kaplan, Stephen. 1995. The Restorative Benefits of Nature: Toward an Integrative Framework. *Journal of Environmental Psychology* 15(3):169–182.

Kaplan, Stephen. 2000. Human Nature and Environmentally Responsible Behavior. *Journal of Social Issues* 56(3):491–508.

Kaplan, Stephen. 2001. Meditation, Restoration and the Management of Mental Fatigue. *Environment and Behavior* 33(4):480–506.

Kaplan, Stephen. 2004. Some Hidden Benefits of the Urban Forest. In *Forestry Serving Urbanised Societies*. Cecil C. Konijnendijk, Jasper Schipperijn, and Karen H. Hoyer, eds. Pp. 221–231. Vienna, Austria: International Union of Forest Research Organizations.

Kaplan, Stephen, and Rachel Kaplan, eds. 1982 [1978]. *Humanscape: Environments for People*. Ann Arbor, Mich.: Ulrich's.

Kaplan, Stephen, and Rachel Kaplan. 1989a [1982]. *Cognition and Environment: Functioning in an Uncertain World*. Ann Arbor, Mich.: Ulrich's.

Kaplan, Stephen, and Rachel Kaplan. 1989b. The Visual Environment: Public Participation in Design and Planning. *Journal of Social Issues* 45(1):59–86.

Kaplan, Stephen, and Rachel Kaplan. 2003. Health, Supportive Environments, and the Reasonable Person Model. *American Journal of Public Health* 93(9):1484–1489.

Kaplan, Stephen, Rachel Kaplan, and John S. Wendt. 1972. Rated Preference and Complexity for Natural and Urban Visual Material. *Perception and Psychophysics* 12(4):354–356.

Kuo, Frances E. 2001. Coping with Poverty—Impacts of Environment and Attention in the Inner City. *Environment and Behavior* 33(1):5–34.

Kuo, Frances E., and William C. Sullivan. 2001a. Environment and Crime in the Inner City—Does Vegetation Reduce Crime? *Environment and Behavior* 33(3):343–367.

Kuo, Frances E., and William C. Sullivan. 2001b. Aggression and Violence in the Inner City—Effects of Environment via Mental Fatigue. *Environment and Behavior* 33(4):543–571

Kuo, Frances E., William C. Sullivan, Rebekah Levine Coley, and Liesette Brunson. 1998. Fertile Ground for Community: Inner-City Neighborhood Common Spaces. *American Journal of Community Psychology* 26(6):823–851.

Kweon, Byoung-Suk, William C. Sullivan, and Angela R. Wiley. 1998. Green Common Spaces and the Social Integration of Inner-City Older Adults. *Environment and Behavior* 30(6):832–858.

Lesage, Pauline, and Russell K. Portenoy. 2002. Management of Fatigue in the Cancer Patient. *Oncology (New York)* 16(3):373–378, 381.

Lewis, Charles A. 1996. *Green Nature Human Nature: The Meaning of Plants in our Lives*. Urbana: University of Illinois Press.

Luks, Allan. 2003. How Alive Is the Helping Connection? Spirituality and Health. http://www.spiritualityhealth.com/newsh/items/ article/more_5989.html. Accessed Dec. 10, 2003.

Luks, Allan, and Peggy Payne. 1991. *Healing Power of Doing Good: The Health and Spiritual Benefits of Helping Others*. New York: Fawcett.

Meyerowitz, Beth E., F. C. Sparks, and I. K. Spears. 1979 Adjuvant Chemotherapy for Breast Carcinoma: Psychosocial Implications. *Cancer* 43(5):1613–1618.

Mock, Victoria. 2001. Fatigue Management—Evidence and Guidelines for Practice. *Cancer* 92(6):1699–1707 Suppl.

Postman, Neil. 1985. *Amusing Ourselves to Death: Public Discourse in the Age of Show Business*. New York: Viking.

Ray, Paul, and Sherry R. Anderson. 2000. *The Cultural Creatives: How 50 Million People Are Changing the World*. New York: Three Rivers Press.

Ryan, Robert L. 2000. A People-Centered Approach to Designing and Managing Restoration Projects: Insights from Understanding Attachment to Urban Natural Areas. In *Restoring Nature: Perspectives from the Social Sciences and Humanities*. Paul H. Gobster and R. Bruce Hull, eds. Pp. 209–228. Washington, DC: Island Press.

Ryan, Robert L., Rachel Kaplan, and Robert E. Grese. 2001. Predicting Volunteer Commitment in Environmental Stewardship Programmes. *Journal of Environmental Planning and Management* 44(5):629–648.

Schroeder, Herbert W. 2000. The Restoration Experience: Volunteers' Motives, Values, and Concepts of Nature. In *Restoring Nature: Perspectives from the Social Sciences and Humanities*. Paul H. Gobster and R. Bruce Hull, eds. Pp. 247–264. Washington, D.C.: Island Press.

Seligman, Martin E. P. 1975. *Helplessness: On Depression, Development, and Death*. San Francisco: Freeman.

Shafir, Eldar, and Robyn A. LeBoeuf. 2002. Rationality. *Annual Review of Psychology* 53:491–517.

Taylor Andrea Faber, Frances E. Kuo, and William C. Sullivan. 2002. Views of Nature and Self-Discipline: Evidence from Inner City Children. *Journal of Environmental Psychology* 22(1–2):49–63.

Trust for Public Land. 2003. LandVote 2003. http://www.tpl.org/tier3_cdl.cfm?content_item_id=12030&folder_id=2406. Accessed Dec. 10, 2003.

U.S. Forest Service. 2003. Living Memorials Project. http://www.fs.fed.us/na/durham/living_memorials/ about/index.htm. Accessed Dec. 10, 2003.

Williams, Deborah. 2003. 2003 Garden Competition Awards. *New York City Housing Authority Journal* 33 (10): 8. http://www.nyc.gov/html/nycha/pdf/j03octe.pdf. Accessed Dec. 10, 2003.

13

Concluding Remarks: Nature and Health in the Urban Environment

Jules Pretty and Peggy F. Barlett

What effect does the presence of living things around us have on our daily lives? Green vegetation and blue sky can ease a difficult day, and if there is water in the scene, then we tend to like it even more. Much, of course, will depend on what else is important, but for most people around the world, contact with the natural world generally makes us feel good. This idea that the quality of nature in our home neighborhood scene will affect our mental health is not a new one, but it has quite rarely combined with the planning of our urban and rural environments. Still less have we understood the medical and psychological costs of nature estrangement, though we are beginning to understand the costs to us of ecologically unsustainable lifeways.

In this book, the authors have explored the ways in which pioneering groups, seeking a more sustainable relationship to the earth, have reconnected with the natural world and thereby discovered new dimensions of personal and community health. Echoing the patient hours documented by Annie Dillard as she learned the habits of muskrats on Tinker Creek, we have read of the joy and fascination, the individual meaning and motivation, of urban people discovering new avenues for deeper connections to place. As Andy Goldsworthy's art awakens us in his movie *Rivers and Tides* to the ephemeral beauty of currents that can carry a leaf, jostle a marigold, or open a rock cairn, these accounts are part of a wider awakening of a new relationship with the natural world, embodied in sustainability experiments in arenas such as community gardens and forest restoration.

Yet these new threads of experience carry some urgency, given human population and urban growth. Since the advent of the industrial revolution, an increasing number of people have found themselves living in wholly urban settings. Indeed, within the next decade, the number of people in urban areas will exceed those in rural contexts for the first time in human history. In 1960, the total world population was some 3 billion; by 2010 there will be more than 3 billion people dwelling just in urban settlements. What we make of such settings is an urgent task. By definition, an urban setting has less nature than a rural one, and if less green nature regrettably means reduced mental and physical well-being—or at least less opportunity to recover from mental stresses—there is an imperative to provide opportunities for more connection with nature.

Today, concerns about stress and diseases of mental ill health are becoming more common and the costs are enormous. The World Health Organization (2001) estimates that depression and depression-related illness will become the greatest sources of ill health by 2020.[1] This prediction reflects the fact that many other activities, such as smoking, overeating, and high alcohol consumption, are coping mechanisms for depression and have their own serious consequences. Stress is now a major problem for people living in modern societies. Similarly, many of the urgent physical health challenges—obesity, heart disease—are connected to sedentary, indoor urban lifeways.

In most health care systems, the predominant focus for both treatment and expenditure has come to be the people who are ill. The same is also true for our environments: we tend to become concerned only when something important is harmed. Yet the best approach, and the cheapest, is to focus efforts upstream and try to create healthy environments in which people can flourish rather than flounder. Thus, we should be concerned with not just preventing ill health but creating positive health contexts for all. In chapter 12, Rachel Kaplan and Stephen Kaplan point out that contact with nature can promote psychological restoration, offering opportunities for stimulation, fascination, and rest from mental fatigue. Such dimensions of personal well-being can affect community life, as restored individuals are more likely to be cooperative and helpful—perhaps even to take care of the environment around them. They warn that environments without nature contact can leave urban dwellers feeling less competent than usual, being exceptionally irritable, impaired in making plans, or error prone.

The natural settings that help reduce mental fatigue and stress need not be remote wildlands, but can be everyday, often unspectacular nearby places, such as parks, street trees, vacant lots, and backyard gardens (Kaplan, Kaplan, and Ryan 1998). As the chapters of this book demonstrate, contact with nearby nature can foster a clear-headed, resilient, and cooperative individual who can be expected to respond in a reasonable manner to daily challenges. In contrast, a dysfunctional built environment can often be a source of stress and a malign influence over social networks and support mechanisms.

Urban Form, Engagement with Nature, and Social Connections

William Sullivan in chapter 10 and Howard Frumkin in chapter 11 explore ways that building form can strengthen healthy habits, and they call for attention to nearby nature in all urban planning (see also Frumkin, Frank, and Jackson 2004). Problems arising from physical features of the built environment include sick building syndrome caused by materials used in some buildings and ill-designed air-conditioning systems, long-distance commutes to work, and suburban communities with self-contained homes that encourage little contact with neighbors. Positive social features include access to an immediate family environment or extended networks of friends and neighbors, as well as presence of green spaces, meeting places, and opportunities for exercise, all of which lead to improvements in mental, physical, and spiritual well-being (Garreau 1992; Maller et al. 2002; Newman 1980; Pretty and Ward 2001).

Some of the most obvious effects occur when built environments are transformed. After slum clearances, for example, residents gain from improvements in physical assets and services, but lose out when social networks deteriorate and distinctive cultures break down. As Hugh Freeman puts it, such clearances often involve not just the destruction of buildings and even of neighborhoods, but also the destruction of functioning social systems, with characteristic cultures of their own and important social networks that could never be reproduced artificially (1984). One study of social change among the 20,000 people originally settled in the 1920s Dagenham neighborhood in east London found that there were wide variations in sociability according to the make-up of the streets. People living in small, narrow streets and cul-de-sacs had more social connections and reciprocal arrangements than those in wider, busy streets, where few people could get to know their neighbors or describe them as friendly. When these small streets were replaced by large, modern housing developments, these social support networks based on geographical proximity entirely broke down, leading to an atomized community with less buffering capacity for those under stress. At atomized community is less creative and less politically empowered as well.

Another study of a 43-block project in St. Louis, Missouri, built in the mid–1950s to house 12,000 people, found that although residents had a similar number of friends as nonproject dwellers, these seemed to bear little or no relation to the physical proximity of families to each other (Newman 1980). Neighbors had become much more hostile, and the quality of life had fallen, even though individuals were generally satisfied with their own apartments. The problem was that the project offered no common facilities around which neighborly relationships could develop. The space between the blocks was soon called "wasted space" by residents. By 1972, only 18 years after the project had been opened, all the blocks were demolished after years of vacancy rates exceeding 70 percent. Ironically, the design won architectural praise, but only before the people had to live in it (Yancey 1971 in Halpern 1995).

In chapter 10, William Sullivan draws on the anthropology of human origins to argue that as a species, we may be able to survive but not thrive in such barren urban settings. Human environments so radically disconnected from the natural world are a sharp break from the *longue durée* of human evolution. Further research in different countries and contexts would shed light in interesting ways on whether and to what extent different cultural framings of the barren urban neighborhood might affect the negative effects of being cut off from the natural world. Can some kinds of social supports help? How much can steady employment or daily praise ameliorate the effects of a neighborhood of concrete? Sullivan recommends that there be a green infrastructure layer to all urban planning. He and his colleagues at the University of Illinois seek to encourage public officials to provide "nature at every doorstep." The findings of others in this book support this conclusion.

In contrast to studies of social breakdown in urban renewal projects, Susan Stuart (in chapter 3) documents how therapeutic gardens offer emotional respite and moments of restoration, new diet and nutritional benefits, exercise, and opportunities for recreation. The experience of even small gardens in shelters for families suffering from domestic violence suggests that important effects can occur with only short-term contact. Although one might expect battered women to be too highly stressed to connect with the natural world, especially given their brief stays in shelters, the evidence points to the contrary. We see the pleasures of sensory, embodied learning—dirt, smells of the garden, tastes of fresh food—and an enhanced openness to new foods. Even pessimistic staff embraced the therapeutic gardens project and found that they benefited as well. The intersection of the built and natural environment can therefore be restorative or harmful, and therapeutic gardens are a component of urban planning deserving of greater attention.

A healthy urban community includes a supportive web of social relations and trust. Greenspace restoration volunteers appreciate the opportunity to make a difference, working for the benefit of the community, as reported by Robert Ryan and Robert Grese in chapter 7. They become loyal to the sites in which they work and with longer involvement become even more willing to work with others to defend and protect natural areas. While such efforts are never free of conflict or perfectly harmonious, they often build social capital and more vibrant neighborhood life. Efforts to sustain community-supported agriculture or farmers markets may also suffer from challenges but are new ways in which voluntary organizations strengthen face-to-face communities within cities (DeLind 1999; Andreatta 2000).

Such opportunities for civic engagement and social connectedness support well-being by providing a web of social relations for urban residents. In addition to these social benefits, however, there is evidence that a supportive web of social relations supports physical health as well (Baum 1999; House, Landis, and Umberson 1988; Wilkinson 1999). Death rates for individuals with low levels of social integration are higher when facing a stroke or coronary heart disease (Maller et al. 2002:13; Baum 1999). Some research even suggests that the opportunity to walk in parks and to experience nearby nature boosts the body's immune system (Parsons et al. 1998) and is a "vital component of health that has for too long been ignored" (Maller et al. 2003:20; Frumkin 2002a). We hope the chapters here will stimulate further research to elucidate connections between satisfying and supportive urban social life, the built environment, and relationships with the natural world.

Fostering Nature Contact in the City

To enhance opportunities for restoring nature contact within the city, this book documents a range of useful contexts. Chapters 1, 2, 10, 11, and 12 all offer ways of categorizing nature contact, but we highlight here three levels that draw our attention (Pretty 2004):

• Viewing nature, as through a window, in a book, or in a painting
• Being in the presence of usually nearby nature, which is incidental to some other activity, such as walking or cycling to work, reading on a garden seat, or talking to friends in a park
• Active participation and involvement with nature, such as gardening or farming, horseback riding, or tree planting

The View from the Window

The evidence for the benefits of windows comes from both the workplace and home and from traveling to work. Windows in the workplace buffer the stresses of work, and over long periods people with windows have been shown to have fewer illnesses, feel less frustrated and more patient, and express greater enthusiasm for work (Tennessen and Cimprich 1995; Kaplan 2001; Leather et al. 1998; Ulrich 1984). People are better able to think with green views, including university students. Those in offices without windows often compensate by putting up more pictures of landscapes or by keeping indoor plants (Heerwagen and Orians 1993). Those who cannot compensate can respond by becoming more stressed, mentally fatigued, and aggressive. One study of Alzheimer patients in five homes found that those in the three with gardens had significantly lower levels of aggression and violence than those in the two with no gardens (Ulrich 1993). Ulrich also reports on a Swedish psychiatric hospital in which patients over a 15-year period had often complained about damaged paintings on the walls. However, damage was done only to abstract paintings, and there was no recorded attack on any depicting nature and landscapes (Ulrich 1993). At home, the view is equally important. Chapter 10 demonstrates that a little bit of green grass, shrubbery, or a tree seen out the window can ameliorate the barren urban environment of Chicago housing projects and make a measurable difference to people's lives. The medical studies reviewed in chapter 11 that showed better pain control with landscape picture distraction and sounds of birds and water suggest that there are opportunities to spend less money on painkilling drugs for patients, with substantial benefits in well-being as well (Diette et al. 2003).

In the Presence of Nature
A study of people exposed to different types of roadside corridors on a potential commute to work found that those on the urban drive dominated by human artifacts were more stressed than those driving through the nature-dominated scenes of forests or golf courses. The nature drive also seemed to have a protective effect against future stresses that might arise during the day (Parsons et al. 1998). The lack of concordance between these findings and what civic and park authorities tend to do draws attention to the urgent need for social science research to engage with urban planning and urban policy.

This evidence suggests that green spaces and nearby nature should be seen as a fundamental health resource (Frumkin 2001; Frumkin, Frank, and Jackson 2004; Maller et al. 2002). Another simple idea has been to put an aquarium full of fish in the waiting room at dentists' offices. Those exposed to this kind of nature are more relaxed than patients awaiting treatment in a room without an aquarium (Beck and Meyers 1996; Katcher and Wilkins 1993). Nearby natural settings can confer health benefits for patients of hospitals (Cooper-Marcus and Barnes 1999; Whitehouse et al. 2001). As noted in chapter 3, such benefits appear to have been recognized as early as the Middle Ages, with garden cloisters and vegetable gardens used as part of the healing process. In the Victorian period, gardens were routinely located in hospitals for the benefit of patients, and hospitals themselves located in pleasant surroundings. Some argue that modern health systems, with a focus on

treatment of diseases rather than patient comfort and care, have abandoned useful principles regarding connections with nature and place
(Lindheim and Syme 1983). Empirical studies have shown that patients
regularly report positive changes in mood when visiting gardens (Cooper-
Marcus and Barnes 1999).

Such principles are being applied in the Eden Alternative nursing
homes in Texas, where healing gardens, greenhouses, atriums, and plants
have been deployed. After conversion, there were 57 percent fewer bed-
sores, an 18 percent reduction in patients restrained, a 60 percent reduction in behavioral incidents, and a 48 percent reduction in staff
absenteeism. The costs of such nature-based treatments are expected to
be much less than expenditure for drugs and surgery to achieve the same
outcomes (Eden Alternative 2004). The implications of these experiments and also studies of day care facilities for children suggest that we
pay a significant price when we live without contact with nearby nature
(Wells 2000; Wells and Evans 2003).

Direct Participation with Nature

The third category of engagement with nature comprises direct participation in some activity in green spaces. This differs from the second category, as it implies a positive decision to go to places where there is green
nature rather than be incidentally exposed to it while doing something
else. Even short exposures to nature, such as a 30-minute walk, can be
highly beneficial (Taylor, Kuo, and Sullivan 2001). Research does not yet
tell us whether cumulative short exposures, such as looking out of the
window or short walks, equate to longer, less frequent exposures to
nature, such as a weekend nestled in an urban forest (Hartig et al. 2003).
One consequence of a better understanding of the full range of urban
reengagement with place is the opportunity to explore such issues more
carefully. We also wonder if there is an enhanced or different effect of
exposure to specific places when there are memories, stories, or rituals
associated with them (Gallagher 1994; Tuan 1977).

The importance of private and community gardens and the growing
movements to expand such areas in various parts of the United States
contrast with the longer history in Europe. In the United Kingdom, there
are now some 300,000 occupied garden allotments on 12,000 hectares

of land. These allotments today yield some 215,000 tons of fresh food each year, its own contribution to health. But probably more important are the opportunities they provide for regular contact with nature and for constructive social interaction. There are now several hundred city farms or community gardens in the United Kingdom (Pretty 1998). They transform derelict or vacant land into desirable areas for local people to visit and enjoy, often providing quiet, tranquil places for the community, spaces that can also increase wildlife. In some cases, they also provide the opportunity for mental health patients to engage in work that builds self-esteem and confidence and for unemployed people to use their time productively in their own community. As Malve von Hassell describes (chapter 4), gardens offer different forms of engagement to different ages and interests, providing herbs for healing, a more varied diet, or a shady respite where children can play.

The American National Gardeners Association estimates that some 35 million people are growing their own food in backyard gardens and allotments in the United States. Their contribution to the informal economy is estimated to be about $12 to $14 billion per year. Why do they do it? As this book shows, private gardeners enjoy better-tasting and more nutritious food, and also save money, obtain outdoor exercise, and engage in a form of therapy. Perhaps more important, it makes them feel better. This is particularly true of community gardens and farms that, by contrast, seek to enhance both food production and social benefits. Some participants also see themselves as resisting the local power structure and helping to explore an alternative economy, separate from the intrusions of corporate or governmental control. Further work is needed on the political economy of community gardens and allotment gardens and the range of effects on social networks, identity, and well-being.

An important unanswered question for those concerned about sustainability is the extent to which the benefits of such direct interactions continue off-site. Data from Peggy Barlett's study (chapter 2) suggest that new knowledge and experiences in nature can provoke long-term changes in thinking. How often, however, is this true, how long does it last, and when can it lead to efforts toward social and political transformation? Rachel Kaplan and Stephen Kaplan note that sometimes in community-based nature activities, a commitment to the cause comes first. People seek to make a social contribution and in doing so come to discover a new relationship with place. For others, attachment to the place or type of nature comes first, and efforts to defend them come later. It is also true that people with a certain set of positive environmental values may be predisposed toward the restorative potential of nature and that these values help to shape environmental attitudes (Kaiser, Wölfing, and Fuhrer 1999; Kals, Schumacher, and Montada 1999; Schultz and Zelezny 1999).

Ryan and Grese (chapter 7) show us how the environmental restoration movements have shifted the actions of typical environmentalist groups from land protection, ecological education, and political organizing toward a new, healing aspect: an effort to bring back a fuller range of species and more self-sustaining local ecosystems. Healing small pieces of forest or prairie connects with a new vision of human life in urban areas, and one that connects as well with human health through meaningful labor, learning, and political engagement. Desires to "help the environment and feel useful" draw together the threads of environmental and human health in interesting new ways.

Combining Nature and Exercise

Physical activity is now known to be a codeterminant of health (Centers for Disease Control 1996; Department of Culture, Media, and Sport 2002). It greatly reduces the risk of dying from coronary heart disease and also reduces the risk of developing diabetes, hypertension, and colon cancer. It fosters healthy muscles and bones, helps maintain independence in older adults, and has a substantial influence on people's sense of well-being (Pretty, Griffin, and Sellens 2004).[2] In Europe, there has been a dramatic fall in physical activity over the past 50 years, as the energy output per day in adults aged 20 to 60 years has dropped the equivalent of running a marathon each week (a decline of 500 kcal a day). Jobs have become less physical, people are more likely to take the elevator than walk the stairs, and adults and children are more likely to travel to work or school by car than to walk or bicycle.[3]

As physical activity can positively affect mental well-being and self-esteem (Scully et al. 1999), there may be a synergistic benefit in adopting physical activities while at the same time being directly exposed to nature. We have called this "green exercise" (Pretty et al. 2003). The behavior of many groups of people seems to suggest that they already appreciate the benefits of protecting the environment, undertaking physical activity, and combining the two. Despite the increased daily disconnections between a predominantly urban population and nature, and the increase in sedentary lifestyles imposed or adopted by the majority of the population, people still express a desire for lifestyle change in a variety of direct and indirect ways. The pioneering grassroots sustainability efforts recounted in this book suggest ways to enhance opportunities for healthful exercise, approaches that are particularly appealing and meaningful.

Team sports provide another avenue for exercise outdoors, though public space for playing fields and parks do not always coexist peacefully. Large numbers of people in the United Kingdom regularly engage in physical activity in their communities; for example, 400,000 people play soccer each weekend in 33,000 registered amateur clubs. The United Kingdom has a network of some 110,000 community amateur sports clubs run by 1.5 million volunteers. In some areas, new construction threatens organized local sports with the loss of playing fields, and the number of sports clubs has declined by 40,000 since 1996. Howard Frumkin and colleagues in the United States have found that the demand for soccer fields and other organized sports venues is one of the biggest challenges to forest preserves and more natural environments in the city. Similar controversies arise when bicycling enthusiasts seek to pave trails in woodlands, although the benefits of exercise for urban populations are significant. Research presented here suggests the importance of finding opportunities for both healthful nature contact and for vigorous exercise and also for exploring more carefully the differential benefits of the two.

Collective Action for Sustainable Urban Environments

Vigorous exercise in smog-filled air, however, is not a contribution to urban health (Frumkin 2002b). Playing in the creek if water quality is poor can be a threat. Emerging efforts to refashion daily life impacts on the surrounding natural environment and build a healthier urban ecosystem are important components of developing healthier urban places for residents as well. The arenas of action documented in this book turn our attention to efforts to develop new institutional and public policies in support of rebuilding connections to place.

The urban foodshed movement described by Elizabeth Barham, David Lind, and Lewis Jett (chapter 6) emerged out of concerns for health—both of the farm environment and the food we eat. Building a new connection to place through food counters the pervasive estrangement from the land for most urbanites. Local food groups unite diverse agendas, bringing together concerns about migrant worker pay, and a desire for food without pesticide residues. Such coalitions of interests extend sustainability impacts beyond consumers' diets to have effects on farm workers and their families as well. Food provides an entrée to issues of local employment opportunities and socially beneficial land uses, though there is no guarantee that locally grown food is necessarily connected to a more environmentally sustainable or socially just community. As chapter 6 describes, however, the local food movement reorients values embedded in the production and consumption of food.

Deeper connection to place can lead to political struggles with entrenched interests. Barbara Lynch and Rima Brusi (chapter 8) show us how the Puerto Rican garden movement in New York challenges the city's absolute rights to legitimate claims to land. Community gardens, public parks, and urban stream buffers are all struggles on behalf of scarce urban space in a form of resistance to market forces. Paradoxically, they are implicated in these forces as well: nice gardens and wild spaces enhance the neighborhood and foster gentrification.

The ways in which local food systems pull together diverse constituencies are not rare among the grassroots groups explored in these chapters. Susan Andreatta's experience with Project Green Leaf in North Carolina (chapter 5) provides a model for how 44 low-income families were brought into one community-supported agriculture venture through the creative use of federal program support and volunteer drivers to deliver the food. The chapters on community gardens bring together multiple agendas across lines of class and race. A striking dimension of many of the accounts in this book is the way more egalitarian social relations can be built through nature connection. Boundaries of hierarchy are softened and at times transcended between younger and older university faculty (chapter 2), staff and residents at shelters (chapter 3), working-class and middle-class New Yorkers (chapter 4), and community-supported agriculture shareholders and farmers (chapter 5). More research to understand the durability of such alliances and the long-term effectiveness of the strategies used to balance conflicting agendas would be useful.

Public policy impacts become more likely as numbers grow. Several chapters highlight that local organizations have evolved into larger networks of groups, such as the Volunteer Stewardship Networks of those protecting and restoring green spaces and the Regional Food Councils that seek to promote food security, sometimes on a statewide level. Such linkage shows the transition from personal experience to political clout. The reconnection with the natural world becomes woven into institutional change. As grocery chains, hospitals, schools, and restaurants seek to purchase local food, they can join with governmental programs such as food stamps and WIC to foster new relationships to place.

Faith communities from many traditions are part of the reconnection to place, often as they seek to incorporate environmental responsibility into their own practices (Taylor 2004). Higher education has also begun to create place-based currricula that emphasize local knowledge and experiential learning (Andelson 2004). Schools as diverse as Grinnell College, Appalachian State University, and the University of Montana have joined several institutions in the United Kingdom to highlight sustainability issues with a new emphasis on place and connection to the natural world. Such efforts from faith communities and educational institutions begin to counter the modernist celebration of ignorance about the natural world and articulate a new paradigm. Many of these efforts combine the health benefits of nature contact with new efforts for livelihood, food security, or struggles for justice. The forms of reinhabitation of place feed back into the meaningfulness of connections with nature.

Identity and Meaning: Place and Nature

Why do people spend a Saturday wrenching invasive plant species out of a park or "planting an extra row for the hungry"? We have seen that reconnection with the natural world can be a satisfying, enriching experience for the individuals involved. "Volunteering has opened up a new world for my family," responds a worker interviewed by Robert Ryan and Robert Grese (chapter 7). The efforts recounted in chapters 2 and 3 show some of the avenues of entry into new relationships with nature. In the words of a university teacher whose walk home suddenly includes a sense of responsibility for a nearby creek, "In my neighborhood . . . it's Emory's creek," we see new attachments have formed. Said residents at a California shelter, "It was really fine when the garden began. When we were pulling things out." "It is something to see your results. You see the seed, then the flower, and then the *chiles* come." New learning draws in some people, emotional attachment draws in others, and identity shifts as a result (Castells 2004:169; Thomashow 1995:4).

Contact with nature and place can contribute fundamentally to the way we establish self-identity. Identity is a relationship in which something is shared, and linkage with nature and communities partially helps to do this (Fox 1995; Milton 2002). To a certain extent, who and what we are has historically been constructed through relationships with both people and nature. Thus, if we lack these relationships and connections in contemporary urban settings, we may lose a potential part of our sense of personal identity and self-esteem. We are partly shaped, then, by the environment and by attachments developed during specific lifetime experiences and interactions (Fredrickson and Anderson 1999) and partly by our genetic makeup as well. Personal benefits can include psychological well-being, changing self-image, and growing self-esteem. Social benefits we have seen include family stability, community pride, and cultural identity (Pretty 2002).

Individual identity is supported by shared values and collective knowledge, and narratives can foster the group's vitality. The particularities of place that support a rich social matrix are often connected to the stories and meanings embedded in the locale (Langenbach 1984; Nabhan and St. Antoine 1993; Okri 1996; Schama 1996; Tall 1996). Ralph Metzner (2000) uses the term *reinhabitation* to describe the need to dwell in a place in a balanced way, with respect for the stories of the other inhabitants.

Accounts in many of the chapters of this book tell of restoration not only of civility and mental functioning but of cultural tradition. In community gardens and shelters, in public rituals and casual socializing, dimensions of lost foodways or play in nature are rebuilt. Barham's account (chapter 6) shows that regional food labeling efforts can contribute to the preservation of culture, even as it teaches new bioregional thinking. Food itself can orient the person in terms of self and identity, place and region, and politics, both global and local. Lynch and Brusi (chapter 8) highlight that a garden in a vacant lot can embody multiple meanings and traditions. New York's Lower East Side boasts the clashing symbols of the City Parks Department maple leaf (certifying park-like features in a community garden) and the Puerto Rican flag, with its celebration of *casita*, yard, and Caribbean heritage. Gardens provide food and opportunities to socialize but can also enhance a displaced Puerto Rican identity in New York, both "nostalgia and therapy." Even as neighbors clash over the appropriateness of fences or chickens, they highlight for us that connection to the natural world involves the creative tension between the built and the unbuilt, notions of the natural and the artificial, and the relations of humans and other species.

One form of meaning building is the creation of new rituals and playful forms of collective celebration. From the Rites of Spring Pageant described by von Hassell that pull hundreds of New Yorkers into a flamboyantly artistic, day-long pageant, to the end-of-season breakfast, cooked by Andreatta's urban neighbors for the local farmers they have come to know, such emerging rituals are a theme in many chapters. Even the simple "game" of tramping down wild prairie seeds by running over them creates meaning for the children who help to do this restoration work. We have seen that reconnection with the natural world can be a joyful, satisfying, enriching experience for the individuals involved. The studies in this book draw us to more questions about the full variance of individual experience, collective expression, and its health impact.

Robert Rotenberg (chapter 9) draws our attention to the important role of culture in framing experiences in nature and expanding that experience through an emotional vocabulary. As we deepen our appreciation of humankind as embedded within larger systems of life, the question arises of not only how we might accept the loss of a control over the natural world many presume to have, but even how we might celebrate the sublime, the awe and terror felt in the contact with nature.

Rotenberg calls for a civic discourse that values the extraordinariness of the sublime, seeing it as essential for a full human life as is the appreciation of beauty. How might we rethink parks and public policy—and even our pervasive concern for safety—if we deeply appreciated the sublime?

Concluding Comments

This book has woven together the evocative accounts of personal experience of reconnection with nature with the histories of the groups that foster them. Emerging from environmental concerns, moving toward a paradigm of sustainability, our attention has been drawn to the depth and breadth of new attachments to place. That many of these encounters with the natural world are described with satisfaction, even joy, reflects a hunger, a readiness on the part of many urban dwellers to move beyond the modernist paradigm and embrace a more engaged relationship with the living systems that support life in cities.

Joining together to restore or protect habitat for herons or wildflowers, to plant roses or pumpkins in a community garden, or to support a local farmers market, new arenas of action and new networks of friends are created. The search for sustainability renews our understanding of dimensions of human well-being, the importance of connection with the natural world around. Community well-being and social capital are nourished as well.

To grasp this emerging cultural pattern requires the intersection and collaboration of natural sciences, social sciences, humanities, landscape architecture, urban planning, medicine, and public health. Such cross-disciplinary dialogue is urgently required in the face of pressures from global population, migration, urban expansion, ecosystem degradation, and social alienation that call out for new ways to design healthy urban environments. Beyond healing the ill, these accounts of reconnection to place suggest important opportunities to prevent illness and to create health-promoting contexts within the city. We see in these grassroots efforts an emerging vision for healthier and more sustainable urban lifeways. The natural world, both compelling and restorative, beckons us to a new commitment.

Can this be achieved in the cities of the future? Can we all benefit from close engagement with nature and places? It may be possible, but it will require positive policy changes combined with community action to help shape such novel approaches to places and their effects on us.

Notes

1. There are many different ideas about what constitutes mental health. For a long time, it has been taken to mean the absence of a recognizable illness. Yet this type of deficit model does not explain how mental health and psychological well-being also positively influence us—helping to shape how we think and feel, how we learn and communicate, how we form and sustain relationships, and critically how we cope with shocks and stresses (Health Education Authority 1997). Everyone has mental health needs, not just those with an illness. We recognize that this view is not everywhere accepted, and mental ill health can sometimes be seen as the fault of the sufferer, arising from some lack of resolve or backbone. And for centuries, the policy response has been to stigmatize or even lock up the sufferers, to protect the rest of society from them.

2. Compared with active people, those who are sedentary have up to a twofold increased risk of dying, with levels of cardiovascular fitness strongly associated with overall mortality. One study found that men reduced their risk of death by 33 percent if they walked 15 or more kilometers per week, by 25 percent if they climbed 55 or more flights of stairs a week, and by 53 percent with 3 or more hours per week of moderate sports activity (Paffenbarger, Lee, and Leung 1994). There also appears to be a protective effect in later life, as the effects of activity early in life persist into the seventies and eighties.

3. Some 63 percent of men and 75 percent of women in the United Kingdom do not take enough physical activity to benefit their health. In almost all activities (except swimming and yoga), female participation is lower than male. In the group aged 16 to 24 years, 42 percent of men and 68 percent of women are inactive, and these proportions rise steadily as people age. One of the major problems is that although 80 percent of people in the United Kingdom correctly believe that regular exercise is good for their health, a majority wrongly believe that they exercise enough to stay fit.

References

Andelson, Jonathan. 2004. *The Pedagogy of Place.* Grinnell College Summer Faculty Workshop. Grinnell, Iowa: Center for Prairie Studies.

Andreatta, Susan. 2000. Marketing Strategies and Challenges of Small-Scale Organic Producers in Central North Carolina. *Culture and Agriculture* 22(3):40–50.

Baum, Fran. 1999. Social Capital and Health: Implications for Health in Rural Australia. In *Leaping the Boundary Fence: Using Evidence and Collaboration to Build Healthier Communities*. Helen Pampling and Gordon Gregory, editors. Pp. 96–109. Adelaide: National Rural Health Alliance.

Beck, A. M., and N. M. Meyers. 1996. Health Enhancement and Companion Animal Ownership. *Annual Review of Public Health* 17:247–257.

Castells, Manuel. 2004. *The Power of Identity*. 2nd ed. Malden, Mass.: Blackwell.

Centers for Disease Control and Prevention. 1996. *Physical Activity and Health: A Report of the Surgeon General*. Washington, D.C.: U.S. Government Printing Office.

Cooper-Marcus, C., and M. Barnes. 1999. *Healing Gardens: Therapeutic Benefits and Design Recommendations*. New York: Wiley.

DeLind, Laura B. 1999. Close Encounters with a CSA: The Reflections of a Bruised and Somewhat Wiser Anthropologist. *Agriculture and Human Values* 16:3–9.

Department of Culture, Media, and Sport. 2002. *Game Plan: A Strategy for Delivering Government's Sport and Physical Activity Objectives*. London: Department of Culture, Media, and Sport Cabinet Office.

Diette, G. B., N. Lechtzin, E. Haponil, A. Devrotes, and H. R. Rubin. 2003. Distraction Therapy with Nature Sights and Sounds Reduces Pain during Flexible Bronchoscopy. *Chest* 123:941–948.

Dillard, Annie. 1974. *Pilgrim at Tinker Creek*. New York: Harpers.

Eden Alternative Green House Project. 2004. http://www.edenalt.com/ and http://thegreenhouseproject.com/. Accessed Aug. 16, 2004.

Fox, Warwick. 1995. *Toward a Transpersonal Ecology*. New York: State University of New York Press.

Fredrickson, Laura M., and Dorothy H. Anderson. 1999. A Qualitative Exploration of the Wilderness Experience as a Source of Spiritual Inspiration. *Journal of Environmental Psychology* 19:21–39.

Freeman, Hugh, ed. 1984. *Mental Health and the Environment*. London: Churchill Livingstone.

Frumkin, Howard. 2001. Beyond Toxicity: Human Health and the Natural Environment. *American Journal of Preventative Medicine* 20(3):47–53.

Frumkin, Howard. 2002a. Urban Sprawl and Public Health. *Public Health Reports* 117:201–217.

Frumkin, Howard. 2002b. The Clean Air Campaign Enhances Smog Related Health Information. *Atlanta Journal and Constitution*, Apr. 25.

Frumkin, Howard, Lawrence Frank, and Richard Jackson. 2004. *Urban Sprawl and Public Health: Designing, Planning, and Building for Healthy Communities*. Washington, D.C.: Island Press.

Gallagher, Winifred. 1994. *The Power of Place*. New York: Harper Perennial.

Garreau, Joel. 1992. *Edge City: Life on the New Frontier*. New York: Anchor Books.

Halpern, David. 1995. *Mental Health and the Built Environment: More Than Bricks and Mortar?* London: Taylor and Francis.

Hartig, T., G. W. Evans, L. D. Jamner, D. S. Davis, and T. Garling. 2003. Tracking Restoration in Natural and Urban Field Settings. *Journal of Environmental Psychology* 23:109–123.

Health Education Authority. 1997. *Mental Health Promotion: A Quality Framework*. London: Health Education Authority.

Heerwagen, Judith H., and Gordon H. Orians. 1993. Humans, Habitats and Aesthetics. In *The Biophilia Hypothesis*. Stephen R. Kellert and Edward O. Wilson, eds. Pp. 138–172. Washington, D.C.: Island Press.

House, J. S., K. R. Landis, and D. Umberson. 1988. Social Relationships and Health. *Science* 241:540–545.

Kaiser, Florian G., Sybille Wölfing, and Uns Fuhrer. 1999. Environmental Attitude and Ecological Behavior. *Journal of Environmental Psychology* 19:1–19.

Kals, E., D. Schumacher, and L. Montada. 1999. Emotional Affinity toward Nature as a Motivational Basis to Protect Nature. *Environment and Behavior* 31:178–202.

Kaplan, Rachel. 2001. The Nature of the View from Home: Psychological Benefits. *Environment and Behavior* 33:507–542.

Kaplan, Rachel, Stephen Kaplan, and Robert L. Ryan. 1998. *With People in Mind: Design and the Management of Everyday Nature*. Washington, D.C.: Island Press.

Katcher, Aaron, and Gregory Wilkins. 1993. Dialogue with Animals: Its Nature and Culture. In *The Biophilia Hypothesis*. Stephen R. Kellert and Edward O. Wilson, eds. Pp. 173–197. Washington, D.C.: Island Press.

Langenbach, Randolph. 1984. Continuity and Sense of Place: The Importance of the Symbolic Image. In *Mental Health and the Environment*. H. Freeman, ed. Pp. 455–469. London: Churchill Livingstone.

Leather, P., M. Pyrgas, B. Beale, B. Kweon, and E. Tyler. 1998. Plants in the Workplace: The Effects of Plant Density on Productivity, Attitudes and Perceptions. *Environment and Behavior* 30:261–282.

Lindheim, R., and S. L. Syme. 1983. Environments, People and Health. *Annual Review of Public Health* 4:335–339.

Maller, Cecily, Mardie Townsend, Peter Brown, and Lawrence St. Leger. 2002. *Healthy Parks Healthy People: The Health Benefits of Contact with Nature in a Park Context*. Victoria, Melbourne: Deakin University and Parks.

Metzner, Ralph. 2000. *Green Psychology. Transforming Our Relationship to the Earth*. London: Part St. Press.

Milton, Kay. 2002. *Loving Nature: Towards an Ecology of Emotion*. London: Routledge.

Nabhan, Gary Paul, and Sara St. Antoine. 1993. The Loss of Floral and Faunal Story: The Extinction of Experience. In *The Biophilia Hypothesis*. Stephen R. Kellert and Edward O. Wilson, eds. Pp. 229–250. Washington, D.C.: Island Press.

Newman, Oscar. 1980. *Community of Interest*. New York: Anchor.

Okri, Ben. 1996. *Birds of Heaven*. London: Harmondsworth/Penguin.

Paffenbarger, R. S., I-M. Lee, and R. Leung. 1994. Physical Activity and Personal Characteristics Associated with Depression and Suicide in American College Men. *Acta Psychiatrica Scandinavica Supplementum* 377:16–22.

Parsons, R., L. G. Tassinary, R. S. Ulrich, R. S. Hebl, and M. Grossman-Alexander. 1998. The View from the Road: Implications for Stress Recovery and Immunization. *Journal of Environmental Psychology* 18:113–140.

Pretty, Jules N. 1998. *The Living Land*. London: Earthscan.

Pretty, Jules N. 2002. *Agri-Culture: Reconnecting People, Land and Nature*. London: Earthscan.

Pretty, Jules N. 2004. How Nature Contributes to Mental and Physical Health. *Spirituality and Health International* 5:68–78.

Pretty, Jules N., Murray Griffin, and Martin Sellens. 2004. Is Nature Good for You? *Ecos* 24:2–9.

Pretty, Jules N., Murray Griffin, Martin Sellens, and Chris J. Pretty. 2003. *Green Exercise: Complementary Roles of Nature, Exercise and Diet in Physical and Emotional Well-Being and Implications for Public Health Policy*. CES Occasional Paper 2003–1. Colchester, Essex: University of Essex.

Pretty, Jules N., and Hugh Ward. 2001. Social Capital and the Environment. *World Development* 29(2):209–227.

Schama, Simon. 1996. *Landscape and Memory*. London: Fontana Press.

Schultz, P. W., and L. Zelezny. 1999. Values as Predictors of Environmental Attitudes: Evidence for Consistency across 14 Countries. *Journal of Environmental Psychology*. 19:255–265.

Scully, D., J. Kremer, M. Meade, R. Graham, and K. Dudgeon. 1999. Physical Exercise and Psychological Well-Being: A Critical Review. *British Journal of Sports Science* 32:11–20.

Tall, Deborah. 1996. Dwelling: Making Peace with Space and Place. In *Rooted in the Land: Essays on Community and Place*. William Vitek and Wes Jackson, eds. Pp. 104–112. New Haven, Conn.: Yale University Press.

Taylor, Andrea Faber, Frances E. Kuo, and William C. Sullivan. 2001. Coping with ADD: The Surprising Connection to Green Play Settings. *Environment and Behavior* 33:54–77.

Taylor, Bron. 2004. Introduction and Reader's Guide: The Encyclopedia of Religion and Nature. www.ReligionandNature.com. Accessed July 31.

Tennessen, C. M., and B. Cimprich. 1995. Views to Nature: Effects on Attention. *Journal of Environmental Psychology* 15:77–85.

Thomashow, Mitchell. 1995. *Ecological Identity*. Cambridge, Mass.: MIT Press.

Tuan, Yi-Fu. 1977. *Space and Place*. Minneapolis: University of Minnesota Press.

Ulrich, Roger S. 1984. View through a Window May Influence Recovery from Surgery. *Science* 224:420–421.

Ulrich, Roger S. 1993. Biophilia, Biophobia and Natural Landscapes. In *The Biophilia Hypothesis*. Stephen R. Kellert and Edward O. Wilson, eds. Pp. 73–137. Washington, D.C.: Island Press.

Wells, Nancy. 2000. At Home with Nature: Effects of "Greenness" on Children's Cognitive Functioning. *Environment and Behavior* 32:775–795.

Whitehouse, S., J. W. Varni, M. Seid, C. Cooper-Marcus, M. J. Ensberg, J. R. Jacobs, and R. S. Mehlenbeck. 2001. Evaluating a Children's Hospital Garden Environment: Utilisation and Consumer Satisfaction. *Journal of Environmental Psychology* 21:301–314.

Wilkinson, Richard G. 1999. Putting the Picture Together: Prosperity, Redistribution, Health, and Welfare. In *Social Determinants of Health*. Michael Marmot and Richard G. Wilkinson, eds. Pp. 256–274. New York: Oxford University Press.

World Health Organization. 2001. *World Health Report*. Geneva: WHO.

About the Authors

Susan L. Andreatta   received her master's in anthropology from Iowa State University in 1986 and her Ph.D. in anthropology in 1994 from Michigan State University. She is an associate professor of anthropology at the University of North Carolina at Greensboro and director of Project Green Leaf. Her research and outreach strengthen rural and urban connections by connecting the public to farmers markets, farms, and farmers. As a farmer advocate, she has published on farmers markets and community-supported agriculture. Two publications that illustrate her work are "Managing Farmer and Consumer Expectations: A Study of a North Carolina Farmers Market." (*Human Organization* 2002) and "Marketing Strategies and Challenges of Small-Scale Organic Producers in Central North Carolina" (*Culture and Agriculture* 2000).

Elizabeth Barham   holds master's and Ph.D. degrees in development sociology from Cornell University. She is an assistant professor within the Rural Sociology Department of the University of Missouri–Columbia. Her research interests are related to local-global linkages and the sociology of food and agriculture. Her central research theme is the social significance of food labeling, in particular labels of origin. She has carried out case study research related to this theme in Québec, France, Spain, and Portugal. She is particularly interested in issues of globalization, the sociology of agriculture, food, nutrition, and community. Recent publications include "The Lamb That Roared: Origin Labeled Products as Place Making Strategy in Charlevoix, Quebec" (2006) and "Translating Terroir: The Global Challenge of French AOC Labeling" (*Journal of Rural Studies* 2003).

Peggy F. Barlett   is professor of anthropology at Emory University in Atlanta and is active in helping the university embrace environmental stewardship. While growing up, she became attached to the oak woodlands of the Washington, D.C., area but has found familiarity with Atlanta's streams and wild spaces to be rejuvenating. She is editor of *Sustainability on Campus: Stories and Strategies for Change* (2004, with Geoffrey W. Chase) and *Agricultural Decision-Making: Anthropological Contributions to Rural Development* (1980). She is author of *American Dreams, Rural Realities: Family Farms in Crisis* (1993) and *Agricultural Choice and Change: Decision Making in a Costa Rican Community* (1982). She received the Ph.D. from Columbia University in 1975.

Rima Brusi was born in Puerto Rico in 1970 and did undergraduate work in psychology at the University of Puerto Rico. She received the Ph.D. from Cornell University in 2003, choosing anthropology for graduate work largely as the result of work with Manuel Valdes-Pizzini on social displacement along the Puerto Rican coast. Concerns with the coastal landscape figured strongly in her dissertation research, a study of the transformation of La Parguera in the Puerto Rican southwest from a fishing town into a tourist attraction and the site of a real estate boom. She currently lives in Boqueron, a coastal village in Puerto Rico, and is assistant professor at the University of Puerto Rico-Mayaguez.

Howard Frumkin is an internist, environmental and occupational medicine specialist, and epidemiologist, having received his M.D. from the University of Pennsylvania and his M.P.H. and Dr.P.H. from Harvard. He is professor and chair of environmental and occupational health at the Rollins School of Public Health of Emory University and professor of medicine at Emory Medical School. A native of Poughkeepsie, New York, he has lived in the Olmsted-designed Druid Hills section of Atlanta for 14 years. His research and teaching focus on environmental health. His books include *Urban Sprawl and Public Health* (2004, with Larry Frank and Dick Jackson), *Environmental Health: From Local to Global* (2005), and *Safe and Healthy School Environments* (forthcoming, coedited with Leslie Rubin and Robert Geller).

Robert E. Grese grew up in Tennessee and studied landscape architecture at the University of Georgia and the University of Wisconsin–Madison. He has taught landscape architecture at the University of Michigan since 1986 and currently serves as director of Nichols Arboretum and Matthaei Botanical Gardens. He is the author of *Jens Jensen: Maker of Natural Parks and Gardens* (1992) and has written widely on the prairie style of landscape gardening. A long-time advocate of native plants and ecologically based design, natural areas stewardship, and ecological restoration, he helped to establish the Volunteer Stewardship Network of Southeast Michigan and is active in a wide variety of community-based groups.

Malve von Hassell is an independent anthropologist and author of *The Struggle for Eden: Community Gardens in New York City* (2002) and *Homesteading in New York City, 1978–1993: The Divided Heart of Loisaida* (1996). She received her Ph.D. in anthropology from the New School for Social Research in 1987. She lives on the South Fork of Long Island with her son; together they love to explore the woods and wetlands in the area, grateful to live on a road that turtles cross in the summer and gets flooded by bay water in the winter.

Lewis Jett is a native of West Virginia, where he was raised on a family farm that produced beef cattle and vegetables for direct market. He attended West Virginia University for his B.Sc. and Virginia Tech for his M.S. and Ph.D. in horticulture. He is currently state vegetable crops extension specialist and assistant professor in the Department of Horticulture at the University of Missouri–Columbia. He conducts research on techniques to improve stand establishment of vegetables and methods to extend the growing season of warm-season vegetable crops using hoophouses or high tunnels.

Rachel Kaplan and **Stephen Kaplan** have long been connected to the same places, starting at Oberlin College in the 1950s. They received their Ph.D.s in psychology from the University of Michigan, where they are both professors. Stephen is also professor of computer science and engineering, and Rachel is the Samuel T. Dana Professor of Environment and Behavior at the School of Natural Resources and Environment. Major themes of their research and publications are fostering reasonable behavior in a difficult animal, the role of natural environments in human effectiveness and sanity, and participatory approaches to bringing out the best in experts and citizens. The Kaplans have coauthored four books, including *The Experience of Nature* and *With People in Mind: Design and Management of Everyday Nature* (with R. L. Ryan). The firsthand validation of their writings often occurs while paddling in a kayak, walking, or even in the view from the window.

David Lind is a doctoral candidate in the Department of Rural Sociology at the University of Missouri–Columbia. For his master's degree, he conducted a case study of contract broiler growers in a Louisiana parish and has coauthored a paper on the social life of the tortilla. He has discovered the social and environmental particularity of Columbia, Missouri, not his natal hearth, through a part-time job delivering milk to local homes for a small dairy farmer. The route and its placedness have also inspired his academic imagination. He is currently conducting research that explores the alternative, community-based food system constructed through the local milk route.

Barbara Deutsch Lynch environmental sociologist and director of urban and regional studies at Cornell University, is a Brooklynite who caught tadpoles in the Brooklyn Botanical Garden, fed ducks and climbed trees in Prospect Park, ice-skated on the Central Park lake, and communed with lesser pandas in the Bronx Zoo. She has written on land and water questions in the Andes and the Greater Antilles and on Caribbean environmental perspectives, and she is currently editing a volume on that topic with political scientist Sherrie Baver. Returning to her native city as a visitor, Lynch is studying Latino contributions to environmental practice and discourses. She received a Ph.D. from Cornell University.

Roderick Frazier Nash is Professor Emeritus of History and Environmental Studies at the University of California, Santa Barbara. A founder of the field of environmental history, he is the author of *Wilderness and the American Mind* (4th ed., 2001), *The Rights of Nature: A History of Environmental Ethics* (1989), and *American Environmentalism: Readings in Conservation History* (1990).

Jules Pretty is head of the Department of Biological Sciences at the University of Essex. He grew up in west Africa and lives in the rolling rural landscape of East Anglia in the United Kingdom, where his family can trace their roots for nearly 500 years. He is author of *Agri-Culture: Reconnecting People, Land and Nature* (2002), *The Living Land* (1998), and *Regenerating Agriculture* (1995).

He is coauthor of *Fertile Ground* (1999), *The Trainers Guide for Participatory Learning and Action* (1995), *The Hidden Harvest* (1992), and *Unwelcome Harvest* (1991). He is also editor of *Guide to a Green Planet* (2002). He is deputy chair of the government's Advisory Committee on Releases to the Environment and has served on numerous government advisory committees. He received a 1997 award from the Indian Ecological Society for International Contributions to Sustainable and Ecological Agriculture and was runner-up for the 2002 European Sicco Mansholt Prize for agricultural science. He was appointed A.D. White Professor-at-Large by Cornell University for six years from 2001, served on the international jury for the Slow Food Award in 2002, and is chief editor of the *International Journal of Agricultural Sustainability*. He is a fellow of the Institute of Biology and the Royal Society for Arts.

Robert Rotenberg is an urban anthropologist and holds a Ph.D. in anthropology from the University of Massachusetts in Amherst (1978). He is currently Vincent DePaul Professor of Anthropology at DePaul University in Chicago. He is the author of *Time and Order in Metropolitan Vienna* (1992) and *Landscape and Power in Vienna* (1995), and the coeditor (1993, with Gary W. McDonogh) of *The Cultural Meaning of Urban Space*. He calibrated his own sense of the sublime while whitewater rafting on the category 5 Zambezi River in Botswana. His home garden is a tangle of kitchen herbs.

Robert L. Ryan is an associate professor at the Department of Landscape Architecture and Regional Planning, University of Massachusetts, Amherst. He holds a master's in landscape architecture and urban planning degrees from the University of Michigan and a Ph.D. in natural resources (environment and behavior concentration) from the same institution. He is coauthor with Rachel Kaplan and Stephen Kaplan of *With People in Mind: Design and Management of Everyday Nature* (1998). His current research looks at people's attachment to place in rural New England.

Susan M. Stuart received a B.A. in history (1972) from the University of Nebraska and masters' degrees in Latin American studies (1976) and public health (1977) from the University of California, Los Angeles. She learned to garden alongside her mother and father in the Sandhills of western Nebraska before joining the high plains diaspora. She has long since learned to embrace winter gardening in coastal California and shares her fava beans, arugula, lemons, and figs with a teenage son, Jonah, and her husband, David, in Santa Cruz. She served as project manager of Project GROW and as staff of the Center for Food and Justice, a division of the Urban and Environmental Policy Institute of Occidental College in Los Angeles.

William C. Sullivan lives with his son in Urbana, Illinois, where he is associate professor and director of the Environmental Council at the University of Illinois. He is a founder and codirector of the interdisciplinary Human-Environment Research Laboratory in the Department of Natural Resources and Environmental Sciences. Sullivan earned a Ph.D. from the University of Michigan, where he was a student of Rachel Kaplan and Stephen Kaplan. He grew up in Glen Ellyn, Illinois, and has spent his life in the Midwest (Illinois, Kansas, and Michigan).

Index